Emerging Voices

Emerging Voices

South Asian American women redefine self, family, and community

Editor
Sangeeta R. Gupta

ALTAMIRA
PRESS

Walnut Creek/London/New Delhi

For information address:

AltaMira Press
A Division of Sage Publications, Inc.
1630 North Main Street, Suite 367
Walnut Creek, CA 94596

Sage Publications Ltd
6 Bonhill Street
London EC2A 4PU
United Kingdom

Sage Publications India Pvt Ltd
M-32 Market
Greater Kailash-I
New Delhi-110 048, India

Printed in New Delhi, India

Library of Congress Cataloging-in-Publication Data

Emerging voices: South Asian American women redefine self, family, and community/editor, Sangeeta R. Gupta.
    p.   cm.
    Includes bibliographical references and index.
    ISBN 0-7619-9295-2 (cloth). —ISBN 0-7619-9296-0 (pbk.)
    1. East Indian American women—Ethnic identity. 2. Pakistani American women—Ethnic identity. 3. East Indian American women—Family relationships. 4. Pakistani American women—Family relationships. 5. East Indian American women—Social conditions. 6. Pakistani American women—Social conditions. I. Guptā, Saṅgītā.
    E184.E2E64   1998   305.48'8914073—dc21   98–37064

99 00 01 02 03 04 05 06 07   8 7 6 5 4 3 2 1

Interior Design and Production by Siva Math Setters, Chennai
Cover Design by Bharati Mirchandani

This book is dedicated to

my mother

and
her generation of pioneering immigrant women
who forged a new life for themselves and future
generations of South Asians
in the United States

Contents

✦

Acknowledgments

I would like to thank Kamna, Karen, Kauser, Lalita, Lubna, Mantosh, Pooja, Sabah, and Sudha who have patiently worked with me and whose encouragement and support helped to bring this book together.

I would also like to thank the following individuals at UCLA: Ronald Mellor, Department of History; Sue Fan, Center for Pacific Rim Studies; Katherine Norberg and Dawn Waring, Center for Study of Women; Don Nakanishi, Asian American Studies Program; and Raymund Parades, Assistant Vice-Chancellor of Academic Development who generously provided support for the 1994 South Asian Women's Conference which provided the basis for this book. I would also like to thank Stanley Wolpert, D.R. Sar Desai, Shela Patel, and Barbara Bernstein from UCLA's History Department for their faith in and support of this project through its several incarnations. A special 'thank you' needs to be added for Stanley Wolpert, my advisor, in recognition of his unwavering belief in me and his consistent support and encouragement of all my endeavors. Kamran Scot Aghaie, Linda Line Alipuria, Vasanthi Ananth, Craig C. Brandau, Georgina Dodge, Christian Ghasarian, Sapna Kumar, and Valerie Matsumoto, Michel Potts and Rekha Rao also deserve thanks for their valuable and insightful comments on various sections of this volume.

To Omita Goyal, Acquisitions Editor at Sage Publications, thanks for her professional dedication and hard work—it was certainly a pleasure to work with her! I would also like to thank Tejeshwar Singh for his support of this project and Jaya Chowdhury for her hard work.

And finally, I would like to thank my mother and sister, Salim Chagan, Shela Patel, Rena Prayaga, Linda Rudolph, Regina Saum, Asha Singh, and Chitra Subbarayen. Their friendship, love, and support enabled me to walk on the road of self-discovery and find my own emerging voice.

Introduction

Sangeeta R. Gupta

As a child of immigrant parents, I, like most of my generation, grew up on the edge of two, often conflicting, worlds. The boundaries between these worlds usually blurred, sometimes juxtaposed and often overlapped. I had one foot planted in the traditional world of my parents and grandparents within the home, the other rooted in the world outside the front door. The journey to adulthood and finding one's place in the world is difficult enough, but children of immigrants must also find a bicultural identity that will reconcile one culture with the other. This book is inspired by my personal journey as a South Asian American woman who grew up in the United States and struggled to build a bridge between several different cultures: South Asian, Asian-Indian, American and South Asian American. This process continues into my adulthood and now takes on a new dimension as my family members and I try to transmit a meaningful blend of 'values', 'traditions', and 'culture' to the third generation of our family.

Another group also affected, although in different ways, by the immigrant experience consists of the adult women who came to the US with their husbands and, sometimes, young children. These women are also renegotiating their identities as women, wives, and mothers. They struggle with their own sense of 'self' as they themselves adjust to a culture very different from that of their childhood and as they bring up their children in this rapidly changing and sometimes confusing world. My mother is one of these immigrant women and my sister and I, amidst our own journey to adulthood, have watched her struggle and change over the years as she redefined herself as a woman, a wife, and a mother. At times her experiences seemed to mirror ours. We have often grown together as women—as individuals as well as members of our immediate and extended families—and we have found our own unique place in our community and in the larger mainstream society.

This volume explores how *some* women from India and Pakistan have experienced immigration in various aspects of their lives. Their experiences span different generational, religious and regional points of view; furthermore, their status as single, married or divorced women, as mothers, sisters or daughters, and as homemakers or professional women, adds additional layers to their lives as immigrants. The authors in this collection do not claim to represent all South Asian women nor do they imply that there is just one experience for all women from this region. This volume explores the issues and circumstances that make their experiences different and, yet, similar to those of other women immigrants and their daughters. The various chapters will also examine how these experiences differ from those of the male immigrants. Why are women's experiences different? I believe that gender role expectations—from South Asian cultures along with the mainstream Western culture—form the foundation of their various struggles. These expectations affect various generations of women in different ways. While first generation parents want their children to adopt some aspects of Western culture such as education or occupation (what we may call structural assimilation), they also expect their offspring to shed this 'foreign' influence at will under other circumstances (especially in issues of dating and marriage). Thus, parents do not want their children to completely submerge themselves in this mainstream culture by adopting all Western social patterns of behavior, referred to as cultural assimilation. These conflicting expectations put tremendous pressure on the second and subsequent generations to be 'American' outside the home and South Asian inside the home. This pressure is especially felt by young women who, like most women around the world, are considered the bearers of tradition and thus are expected by their communities to preserve 'the culture' and pass it on to the next generation. But what exactly are they passing on? Is it the South Asian culture that is so dear to their parents, or, are they blending their South Asian heritage with mainstream American culture? The pieces in this volume will address some of these issues from various points of view.

Terminology

The term 'Asian-Indian' is used in the US census to identify individuals from India. It is also used to denote the US-born second generation by describing them as native-born Asian-Indians. I believe it is problematic to use the terms 'Asian-Indian' or 'Pakistani' for the second generation and not also name them as Americans. Researchers may, for the sake of simplicity, use first and second generation Asian-Indian to denote these two groups, however, many members of these groups refer to themselves as Indo-American/Indian-American or as Pakistani-American.

In this chapter, I will use 'Asian-Indian' and 'Pakistani' to describe the first or immigrant generation and 'Indian-American' and 'Pakistani-American' to describe their US-born children. 'Asian-Indian' will also be used to describe the individuals who came from India prior to 1947. To enable each author to maintain her own voice, the terminology has not been standardized throughout this volume.

Historical overview of Asian-Indian immigration

Until recently, immigration studies in the United States have mainly focused on either European immigration or the involuntary African migration. Comparatively, little research has been conducted on Asian immigration and even less on the immigrants from colonial India. 'Colonial India' (hereafter shortened to India) at this point refers to the entire subcontinent for the pre-1947 immigrants and thereafter, the region is referred to as South Asia. Although a few scholars have researched the pre-1965 Asian-Indian population, they have usually concentrated on the political or economic activities of these predominantly male immigrants. These works have not examined the cultural change inside the family nor the role of women within the immigrant experience. No one has documented the history—or *her* story!—of South Asian women immigrants. This collection will explore the experiences of some of the women who immigrated to the US after 1965 (when the Immigration Act of 1965 abolished the national-origins quotas, established 'preference categories' and inadvertently, lifted the heavy restrictions on Asian immigration) as well as take a look at other women who either immigrated with their parents at a very young age or were born in the United States.[1]

Immigration is not a new phenomenon to the population of India. Asian-Indians have participated in what anthropologist Bruce La Brack calls 'assisted immigration' to various parts of the British Empire for generations. These migrations were usually for economic reasons. There were two types of Asian-Indian immigrants after 1800: indentured or bonded, and freeman or passenger. The indentured Asian-Indians went to Fiji, Guyana, Mauritius, Surinam, and were also among the early immigrants to various locations in Africa. The 'freeman' or 'passenger immigrants', who often constituted a 'second wave' after the initial indentured migration, went to the above locations in addition to Canada, the US, and Australia.[2] Those who came to the US, overwhelmingly Jat Punjabi Sikhs, wanted to earn some money and go back to India and are, therefore, considered sojourners and not permanent immigrants. Due to the temporary nature of their stay, they did not need to focus on adaptation or assimilation but only needed to adjust enough to get by and they may have been more inclined to tolerate certain situations and restrictions in their early years in the United States. Like other Asian immigrants, these early immigrants from India faced a great deal of racism. Much of the hostility towards Asian-Indians can be directly linked to their status (or lack thereof) in the British Empire.

Under British law, Indian men and women were British subjects and therefore should have had the right to go anywhere within the Empire. Ideally, this privilege would have enabled Indians to immigrate to wherever the British flag flew, including Canada (a member of the Commonwealth). However, Asian-Indians around the world soon realized that, whereas they were expected to support the machinery of the British Empire, they could not reap the same benefits as their 'white' counterparts. Therefore, when Asian-Indians traveled abroad the British government usually did not enforce their rights as British citizens. This lack of protection left them vulnerable to economic, social, and legal discrimination, and even to physical attacks, in their new homes.

When discussing sojourners, it is important to consider how the legislative acts of host countries affected their lives, especially when immigration was curtailed and families separated, sometimes for decades. Ranjani Kanta Das, conducting research among Canadian and US immigrants from approximately 1919 to 1922, states that these governments deliberately adopted policies that would separate Indian families in an effort to force the men to return to India. Das believes that the immigrants understood this and 'nothing so embittered them as this policy of exclusion; for it is not only injustice to them, but also to their innocent wives and children'.[3] While Das' statement has merit, limiting immigration to male laborers is a policy consistent with the politics surrounding a transitory and temporary labor force. In the eyes of these Western countries, Asians, in general, could come as long as they were needed as a source of cheap labor. However, they were not welcome to stay as permanent residents and were certainly not expected to become citizens. By excluding their wives and children, it was believed that the men would eventually leave, and some did. However, enough Asian-Indians stayed to establish a small US community.

Canada and the United States

There were several significant groups of immigrants from India, each different enough to warrant separate attention. Although a few Indians came to North America in the late 1800s, their numbers were too small to discuss them as a distinct group. As stated earlier, the first wave of Indian laborers came to Canada and the US as sojourners, and not as permanent immigrants, in the early 1900s. The second group came after US immigration laws were changed in 1946; at this time, many of the original immigrants were reunited with their families. The majority of the first two groups were uneducated laborers from the rural areas of India, primarily from the state of Punjab.[4] The third and largest group came after immigration laws were once again changed in 1965 and are the much-touted highly educated, urbanized professionals. In the 1980s, relatives of this post-1965 group started arriving under the preference categories which facilitated family reunification. This group, not *as* highly educated as their sponsors (65 percent of those coming before 1980 had a bachelors degree or higher while only 53 percent of those immigrating between 1980 and 1990 had similar educational credentials), did not fit the 'model minority' image of the post-1965 group and consequently their experiences are also different.[5]

The main concentration of Asian-Indian laborers began arriving around 1904 in both the US and Canada.[6] Between 1904 and 1908, a total of 5,198 Asian-Indians arrived in Canada (95.5 percent men, 0.3 percent women and 0.2 percent children).[7] Although pressured to stop the immigration, Canadian Prime Minister Sir Wilfred Laurier took an unpopular, but legally correct, position and insisted that Canada could not exclude British subjects of any race.[8] However, within four years of the arrival of the first Punjabi Sikhs, the Canadian government passed legislation which effectively barred further immigration from the Indian subcontinent. For the next 34 years, Canada would admit only 868 Asian-Indians, mostly wives and dependent children of the previous immigrants.[9]

Moving south

There is disagreement among researchers regarding the origins of Asian-Indian immigration to the United States. Some state that it was a by-product or overflow from Canadian immigration. According to another theory, it was a result of Canadian immigration laws which became increasingly exclusionary, and the hostile and sometimes violent reception from Canadians that turned many Asian-Indians towards the United States. However, La Brack contends that, originally, immigration to the US occurred side-by-side with immigration to Canada.[10] When Canadian doors were closed to Asian-Indians, their numbers to the US eventually increased. La Brack's views are supported by the fact that the US-based Asiatic Exclusion League (AEL) helped the citizens of Vancouver pressure their officials to stop Asian immigration. The Pacific Coast of the US had recently experienced its own Asian immigration 'crisis' and responded by enacting the Chinese Exclusion Act of 1882 and the Gentleman's Agreement with Japan in 1907. These two measures barred Chinese and Japanese laborers from immigrating to the United States. The Chinese Exclusion League became The Chinese and Japanese Exclusion League and was later renamed the Asiatic Exclusion League (AEL) so that Asian-Indians could be added to the list of Asians targeted for exclusion from the US. Therefore, there must have been sufficient numbers of Asian-Indians in the US to warrant the attention of the AEL.

Although Das states that Asian-Indians came to California because they were attracted by the opportunity to farm,[11] the general consensus is that they moved into agricultural jobs as other avenues of employment were closed to them. Soon, however, the residents of California felt that Asians were becoming too successful at farming (for the Jat Punjabi Sikhs, much of California had soil conditions similar to the Punjab and also, they were willing to cultivate land that others considered un-farmable) and in 1913 the Alien Land Act was passed and only aliens eligible for citizenship were able to lease or own land (East Asians had already been deemed ineligible for US citizenship). In 1917, bowing to public pressure and trying to avoid the appearance of overt racism towards any particular group, the US government passed the

1917 Immigration Act with a 'barred zone' provision which stated that individuals from particular geographical zones could not immigrate. Without listing specific countries, the US could still achieve its objective of excluding 'undesirable' races. The countries affected by this provision were India, Siam, Indo-China, parts of Siberia, Afghanistan, Arabia, and most of the islands of the Malay Archipelago.[12]

'White' v. 'Caucasian'

With Asian-Indian immigration effectively stopped by the 'barred zone' provision, the status of those already in the US was now in question. The 1790 Naturalization Act had restricted citizenship to 'whites' and a second law passed after the Civil War extended citizenship privileges to Americans of African ancestry. East Asians were classified as Mongoloids and were, therefore, deemed ineligible for US citizenship. Asian-Indians, on the other hand, were considered Caucasians and members of the Aryan family and as such, they had to be dealt with separately. The Asiatic Exclusion League, while agreeing that Asian-Indians were indeed from the same general family, stated that 'the forefathers of white Americans "pressed to the west, in the everlasting march of conquest, progress and civilization", while the "forefathers of the Hindus went east and became enslaved, effeminate, caste-ridden and degraded. And now we the people of the United States are asked to receive these members of a degraded race on terms of equality"'.[13] The push was on to prevent Asian-Indians from acquiring US citizenship.

With the doors of immigration slammed shut, Asian-Indians realized that they would have to stay in the US (if they left, they may not be able to return) and try to work for change through legislative and judicial systems. Some, however, returned to India and by 1919 La Brack estimates that only 2,600 Asian-Indians remained in California.[14] The predominantly Sikh population felt comfortable challenging what they considered to be unfair laws in the courts and when their right to citizenship was threatened, they fought all the way to the US Supreme Court. Two decisions, the 1910 *US v. Balsara* case and the 1913 *Ajkoy Kumar Mazumdar* decision, upheld that Asian-Indians were Caucasians and therefore 'white'. Using these two rulings, Asian-Indians applied for US citizenship. In 1922 when the Supreme Court ruled, in the *Ozawa* case, that white was synonymous with Caucasian, Indians felt their rights for naturalization were, once again, confirmed. The *Ozawa* case was used to deny citizenship rights to the Japanese who were not considered white based on the racial definition of white. However, a year later, the court would reverse itself. In the *US v. Bhagat Singh Thind* case, the US Supreme Court ruled that 'white' could not be defined by racial, anthropological or scientific methods but by what the 'common man' understood as 'white'. As the 'common man', according to the Court, would not recognize an Asian-Indian as 'white', he was clearly not 'white' and therefore, not eligible for citizenship. Some federal authorities took this ruling one step further and revoked the naturalization of approximately 50 Asian-Indians between 1923 and 1926 claiming that the *Thind* ruling meant that Asian-Indians had never been eligible for citizenship and, therefore, these individuals had obtained their naturalization papers by fraud. Needless to say, this retroactive application of the law astounded many individuals. Until this time, the US, in its entire history, had only revoked the citizenship of six individuals: Germans who had shown disloyalty during the war.

Asian-Indians did not give up and continued to fight this latest development and appealed the stripping of their US citizenship. Sakharam Ganesh Pandit, an attorney who represented Asian-Indians in this battle, was soon targeted himself. A 1926 ruling in his case upheld his naturalization; however, federal authorities continued to contest the naturalization of Asian-Indians through the mid-1930s and appealed the *Pandit* case all the way to the Supreme Court. The case was finally closed when the court refused to hear it.[15] However, the *Thind* decision continued to have far-reaching effects for the Asian-Indians who stayed in the United States.

By adding Asian-Indians to the 'aliens ineligible for citizenship' category, the *Thind* decision also affected their rights to own and lease land. California Attorney General U.S. Webb instructed local district attorneys to begin proceedings to revoke land purchases and publicly stated that Asian-Indians would not be allowed to lease or contract farmland. Clerks in California courts, through their own initiative, decided the *Thind* decision also meant that Asian-Indians could not marry white women and began to refuse marriage licenses to couples they perceived to be 'interracial'.[16] Nobel laureate Rabindranath Tagore reacted to the continuing battle of Asian exclusion by refusing to return to the United States due to the 'utter lack of freedom with which the atmosphere is charged'.[17] On an earlier visit, when subjected to US racist attitudes himself, Tagore had canceled his US tour and returned to India stating: 'Jesus could not get into America because, first of all, He would not have the necessary money, and secondly, He would be an Asiatic.'[18] After the

Thind decision, more Asian-Indians left the US, and with some of the original pioneers dying, the population continued to dwindle. Feeling isolated, the small group of Indians remaining in California created lives within the narrow boundaries allowed by law and often, by stretching those boundaries as far as possible. Many Asian-Indians, like other Asians, found ways to circumvent these restrictions and they continued to farm, some very successfully. For example, Dalip Singh Samra, who came to the US in 1910, became the largest celery grower in California and his grandson, Steven Samra continues this tradition by farming the family lands in Northern California. William Moscher, Sr., like many other Anglo-Americans, disagreed with these restrictions and so, he, against the wishes of his own partner, leased land in his own name for Dalip Singh Samra to farm.[19]

The winds of change

The bombing of Pearl Harbor had far-reaching effects for Asians living in the United States. While Japanese-Americans were interned and their communities devastated, the US government began to re-evaluate its position on Chinese and Asian-Indian immigrants. As Americans reeled from the Japanese attack on their country, they realized that they needed allies in Asia. With renewed interest, they followed the nationalist movements in China and India. China's war-time effort on behalf of the Allies earned its citizens the right to emigrate to the US in 1943 when the Chinese exclusionary laws were repealed and an immigration quota established. The American recognition of China's importance in the war earned Chinese nationals living in the US the right to apply for US citizenship. The US then turned to examine the situation in India more closely and realized that India was on the brink of independence. In addition to this (or because of this), they felt compelled to recognize the substantial effort India was making on behalf of the Allies. It should be mentioned that at this point it was in the best interest of the US to recognize India's war effort and its impending emergence as a very large democracy which could affect the balance of power in South Asia.

In March 1944, Emanuel Celler and Clare Boothe Luce introduced bills in Congress which would repeal the prohibition on Asian-Indian immigration and allow those currently living in the US the right to apply for citizenship. Although there was opposition, the timely intervention of recently elected President Harry S. Truman secured the

passage of the bill in the House in October 1945. After further opposition and delays in the Senate, the new bill was finally signed into law
in July 1946 and a quota to allow 100 Asian-Indian immigrants per year
was established.[20] However, the actual number that came was higher
as wives and children of those already in the US were exempt from the
quota. The beleaguered Asian-Indians living in the US were finally
reunited with their families. This much-needed influx of new immigrants added to the approximately 1,500 Asian-Indians in the country
in 1946 and prevented this minuscule population from dying out.[21]

'The model minority': Post-1965 immigration

World War II also affected US attitude towards its own minorities.
The Fair Employment Practices Commission was created and racial discrimination in defense industries was outlawed in 1941. In 1947, India
became independent and East and West Pakistan were created while in
the US, the Committee on Civil Rights came into being. The following year, California's Supreme Court ruled against anti-miscegenation
laws and the United States Supreme Court struck down 'race-restrictive
housing covenants'.[22] Further change came as the 1954 *Brown v. The
Board of Education* decision marked the beginning of the Civil Rights
Movement in the US. The 'winds of change' picked up speed as Asian
immigrants and their American-born children continued to press for
their rights. The Japanese American Citizens League (JACL) worked
to increase awareness of Asian immigrant contribution to the US and
reminded people that American-born children of Japanese immigrants
had fought against Japan in the recent war and were, therefore, entitled
to the same benefits as other Americans. Californians apparently agreed
as they repealed the Alien Land Laws. Then in 1952, the McCarran-
Walter Act enabled Asian immigrants to apply for citizenship and
immigration restrictions imposed by the 'barred zone' legislation of
1917 were lifted, although the low immigration quotas established in
1946 remained.

The Civil Rights Movement was to have a major impact on Asian
immigration by increasing awareness of racism within the US. The
Cold War also pressured the US government to review its immigration
policies which were still based on the national origin of the appli-
cant. Finally, the Hart-Cellar Immigration Act of 1965 eliminated the
national origin quota system and instead established a system based on

preference categories which favored professionals and highly educated individuals. This act also limited the number of immigrants from both the Western and Eastern Hemispheres to 290,000 people. However, as immediate family members of US citizens (spouses, children and parents) were exempt from the quotas, Asian-Americans were able to rapidly increase their communities by sponsoring these particular family members. Although the 1965 Act represented substantial progress towards racial fairness in immigration policies, the underlying belief was that it would have little or no impact on Asian immigration. In fact, Congress was assured that the Asian population in the US would remain close to its current level of 0.05 percent of the total US population. One of the sponsors, New York Representative Emanuel Cellar, believed that '[s]ince the people of...Asia have very few relatives here, comparatively few could immigrate from those countries because they have no family ties in the US'.[23]

These predictions proved to be completely inaccurate. While the total US population increased by only 11 percent, the various Asian-American communities saw a 141 percent increase between the 1970 and the 1980 censuses. These figures were repeated for the next decade which saw an increase of 10 percent and 99 percent, respectively.[24] The numbers of Asian-Indians immigrating to the US grew from 2 percent of the Asian immigrants in 1960 to 10 percent in 1990 and the numbers of Pakistani immigrants grew from less than 1 percent to 3.3 percent. From 1980 to 1990, 262,841 individuals immigrated from India and 61,364 immigrants came from Pakistan out of a total of 1,946,361 immigrants from Asia.[25] It had not occurred to the sponsors of the 1965 Immigration Act and the government officials who supported it that Asians would take advantage of the new preference categories created for professionals by this legislation. Contrary to expectations, an unprecedented number of highly educated and skilled professional immigrants came from Asia with their families, as settlers, not as sojourners. Intending to establish roots in the United States, Asian-Indians were quick to acquire citizenship—50–60 percent became naturalized citizens by 1980.[26] This group then sponsored their family members who were exempt from the quota of 20,000 immigrants from each country in the Eastern Hemisphere (migrants from the Western Hemisphere were not subject to a quota at this time).[27]

Just as the early immigrants from the Indian subcontinent were overwhelmingly Punjabi, those who came after 1965 also included large numbers from the state of Punjab—an area that had been divided between independent India and the newly created country of East and West Pakistan in 1947. In fact, one-half of the 20,000 Pakistanis who came by 1970 were of Punjabi origin and, like the Asian-Indians, were urban professionals.[28] However, the bulk of the immigration from South Asia continues to be of Asian-Indian origin[29] and their numbers in the US have increased to approximately 815,447 as per the 1990 census. The second largest group of South Asians, of Pakistani origin, numbered 99,974 for the same period.[30] As the number of immigrants from India is significantly higher, the available census data addresses this sub-group of South Asians. Therefore, the comparative analysis I am able to provide is primarily limited to Asian-Indians. With all the South Asian groups increasing in size, perhaps more comparative data will be available in the 2000 census for all the sub-groups with this category.

As stated earlier, few South Asian women came to the United States before 1965. Although there were more women among the post-1965 immigrants, this group was still male-dominated especially in the 35–49 age bracket.[31] The women who did immigrate came primarily as spouses (74 percent of the Asian-Indian women who immigrated between 1980 and 1990 were married), even though they were educated in their own right (45 percent had a bachelors degree or higher) and, therefore, may have been able to apply through one of the preference categories for professional and skilled workers.[32]

Whereas the Koreans, Chinese and Vietnamese who came after 1965 have continued to form ethnic enclaves, this wave of Asian-Indians and Filipinos has scattered throughout the United States. Although they are not inclined towards ethnic communities, Asian-Indians have congregated in a few general areas. According to the 1990 census: 35 percent live in the Northeast; 24 percent live in the southern states; 18 percent live in the North Central or Midwest; and the remaining 23 percent live in the western states. The states with the highest number of Asian-Indians are: California with 159,973; New York with 140,985, New Jersey with 79,440; Illinois with 64,200; and Texas with 55,795. Asian-Indians (95 percent) prefer to live in urban areas which provide greater professional opportunities. This decision is also influenced by the process of chain migration. Other Asian-American groups have also expressed a strong preference for urban areas in comparison to the overall US population where 75 percent live in urban areas.[33]

A woman's perspective

While there are some scholarly works on the Asian-Indian immigrants from the early 1900s, little has been written on their social history. Except for a few essays and taped interviews, women immigrants have not been studied. However, this is changing as a greater acceptance of immigrant and non-immigrant ethnic expression has fostered an environment very different from that encountered by the early pioneers. Also, many Asian-American scholars are interested in researching and preserving the history of their ethnic roots in the United States.

The paucity of material on South Asian women can be directly linked to the fact that women have traditionally been excluded from historical accounts which have focused on the 'Great *Man* of History' premise, thereby writing women out of history. Furthermore, women have almost always been defined according to their relationship to men. In the eyes of traditional South Asian society, like many other societies, a woman is not a person in her own right; she is primarily her father's daughter, a wife or a mother. In addition, 'women's work'—often limited to the home for many women—has usually not been considered as important as a man's work. Women, therefore, did not make a contribution worthy of historical note and could simply be a footnote in *his*-tory. However, as the number of women in the social sciences increases, they are utilizing different methodologies, including life-histories, and different sources, such as women's diaries and letters,[34] which bring out women's voices and thereby, a different nuance to immigration history. We may soon find out what history would be like 'if it were seen through the eyes of women and ordered by the values they define'.[35]

As mentioned earlier, women have, for the most part, been written out of history. Feminist scholars, attempting to rectify the situation, are putting women 'back into history' in order to create a history of *human*kind. Gerda Lerner suggests that this can be accomplished in several ways: (*1*) by analyzing women's contributions in the same manner used for men's contributions; (*2*) a 'women-centered' perspective in which the focus is on experiences specific to women and; (*3*) a 'gender-integrated' history which combines male and female experiences.[36] This book will utilize a 'women-centered' focus with some 'gender-integrated' perspectives added to place the women's experiences. However, as this volume focuses on South Asian *women*, it is not a fully gender-integrated history of both sexes in the United States nor does it provide an extensive history of the South Asian immigrant experience.

In writing women back into history, it is not enough to merely add them to what has already been written. Different methodologies must be utilized as women's experiences differ from men and, therefore, their histories have to reflect this difference. Furthermore, the history of South Asian immigration cannot consist simply of the experiences of the male immigrants or of the female immigrants when they finally came to the United States. It must also include the social, political and economic constraints which prevented women from immigrating with the men who came at the turn of the century and for the first few decades of the 20th century. For the women immigrants who came post-1965 and were separated from their husbands for months or years, it is necessary to look at the effect the forced separation had on their lives. Did the separation from their husbands cause them to behave differently or experience things differently than the women who came with their husbands? Did immigration and the resettling process effect women's self-esteem, identity formation, or their familial relationships? It is important to integrate women and these issues into the current stories of male immigration in order to evaluate the effect of immigration on family dynamics and gender role socialization.

These issues cannot be effectively addressed without including feminist theory in the historical analysis. Sandra Harding has outlined three types of feminist epistemologies: feminist empiricism, feminist standpoint theory and feminist postmodernism.[37] Feminist empiricism, primarily used by researchers in biology and the social sciences, adds women to the existing research projects as it believes that 'both sexes have contributed to the evolution of our species'. Standpoint feminism states that there are many standpoints and that women's experiences cannot simply be placed next to those of men in order to present a 'complete' history. We also need to account for class, caste, race, gender, and religion when placing women's history. And finally, feminist postmodernism argues that there is no universalism among women and women cannot be spoken of in terms of a single homogeneous category. There is no *one* experience for women, Asian women, or South Asian women, even when they have regional, class or educational similarities, just as there is no *one* experience for mainstream American women. South Asian women who immigrated in the 1920s, 1940s, 1960s, and 1980s all have different experiences even within the context of being women immigrants from the same geographical area, for the areas they left and the country they came to were and are in a state of flux and change. This non-static environment shaped their experiences and, therefore, their histories must be considered within these expanded boundaries.

Insider/outsider perspective

All the women who contributed to this volume, except for Karen Leonard,[38] have the unique privilege/burden of being members of the cultural milieu which they are researching. This 'insider/outsider' status often provides easier access to individuals within the respective communities, access which may otherwise be very difficult to obtain, especially when dealing with culturally sensitive issues. I have found that individuals I approach are usually receptive to my inquiries and often eagerly support my research. However, this access does come with a price-tag. South Asian women researchers, whether academic or journalistic, are expected to understand and participate in the cultural nuances of the South Asian communities and to present their data in a way that does not embarrass their cultural peers. They are also viewed by their communities as agents of change—either positive or negative—depending on their subject matter and their analysis and presentation of their data. This can be a difficult position and one which women researchers, especially those working within their own ethnic communities, constantly struggle to manage. Although some scholars believe that researchers should not work within their own communities as their work may be biased, Sociologist Kathleen Gerson states that while 'we cannot completely set aside our personal experiences, even in pursuit of understanding the experiences of others, we are not prisoners of them either. The power of social science analysis is that it allows us to find answers that stand on their own, apart from the predilections of those who seek them.'[39]

Overview of the volume

There was so much interest generated in the community by the South Asian Women's Conference (an international conference which provides a forum for the discussion of issues relevant to South Asian women globally) which prompted this volume that I received an overwhelming number of submissions. The idea of discussing identity formation, adaptation, and acculturation within the South Asian family, and specifically as these issues apply to women, has struck a chord with many individuals. It was a difficult task to select 11 pieces from the many that were submitted. After reviewing each article, the decision was made to tackle the above mentioned issues from a variety of perspectives in order to reach the widest possible audience. I, therefore, decided to incorporate pieces that do not fit into the typical 'academic' category. While some may feel that a multi-disciplinary, multi-generational and multi-perspective volume results in a hodgepodge, I believe that these different viewpoints give a more complete picture of the experiences of these South Asian women. For, as the title of this volume indicates, these voices are finally emerging and it is evident that they all have something important to say. In fact, the non-academic pieces directly connect the reader with some of the data revealed in the more traditionally academic articles. Although it is important to have trained academics conduct research, analyze and report their findings, it is equally important to discover how South Asian women perceive and define themselves. Their voices also need to be heard if we are to understand these communities in a more meaningful way. It is important to find out how these women negotiate personal boundaries which many have found exist too close for comfort, or sometimes, do not exist at all. Therefore, to present a fuller picture, the normative perspective is combined with an 'objective' one in this volume.

The multi-generational approach also strengthens this volume as it enables the reader to see how viewpoints may change over time and provides various perspectives from which to view these groups of women. For it is not only the younger generation who experience issues of identity formation as they live in a dominant culture which differs significantly from their own, but also the women of my mother's generation. These immigrant women grew up in South Asia with a strong female network, married, and then found themselves not only in an alien country thousands of miles away from everything familiar to them, but also without those female connections they had always relied upon. Their relationships with their husbands took on a new dimension as they adapted to and built a nuclear family and raised their children in a world of often bewildering change. Simple things they had always taken for granted became complicated. For example, cooking an Indian meal when the required spices were almost impossible to find. How many of these women, like my mother, initially relied on packets from their families back 'home' which contained these necessary ingredients? How many women, used to wearing the enveloping South Asian garments, grappled with the sometimes much more revealing Western attire? What did they learn about themselves as they tried to explain South Asian customs, especially the ever-fascinating and often exoticized topic of arranged marriages, to their neighbors and colleagues? How did they balance their ever-expanding professional opportunities with their responsibilities at home? How did their husbands adjust to these sometimes rapid and possibly disturbing changes taking place in their previously more predictable partners? Were the husbands an asset or a hindrance as these women redefined themselves? Were social mores being changed and if so, how did all these players react? And equally important, what did these women pass on to their daughters? And their sons? Did their experiences influence or change the second generation? Did these women in fact change? Or did they attempt to recreate the India of their childhood in their own homes and pass on those values to the next generation? These and other questions arose from the research and soul-searching which took place in, and as a result of, the articles in this volume. Due to the insider/outsider perspective of many of the authors in this volume, conducting the research, and evaluating their findings and writing the essays often triggered an introspective analysis of their own bicultural lives.

The thread that ties these pieces together is that many South Asian women, either as researchers or the subjects of research, are searching for what may be an elusive goal, they are searching for an identity. They are asking themselves, 'who are they'? What does being South Asian mean to them? Are they South Asians, Americans or are they South Asian Americans and what does this mean to them? And is being a South Asian woman v. a South Asian man a different experience? If so, how? The vast majority of the women encountered in this volume are on the road of self-discovery, some further along than others, some on it reluctantly and some forging ahead. What ties these women together is the South Asian culture. And although there is no 'one' culture, there are enough similarities so that many women feel a bond, of varying depth, with other South Asian women. Certainly class adds another dimension as Sabah Aafreen's essay in this volume tells us. Religion is another differentiating factor as both Aafreen's and Lubna Chaudhry's pieces reveal. But, beyond that, there is a consciousness of facing a society similar in many ways in that it, often, does not give women the same access to the full range of opportunities which are usually available to the male members of the same socio-economic population. South Asian society and culture is, without a doubt, male-dominated.

This is at the core of the struggles these women face as they search for their identities and for a place in their communities—a place which does not stifle them. How often do women hold something back when they interact with South Asian males or elders in the community? It is almost a game that is played, one all women know about: 'Don't be too bold.' 'Don't state your needs in a firm tone.' 'Don't question too much.' 'Accept.' Accept is a word many South Asian women are familiar with as in 'accept your place'. The women who have written and are written about in this collection are challenging that 'place' they have been told to accept. They are pushing the boundaries of those roles that have been laid out for them. Some pushing more than others. Some challenging more than others. Some accepting more than others. This very diversity in how they define themselves, or how they proceed on their journey is what makes South Asian women dynamic and their identities fluid. This flux comes through in the pieces in this volume. These women's lives are not static, they are in motion and that makes these pieces exciting, insightful, and challenging.

As stated earlier, the path to adulthood for children of South Asian descent living in the US is difficult as they attempt to juggle various ways of being. This point is illustrated in Kauser Ahmed's chapter based on her research among South Asian adolescent girls. Ahmed's chapter reveals that these young girls do want to integrate both their American and South Asian selves—in fact, their self-esteem is higher when they are able to do so. Ahmed states that 'South Asian American girls find the negotiation of relationships between their parents and the outside world to be one of the most difficult aspects of their bicultural lives'. Not surprisingly, Ahmed also found that 'their greatest need. . .was for more open and constructive communication. . .about dating and marriage'.

In Sabah Aafreen's autobiographical essay, a different voice emerges— one that is rarely heard. It is the voice of a lower-middle-class illegal immigrant from India. Aafreen's essay took several forms as this book came together. She began with a defiant voice determined to tell all, then fear of religious retaliation and of shaming her family silenced her voice. Finally, what has emerged is a tentative reaching out as the reader is given access to her struggles, fears and dreams as Aafreen grows up in the US, rebels against an arranged marriage and quietly leaves home to pursue an education which she believed would set her free to determine her own destiny.

The next chapter examines Asian-Indian graduate student views on gender roles. Lalita Subrahmanyan interviewed 11 men and 11 women who had recently come to the US and found that, not surprisingly, the men expressed their preferences for more traditional gender roles whereas the women expressed a desire for gender roles which would allow for more lifestyle options for women—in other words, less traditional gender roles. Interestingly enough, the men believed that the traditional arranged marriage system resulted in more stable marriages whereas the women felt that self-arranged marriages were the answer. Women's paid employment outside the home was another area of contention and confusion. These first generation women were more tentative in their expectations of male participation than the predominantly 1.5 and second generation women in my own study on dating and marriage patterns who expected their partners to share fully 50 percent of all household responsibilities. These graduate students, in some of their observations regarding the Indian and the American family, are expressing polarized views of what they imagine these family systems to be by constructing an 'other' and a self. In doing this, they are presenting an ideal or a myth of the Indian family—a homogeneous reality which they position against their construct of the American family.[40]

A former foreign graduate student herself, Lubna Chaudhry's essay is a personal account which will elicit a response from most South Asian women. Her example of how she feels differently in South Asian attire, as these outfits evoke different boundaries, both for herself and in others, is a common experience for many. Chaudhry's life is that of a cultural hybrid. She lives within several worlds, sometimes on the periphery of one or more, sometimes at their intersection, and sometimes in the midst of one, yet never fully in one as there is usually a level of awareness of other realities. This existence, one many of us share, can be difficult at times. She questions borders in general, between the sexes, generations, nations, or between different realities in one person. It is a thought-provoking piece from which the reader will take away something different each time it is read.

Many readers will also find the conversations in R. Kamna Narain's chapter very familiar. The constant subtle—and sometimes, not so subtle—pressure that South Asian women feel to get married can be observed as we 'eavesdrop' on the frank discussions which take place among the women in this chapter. Having observed and participated in similar discussions among South Asian women in various parts of the country, these statements evoke a feeling of déjà vu. South Asian women are pressured from an early age (usually 21–22) regarding marriage and the number of people doing the pressuring and its intensity increases with each passing birthday. As Narain points out, even if the parents are comfortable with their daughter marrying at a later age, family friends and relatives manage to constantly bring it up. So many people get involved that, at times, it appears to be a community project! It is not surprising then, that Asian-Indian women in the US have the highest rate of early marriages among all Asian-American groups. In the 20–24-year-old category, 60 percent of Asian-Indian women are married compared to 50 percent of Korean and 20 percent of Chinese and Japanese women. Asian-Indian males also marry early. In fact, the overall number of marriages in the Asian-Indian (and Korean) communities are higher than those in any other Asian-American group.[41]

While the marital process is discussed openly, one route to finding a partner, dating, is often a topic avoided by many families. Karen Leonard's chapter, 'The Management of Desire', examines the secrecy surrounding some South Asian social relationships with members of the opposite sex. While it is generally known that a large percentage of young South Asians conceal their premarital romantic relationships from their parents, Leonard brings to light the fact that some of these individuals are taking secrecy much further. They are concealing actual marriages and even children. Leonard states that these individuals 'trust in themselves as agents, as makers of their own destinies', a surprising finding in a community where many young women (and men) bow to parental and community pressure in matrimonial matters. While, as Leonard states, the sample group is very small and not systematically studied—although much can be learned from casual conversations—her research provides some interesting data on a topic that should certainly be pursued.

To continue on the subject of dating and marriage patterns among the 1.5 and second generation of South Asian Americans, we turn next to my own paper. The fact that many women in these communities feel tremendous pressure to get married and that this pressure can sometimes lead to secrecy and deception has been discussed in detail in the previous two pieces. This chapter focuses on what Indian-American women feel about the institution of marriage itself and how it fits into their vision of their own future. If and when they are given a choice, what would they want in a dating and/or a marriage partner? How many of them are sexually active in a culture that frowns on premarital sex? How do they feel about the infamous 'second shift' and the taboo subject of divorce? The women in this research project are single and are describing what they want in a present or future relationship. In the next chapter, Sudha

Sethu Balagopal examines how South Asian wives and mothers are actually negotiating Arlie Hochschild's 'second shift'. The 'double-duty day' is a phenomena common to the vast majority of women who work outside the home or have a career within the home in addition to being wives and mothers regardless of cultural, racial, or national boundaries. Studies indicate that 'men's family involvement has not kept pace with women's increasing commitment to paid employment' and also that married men have two–three hours more leisure time *per day* than married women.[42] South Asian women, like other women, negotiate household responsibilities from various positions within their marital homes. According to Sethu Balagopal, the division of labor 'hinges on whether the Indian husband accepts these changes and whether the Indian wife enforces these changes'. A woman's position appears to be strengthened by her earning potential and also by her mother-in-law's own work history. Men whose own mothers worked outside the home appear to be more comfortable taking on household responsibilities and child care. These findings concur with those of studies conducted among the mainstream US population where Gerson found that 'women's economic resources give them the leverage to insist that men parent more'. They are also supported by the findings of a 1996 *India Today*–MARG study conducted in Mumbai, Calcutta, Hyderabad and Lucknow which states that with 12 percent of urban women in the workforce, men are increasingly expected to participate in child care. However, the study also notes that while Indian men are happy with the increased income, they resent the increasing independence of their wives and the eroding of their decision-making powers.[43]

Mantosh Singh Devji targets another area of South Asian marriages in her research, marital sexuality. In very candid discussions, South Asian women openly state their feelings and experiences of what goes on behind the proverbial closed door. Sexuality, premarital or marital, is a difficult topic for South Asian communities to openly discuss. The women in this chapter are not recalcitrant about their sexual experiences and some are very verbal as to the 'shortcomings' of their husbands in this area. Although some will undoubtedly dismiss their words as 'male-bashing', it is my hope that readers will look beyond the anger some of these women express and the 'blame' they lay at men's doors, and use these stories as a clear indication that an open and honest dialogue on this topic is long overdue.

My second piece in this volume utilizes case studies to examine the subject of divorce in the Asian-Indian and Indian-American communities and how these women continue to rebuild their lives after their hopes and dreams have been shattered, often brutally. As difficult as it is for South Asian communities to acknowledge the existence of divorce, it is an issue that must be faced as 3.2 percent of Asian-Indian women (and 2.9 percent of men) are separated or divorced according to Ghasarian and Levin's analysis of the 1990 census. A further breakdown reveals a higher rate of divorce among American-born Asian-Indians, for both men and women.[44] These figures follow the findings of the 1980 Census which reported that 6.0 percent of the overall Asian-Indian population was divorced and 1.6 percent separated. However, only 2.4 percent and 2.2 percent of those who immigrated between 1975 and 1980 were divorced or separated, respectively. In comparison, 15.6 percent and 3.5 percent of the second generation Indian-Americans were divorced or separated, respectively. It should be noted that the second generation of Indian-Americans had the highest divorce rate of all native-born Asian-Americans.[45] The beginning of a dialogue on divorce will benefit many individuals who often feel stigmatized and isolated at a time when they are in need of understanding and support.

The subject of divorce continues with a personal account from Pooja who shares her story in a frank and moving essay in which she does not look back but focuses on the life ahead of her. Pooja grew up in the United States, went through an arranged marriage, and tried to exist in a mentally and physically abusive relationship. This story of hope and triumph over severe adversity shows that there is life after a tragic marriage. She shares her story with the hope that other women will see that they too can leave an unhappy home, rebuild their lives, and be happy.

The last chapter, by Anannya Bhattacharjee, examines the construction of 'the Asian-Indian community' in the United States. She discusses how women, an integral part of this construction, are also defined and limited by it. As one of the founders of Sakhi, an organization for South Asian women, Bhattacharjee states that Sakhi is viewed as challenging this construction and, therefore, members are labeled as 'homebreakers' when they expose abuse against women. She believes that, for the community, 'any challenge to the family or the Indian community translates. . .into a betrayal of national cultural values'.

It was my intention, at the beginning of this project, to produce a volume which would include chapters on women from all parts of South Asia. Unfortunately, this was not possible as the articles submitted, although numerous, were overwhelmingly on the Asian-Indian population. In fact, articles were only submitted from those individuals of either Asian-Indian or Pakistani origin. It is my hope that future works will be more inclusive.

❧ Notes and References

1. Those immigrating at a very young age are generally referred to as the 1.5 or 'knee-high generation' while those born in the US are the second generation. I will use second generation to refer to both these groups.

2. Bruce La Brack, *The Sikhs of Northern California, 1904–1975* (New York, AMS Press, 1988), 17.

3. Rajani Kanta Das, *Hindustani Workers on the Pacific Coast* (Berlin, Walter De Gruyter & Co., 1923), 109.

4. The first group came from an undivided Punjab and the second from a divided one. This is an important distinction as the joy over independence was tempered with the agony of partition and some immigrants brought these feelings with them to Northern California and inter-community relations were ultimately affected.

5. Christian Ghasarian and Michael Levin, *Asian Indians in the United States* (an unpublished manuscript, 1996), 68.

6. La Brack, 57. See n. 2.

7. James C. Chadney, 'Sikh Family Patterns and Ethnic Adaptation in Vancouver', *AmerAsia Journal* 7(1), Spring 1980, 32.

8. Hugh Johnson, *The Voyage of the Komagata Maru: The Sikh Challenge to Canada's Color Bar* (New Delhi, Oxford University Press, 1979), 4.

9. Joan Jensen, *Passage From India: Asian Indian Immigrants in North America* (New Haven, Yale University Press, 1988), 60 & 76; Chadney, 32. See n. 7.

10. La Brack. See n. 2.

11. Das, 22. See n. 3.

12. Das, 16. See n. 3.

13. Proceedings of the Asiatic Exclusion League, San Francisco, April 1910, p. 223 as quoted in Ronald Takaki, *Strangers From a Different Shore* (Boston, Little, Brown, 1989), 298.

14. Bruce La Brack, 'Occupational Specialization Among Rural California Sikhs: The Interplay of Culture and Economics', *AmerAsia Journal* 9, 1982, 29–56.

15. Gary Hess, 'The Asian Indian Immigrants in the United States: The Early Phase, 1900–65', *Population Review* 25, December-January 1981, 31; Jensen, 260. See n. 9.

16. Jensen, 259. See n. 9.

17. Jensen, 269. See n. 9.

18. As quoted in Takaki, 298. See n. 13.

19. Interviews with Norma Samra (daughter), Paul Samra (son) and Steven Samra (grandson) conducted by the author on 17 August 1996, Elk Grove, CA. Also from interview with William Moscher (Jr.) on 12 February 1998, Elk Grove, CA.

20. Hess, 33. See n. 15.

21. Takaki, 83. See n. 13.

22. Takaki, 406. See n. 13.

23. Takaki, 419. See n. 13.
24. Herbert Barringer, Robert W. Gardner and Michael J. Levin, *Asians and Pacific Islanders in the United States* (New York, Russell Sage Foundation, 1995), 20.
25. Barringer et al., 25–26. See n. 24.
26. Takaki, 445. See n. 13.
27. Takaki, 406–20. See n. 13.
28. Takaki, 445. See n. 13.
29. In the 1980 Census, the respondents who listed themselves as South Asian by ethnicity were: Asian-Indian—387, 223; Pakistani—15, 792; Bangladeshi—1,314 and; Sri Lankans—2,923. Peter Xenos, Herbert Barringer and Michael J. Levin, 'Asian Indians in the United States: A 1980 Census Profile', Papers of the East-West Population Institute; Number 111, July 1980, 6 and Ghasarian and Levin, 22. See n. 5.
30. Ghasarian and Levin, 27. See n. 5.
31. Xenos et al., 99. See n. 29.
32. Ghasarian and Levin, 68. See n. 5.
33. Ghasarian and Levin, 28. See n. 5.
34. Letters from immigrants have been used by historians to document the experiences of the ordinary working person 'to gain some knowledge of the inner social history. . . , of the motives and ways of looking at their world of people who did not lead armies or governments or business firms, but who participated in the greatest movement of people the world has ever known'. C. Erickson, *Invisible Immigrants: The Adaptation of English and Scottish Immigrants in 19th-century America* (London, London School of Economics and Political Science, Weidenfeld and Nicolson, 1971), 1.
35. Gerda Lerner, *The Majority Finds its Past: Placing Women in History* (New York, Oxford University Press, 1979), 168.
36. Lerner. See n. 35.
37. Sandra Harding (ed.), *Feminism and Modernism: Social Science Issues* (Bloomington, Indiana University Press, 1987).
38. As a long-time scholar of the South Asian community, I would argue that Karen Leonard has also encountered the insider/outsider situation when conducting her research.
39. Kathleen Gerson, *No Man's Land: Men's Changing Commitments to Family and Work* (New York, Basic Books, 1993), 12.
40. Benedict Anderson, *Imagined Communities* (London, Verso, revised edition 1991).
41. Barringer et al., 141. See n. 24.
42. Gerson, 5. See n. 39.
43. Gerson, 288 (See n. 39) and Madhu Jain, 'A Search for Intimacy', *India Today*, 31 December 1996, 78–85.
44. Ghasarian and Levin, 53. See n. 5.
45. Barringer et al., 140. See n. 24.

Part I

Redefining Self

1

Adolescent development for South Asian American girls

Kauser Ahmed

The developmental experiences of South Asian and American girls provide important perspectives in understanding the process of integrating American, South Asian,[1] and female identity development. The period of adolescence, in particular, presents unique challenges to these young women. They seek to understand themselves in the contexts of differing and often contradictory cultural imperatives of who they are and who they should be. While adolescent identity exploration can be filled with anxiety as well as exhilaration for women in this society, it holds specific complexities for girls in an immigrant community. Young adolescent girls struggle not only to locate themselves in the landscapes of two cultures, they must contend as well with the particular place of women within those cultures and the impact of multiple forms of biases that are experienced by women of color in the US.

In examining issues related to adolescent development, researchers frequently use the concept of the adolescent's identity, or *self*, as an organizing framework. This concept refers to components of the self, such as self-esteem, self-image, and various other individual attributes. It has also been used as a reference point for exploring how the self operates in other systems, such as the organization of individual identity in the context of relationships. Therefore, in order to understand the process of identity development and adolescence for South Asian American girls, it may be useful to first explore the different ways in which individual identity is constructed in American and South

Asian cultures—in particular, the critical understanding of the self as an autonomous and socially independent being in Western culture and that of the self as part of a larger familial and cultural system within South Asian culture.[2]

Western societies, the United States in particular, are based on principles that valorize the individual. At multiple layers within the society, there is expressed a strong emphasis on the preservation of individual rights, creation of forums for individual self-expression, and at core, a belief in individuals' freedom to construct their own self-definitions. These definitions may rely on the individuals' choices in vocation, personal interests, political affiliation, as well as, or more importantly than, his/her family background or religion. By contrast, the focus of South Asian society is not on the individual and his/her unique rights, rather it is focused on promoting individuals' responsibilities to their communities. Individual identities within South Asian culture are principally defined by the individual's place within a specific social context. This context consists of both the individual's role within the family as well as the status of the family within the larger community.[3]

The roles that individuals inhabit, then, are critical to their own understanding of who they are and their function within their familial and social context.[4] Family relationships reflect the hierarchical and relatively rigid structure of the society. Those in subordinate positions have obligations of obedience and respect to those above them, while those in positions of power are equally duty-bound to protect and care for those they are responsible for. Roles, both familial and social, are closely scripted and detail the nature of the behaviors and attitudes that are expected of each person in relation to others.

Thus, the South Asian self, like its American counterpart, is grounded in the values of the culture in which it exists. While American culture is invested in the exploration and safeguarding of individual experience, South Asian cultures have a similar investment in the incorporation of individual experiences into the fabric of the whole community.

To further examine developmental issues in adolescence for South Asian American women, we will explore the adolescent period with respect to the self and various self-related concepts. We will begin by examining important cultural and early developmental processes that shape the adolescent period, as well as looking at how the self functions in relationships during adolescence and beyond. Following this, we will look at several important components of the adolescent self, including self-expression or *voice*, attractiveness, and academic achievement. Finally, we will examine some factors which have recently been researched as possible facilitators of the adolescent development of South Asian American women. Throughout, we will compare the similarities and differences of the experiences for American and South Asian women, and look specifically at the impact of these issues for South Asian American girls.

Early developmental and cultural issues

Some of the differences in how individual identities are constructed in the two cultures are reflected in the expectations for development from earliest childhood onward. Broadly, the developmental tasks for individuals in Western culture stress increasing mastery over environment and movement towards greater autonomy from a primary 'caregiver'. These developmental expectations are consistent with the ideals for individuals in Western culture: that they be independent and motivated to define their own identity, and that they develop the capacity to form and disengage from relationships with a specific other. From early childhood on, young children in the United States are taught to be self-reliant and expected to be accountable for their behavior. They are weaned, toilet-trained and disciplined earlier than children in South Asia. It is proposed that the task of parenting in the United States is to provide structure and boundaries early in life such that a child develops his/her own sense of competency and confidence in decision-making.

By contrast, the South Asian sense of self is one strongly connected to his/her familial network and is primarily driven not to satisfy individual urges but to accommodate those urges within the needs of the group. The very young in South Asian culture are indulged and pampered well past infancy. For example, children continue to be fed by hand and are groomed by caregivers long past toddlerhood. It has been proposed that not only do South Asian children remain dependent on adult 'caregiving' longer than Western children do, they are also exposed to multiple caregivers.[5] These include aunts and grandmothers who not only provide mothering to the child, but in some sense, prevent an exclusive attachment between mother and child; ultimately, discouraging any strong individual attachments that would supersede loyalty to the group. It is this combination of dependence and diffusion of attachments which sets the stage for the development of a more collectivist, mutable sense of self that is typical of South Asian identity. Thus, the primary attachment in adulthood, as well, is to a group identity first, and second to a cultivation of individual desires or individual relationships. It is within these broad parameters that the tasks of adolescence, or preparation for adulthood, take place within both cultures.

The stage of adolescence

Adolescence, like all developmental phenomena, occurs within the larger social–structural and cultural environment. The process is influenced by the values, attitudes, and expectations particular to that environment.

The hallmark of adolescence in American culture, for both boys and girls, has traditionally been defined as the process of separation from parents and family towards achieving a sense of individuality.[6] American adolescents use this period of development to experiment with changing vocational aspirations, socialize with new peer groups and explore romantic relationships. All these activities are understood as part of a larger process of understanding themselves. Adolescence serves as a period of accommodation on the part of both the individual and the family to the young person's growing needs for emancipation and for renegotiating the terms on which connections between the adolescent and the family can be maintained. While parents of American adolescents may wish to guide them in the choices that they make, it is with the understanding that ultimately, their adolescents have increasing responsibility, not to the parents or the family, but for themselves. The adolescent and young adult must do the work, herself, of deciding who she will be.

In contrast, the phenomenon of adolescence as a period of experimentation and rebellion, may be considered artifactual in South Asian culture for both genders. To South Asian parents, the concept of their offspring 'needing to find themselves' would be difficult to understand. Within the South Asian cultural understanding, identity is already defined by the relationships that exist within the family and the larger cultural community. In traditional South Asian households, the shift from childhood to adulthood is not about the business of separation or individuation. Rather, it is about the clarification of one's many roles within the family and the acceptance of greater responsibility for one's place within that structure.

How then during this time of transition, do young South Asian Americans and their parents balance the different cultural demands that face them? During adolescence, young South Asian Americans have increasing contact with the world outside of the family and experience greater influences from their peer cultures as well as a greater desire to be accepted by their peers. Within certain contexts, such as at school or while socializing with American friends, they experience a pull to define themselves in terms that conform to American cultural norms of dress, language, and attitudes. At the same time, these adolescents feel a powerful demand within the family to retain traditional South Asian behaviors and values.

South Asian parents hope that their offspring can function in the American culture as they do, that is, by adopting appropriately American behaviors and attitudes within the workplace, but retaining a core sense of themselves as South Asian.[7] For their daughters and sons growing to adulthood in this culture, however, the demands to act American without incorporating any American values and ideals is neither realistic nor feasible.

The issues discussed thus far relate to adolescent development for both boys and girls. However, certain issues specifically impact the development of girls. For example, when young girls in South Asia begin adolescence, which coincides with the onset of puberty, they begin undertaking adult responsibilities and roles. Starting from this point, girls give up the relative freedom they have enjoyed and begin to observe the restrictions in movement, dress, and behavior that typify the lives of women in South Asian culture. South Asian girls come into a world in which, from birth, their status is lower than that of males. Boys are perceived to be the future caretakers of parents in their old age and prized as such. Girls, on the other hand, are understood to be temporary members of their own families—their primary roles and responsibilities will be as wives, daughters-in-law, and mothers in the families that they are married into.[8] And while male children carry the aspirations of the family, it is daughters who are the repositories of the family's honor or *izzat*. Their modesty in speech and behavior must be beyond reproach and it is their duty to ensure that no hint of scandal is introduced by their actions. Among the behaviors that can be deemed 'immodest' are included: talking too much, laughing loudly, or, in general, failing to be appropriately demure.

Sudhir Kakar, a prominent Indian psychologist who studies development, argues that young boys by the age of six are made to break from the comfort of maternal attention and closeness in order to learn how to take their place among men.[9] South Asian girls, according to Kakar, are not removed from the intimacy of female caregivers. Their lives remain within this matrix of female connectedness and it is under the tutelage of their mothers, aunts, and other female relatives that they prepare for the future roles that they will play in their husband's home.

Similar ideas are echoed in the work of American psychologist, Nancy Chodorow, in defining the unique paths of female identity development in the United States.[10] She, like Kakar, suggests that boys in the American culture are forced to separate from their primary relationship with their mothers and consequently focus on developing independence from others and autonomy. She argues that because this vital separation does not occur for girls, they continue to define themselves through their relationship with their mother, and continue to value their connections to others more than they cultivate their sense of autonomy.

Chodorow and other feminist developmentalists argue that what has been posited as the 'universal' experience of adolescence, that of individuation and mastery, is specific to Western male development and is neither universal for individuals in other cultures nor for females within this culture. According to these psychologists, American women and girls experience their 'selves' not primarily in terms of distinctness from others but within the context of important relationships with others.[11] In this respect, some of the forces that shape the lives of girls, such as the importance of relationships to self-identity, are similar in the United States and South Asia, although they may differ in how overtly or subtly they are expressed.

The self in relationships

While investment in important relationships is of significance in the lives of women in both cultures, the different assumptions that such relationships are negotiated on reflect differences between the cultures. American relationships are, in the ideal, mutually contracted and mutually designed to meet the needs of both individuals. They operate on the assumption that the relationship is an extension of the partners but does not define either person, and for that reason, each is free to terminate the relationship if it does not satisfy his or her needs. For South Asian women, relationships are set within the context of the hierarchical social structure and are defined by its rules. Each individual seeks to understand and accommodate to the specific requirements of her roles within the social and familial structure. Roles defined by the family, such as the role of daughter or wife, are closely scripted and call for very specific behaviors and responsibilities on the part of each individual and these would not vary regardless of the unique attributes of the individuals inhabiting the role or the specific nature of the relationship.[12]

Thus, an American woman comes to inhabit her 'role' as a wife by first developing a relationship with a man who she feels fits her needs as a husband. Together, they decide how they will negotiate their relationship when it becomes a marriage. It is this negotiation of the relationship that is primary and the role, and the cultural or societal expectations associated with it, secondary. By contrast, a South Asian woman becomes a 'wife' not first by virtue of the relationship she and her partner share, but because of the cultural expectations of one occupying that role. Even if she and her husband have just met, the cultural script guides them in the expectations of marriage and of each other. Only later does a relationship that is unique to the two of them emerge.

Over the course of their lifetimes, Americans exercise tremendous freedom in the management of close relationships, both familial and romantic. While relationships are certainly important to Americans, they are extensions of a core self. In contrast to the flexibility of American relationships, South Asian relationships are tightly restricted. Relationships in South Asian culture establish or preserve kinship and are thus undertaken with great gravity. Preserving the stability of the system, both familial and societal, is a critical responsibility for all its members, as is the imperative to refrain from any actions or desires that jeopardize that stability. In this respect, individuals make few decisions, particularly those related to relationships, that are not strongly influenced by family considerations.[13]

Within both cultures, women give priority to nurturing relationships and assume responsibility for their success or failure. There are rewards and costs to this investment. Euro-American women in the United States often report that sustaining satisfying relationships with family members, friends, and romantic partners is a deep source of personal happiness. South Asian culture values women in their roles as mothers and wives and the women themselves draw strength, during adolescence and adulthood, through strong connections with other female family members. Yet the risks for women in relationships include letting go of the right to express their own wants or grievances for the sake of maintaining smooth relations and caretaking of others at the expense of their own needs. American relational psychologists argue that it is not the cultivation of a self that is invested in relationships that is detrimental to women, rather, it is the inability to leave relationships that are harmful that ultimately places women at risk.

Components of the adolescent self

While there are certainly many components which make up the adolescent self, there are several which have specific relevance for South
Asian American females. These include self-expression, attractiveness,
and academic achievement.

Self-concept and self-expression

One phenomenon specific to adolescent girls' development identified
by American developmental psychologist Carol Gilligan[14] is the process
by which girls are taught patriarchal expectations of a 'good woman'.
These expectations include that a woman should be quiet, unassuming,
and lacking in strong opinions that place her in conflict with others.
Gilligan refers to the process by which young girls lose the freedom and
self-confidence that characterizes childhood in exchange for hesitance
and self-doubt as 'loss of voice'. Gilligan and her colleagues implicate
this lack of 'voice', of a woman's sense of ownership of her own life
and thoughts, in women's greater susceptibility to depression and other
forms of emotional distress.[15]

Some parallels can be drawn between this process and the experience
of South Asian girls during puberty, when young girls are taught the importance of modesty, reticence, and obedience in the lives of women.[16]
Young girls are repeatedly reminded of their need to cultivate *sharam* or
shame in order to safeguard the good name of the family. Specifically
with regard to plans for a young girls' marital future, it is high praise of
a girl and of her family that she be able to say, 'I have no opinion about
the selection of my husband; I completely trust in the judgment of my
parents'.

South Asian American girls live with the pressures to conform to
both sets of relational ideals. Just at the time that adolescent girls in the
United States are launching into the world outside of the family, prepar-
ing for new experiences and developing new relationships, the lives of
South Asian girls are beginning to contract inward into the safety of
the family and crystallize around the roles laid out before them. During adolescence, girls in mainstream America explore new, alternative
relationships outside of the family. Such experiences, particularly the
exploration of dating relationships, are perceived to be integral to the
process of becoming an adult. By contrast, South Asian American girls

typically, are not encouraged to establish strong relationships outside of the family and are actively discouraged from pursuing any interactions that could be construed as romantic. The development of ties between individuals who are not sanctioned by her family are a threat to the integrity of the family unit. The efforts to restrict girls' contact with outside relationships reflects the tremendous concern South Asian parents have with keeping their daughters pure from cultural contamination. The preservation of their daughters' traditional values represents the preservation of the family's own cultural connections.

South Asian American girls find the negotiation of relationships between their parents and the outside world to be one of the most difficult aspects of their bicultural lives. While they love and respect their parents and wish to honor their values, they also find it vital to learn and grow in contexts that would not be sanctioned by their families. In her role as a 'good daughter', a young woman may be called upon to be dutiful and obedient with parents as well as mindful of the expectations of a South Asian female in her interactions with others outside the family. In this way, the definition of a good daughter extends beyond that which takes place within the immediate relationship to encompass how the adolescent represents herself, and by extension, her family, within the world.

In trying to compartmentalize their experiences of being South Asian and American, young women sometimes live two different and separate lives and engage in relationships that are kept hidden from their families. Girls who do attempt to manage both worlds describe living with constant guilt and a sense of fracture in their lives—a feeling that neither their American activities nor their connections with their families provide a space in which they can feel whole.

Attractiveness

A second area of risk for young girls involves the preoccupation with attractiveness and weight as measures of self worth. One of the most important purveyors of gender socialization is through the value that is placed on appearance in many societies. Although it is a societal value that applies to boys as well as to girls, studies have shown that adolescent girls are particularly at risk for developing low self-esteem as they and others evaluate their physical appearance.[17] Girls and women have distorted body images that are based on highly unrepresentative and yet seemingly omnipresent standards of physical beauty. The pressure to conform to such standards can be implicated not only in lower self-esteem in girls but also the development of eating disorders, which are often maladaptive attempts by the girls to retain some control over their lives in the face of societal expectations.

The ideal feminine beauty that is prevalent in South Asian culture focuses as well on the lightness of skin color. Despite the overt rejection of Western values in South Asia, there remains a strain of internalized racism particularly centered around color, with lighter skin clearly favored. For South Asian American girls, pressures to meet unattainable standards of physical beauty can come not only from the dominant culture but from expectations internalized within their own community.

The concentration of energy and attention on the physical attributes of women reflects the objectification of women in both cultures. While South Asian girls are taught that their bodies are inherently dangerous and must be contained and concealed, American culture stresses the importance of promoting one's attractiveness. The emphasis within the culture on the freedom of each individual to be one's own creation promotes the belief that each woman could and should, through effort and ingenuity, embody the ideal of feminine attractiveness. The failure to do so is in some sense a failure to create an acceptable self. South Asian American girls growing up in the United States are exposed to both of these competing and contradictory messages about their own physicality. In addition to the important and difficult task of negotiating relationships with others, South Asian American girls must also come to a healthy relationship with their own bodies.

Academic achievement

Lastly, in the area of academic achievement, it is not clear how their bicultural experiences impact South Asian American girls. The school environment is one of the arenas where American girls have experienced the 'loss of their voices'. As girls begin to doubt how much female achievement is valued within the society, and whether achievement, in fact, compromises feminine identity, their trust in their own capacity to succeed in the world is diminished. But it is not clear how this phenomenon impacts South Asian American girls, who are simultaneously exposed to the cultural messages within the dominant society as well as the values presented at home. While it is questionable how much 'voice' adolescent girls feel that they have within their home environments, it is true that South Asian immigrant culture valorizes scholastic achievement for both genders. Young girls, in fact, are encouraged to adapt to the expectations of the school environment and to succeed in that setting. In this respect, South Asian American girls may find the scholastic environment to be one in which they are freer to be assertive, to speak and act for themselves. It may be the case that South Asian American girls have greater confidence within the school environment because they come to read situational cues and contexts and recognize which contexts provide room and support for certain behaviors. They may use this arena to experiment with different ways of being than are acceptable at home, where daughters in particular are expected to be dutiful and obedient.

However, not all South Asian American girls can adapt or achieve to the extent that their families may wish. Within South Asian American communities, parents engage in social comparison of their children's achievements and adolescents feel a great deal of pressure to bring honor to their families through their successes.[18]

Facilitating factors

Despite the turmoil experienced during this transition, many young South Asian American women express pride in their heritage and a desire to retain connections to the religious and cultural traditions within their community. What then are some factors that facilitate the adolescent process for young South Asian American girls?

In a recent survey of South Asian American adolescents, over 75 percent of the subjects described themselves as wanting ideally to integrate their American and South Asian identities. And of the subjects surveyed, those who had the highest sense of self-esteem and experienced the least feelings of depression were those who indeed did feel successful in combining their dual identities. The study also showed that parents played a critical role in the kinds of values that their adolescents adopted: adolescents whose parents expressed support for them, were more likely to not reject South Asian values and were also more likely to feel positively about themselves. Participants in the survey also indicated that friendships with other South Asian adolescents are very valuable and offered them a context within which they could integrate their different selves. However, they did express frustration with their family's expectation that they can restrict their exposure to and desire for 'Americanness' only to the extent that facilitates functioning within their school environments. The greatest need expressed was for more open and constructive communication between parents and adolescents about dating and marriage.[19]

The discussion outlined above strongly suggests that tasks of adolescence are perceived differently by parents within the two cultures precisely because they serve as paths towards two different definitions of self. Adolescence, as defined by American society, is a period of experimentation and increasing self-definition on the part of a young person in preparation for eventual emancipation from the family. South Asian culture defines adulthood, and the goal of adolescence, not in terms of emancipation but preparedness to assume the roles and responsibilities of one's place both in the family and the culture. The struggles that take place then between South Asian American adolescents and their families during this time reflect not only the concerns of negotiating their relationships, but in a larger framework, the adolescents' and the family's negotiation of two cultures.

Conclusion

Throughout adolescence, South Asian American girls grapple with a maze of cultural messages about who to be as well as the ways in which these trajectories lead one towards being South Asian or American. In reality, neither cultural script alone accurately charts the course for their development. The task of these young women is to seek a course that allows for the healthy integration of their bicultural identity, one that allows them to retain the sustaining aspects of their South Asian heritage while incorporating the opportunities for personal growth in being American. Such a process poses challenges not only to the individual girls but to their families and to the South Asian American communities at large. Continuing dialogue within these communities as well as ongoing research about these issues will be critical for developing answers to these challenges.

◆ Notes and References

1. For the purposes of this paper, South Asian culture will refer to the norms of societies in India, Pakistan, and Bangladesh. While there exist significant linguistic, religious and regional differences within and across these countries, it is generally understood that these immigrant communities face similar cultural issues within the United States. 'American' refers to mainstream America.

2. A. Bharati, 'The Self in Hindu Thought and Action'. In A.J. Marsella, G. DeVos, and F.L.K. Hsu (eds), *Culture and Self* (New York, Tavistock Publications, 1985), 185–230; A. Roland, *In Search of Self in India and Japan* (Princeton, NJ, Princeton University Press, 1988).

3. V.N. Desai, 'Whither Home? The Predicament of a Bicultural Experience'. In Asia Society Galleries (ed.), *Asia/America: Identities in Contemporary Asian American Art* (New York, The Asia Society Galleries and The New Press, 1994); E. Dutt, 'Becoming a 2nd Generation', *India Abroad* 20(2), 1989, 16.

4. S. Derne, *Culture in Action* (Albany, State University of New York Press, 1995).

5. S. Kurtz, *All the Mothers are One* (New York, Columbia University Press, 1992).

6. E.H. Erikson, *Childhood and Society* (New York, Norton, 1950); L. Steinberg, 'Autonomy, Conflict, and Harmony in the Family Relationship'. In S.S. Feldman and G.R. Elliott (eds), *At the Threshold* (Cambridge, MA, Harvard University Press, 1990).

7. J. Naidoo and C. Davis, 'Canadian South Asian Women in Transition: A Dualistic View of Life', *Journal of Comparative Family Studies* 19, 1988, 312–27; Roland. See n. 2.

8. V. Das, 'Reflections on the Social Construction of Adulthood'. In S. Kakar (ed.), *Identity and Adulthood* (Delhi, Oxford University Press, 1979), 89–104; K. Jayakar, 'Women of the Indian Subcontinent'. In L. Comas-Diaz and B. Greene (eds), *Women of Color: Integrating Ethnic and Gender Identities in Psychotherapy* (New York, The Guilford Press, 1994), 61–181.

9. S. Kakar, *Indian Childhood: Cultural Ideals and Social Reality* (Delhi, Oxford University Press, 1979).

10. N. Chodorow, *The Reproduction of Mothering* (Berkeley, The University of California Press, 1978).

11. J.B. Miller, 'The Development of Women's Sense of Self'. In J.V. Jordan, A.G. Kaplan, J.B. Miller, I.P. Striver, and J.L. Surrey (eds), *Women's Growth in Connection* (New York, The Guilford Press, 1991), 11–26; J. Jordan, 'The Relational Self: Implications for Adolescent Development'. *Adolescent Psychiatry* 19, 1993, 228–38.

12. D.G. Mandelbaum, *Women's Seclusion and Men's Honor: Sex Roles in North India, Bangladesh and Pakistan* (Tuscon, AZ, The University of Arizona Press, 1988); Derne. See n. 4.

13. U.A. Segal, 'Cultural Variables in Asian Indian Families'. *Families in Society* 72(4), 1991, 233–41; Jayakar. See n. 8.

14. C. Gilligan, *In a Different Voice* (Cambridge, MA, Harvard University Press, 1982).

15. D.C. Jack, *Silencing the Self* (Cambridge, MA, Harvard University Press, 1991).

16. G.G. Raheja, 'Women's Speech Genres, Kinship and Contradiction'. In N. Kumar (ed.), *Women as Subjects* (Charlottesville, VA, University Press of Virginia, 1994).

17. S. Harter, 'Causes, Correlates and the Functional Role of Global Self-Worth: A Lifespan Perspective'. In J. Kolligan and R. Sternberg (eds), *Perceptions of Competence and Incompetence Across the Lifespan* (New Haven, CT, Yale University Press, 1990), 67–98.

18. G. Kurian, 'Intergenerational Integration with Special Reference to Indian Families'. *Indian Journal of Social Work* 47, 1986, 39–49; Segal. See n. 13.

19. K. Ahmed, 'Acculturation in Relationship Contexts among South Asian American Adolescents'. Unpublished Masters Thesis, University of Denver, 1997.

2

In search of self

Sabah Aafreen

When I was born in Hyderabad, my father decided that I was going to marry his elder brother's son. I grew up in India knowing this and accepting it.

My grandmother, Nanijaan, taught me that a good girl is passive and obedient and a good girl I was.

However, when my parents brought me and my sister, Farah, to Chicago (I was nine years old), our entire world turned upside down.

'Sayba, go sit next to John,' Mrs Smith, my fifth grade teacher said. I was too shy to correct her pronunciation.

'Ugh! She's ugly,' John said.

From then on, John, Bobby, and Joe had a lot of fun terrorizing and humiliating me.

'Beat her up after class, Leslie,' Bobby said.

Leslie, a girl with yellow hair, who everyone thought was pretty, smiled.

Gym was the worst period of the day. I was the slowest runner.

I did not understand the rules of baseball. When team leaders were picked and, they in turn, picked their team members, I was always left over.

'Fat bitch,' Bobby would yell in a volleyball game, 'get out of the way!'

Before falling asleep every night, I found myself breathing hard. I could not control it.

Nanijaan had taught me that if someone doesn't like you, you should please them until they like you. You should not give up.

So I tried.

'Pronounce "quarter",' Chris said.

'Kvaarr-ter,' I said. They all laughed.

When we stood in line to go to lunch, Julie was standing behind me. She touched my shoulder and yelled, 'Sayba's germs! Thumbs up!'

Then she touched the boy behind her.

The kids behind him had their thumbs up.

'Straighten up the line again,' Mrs Smith said.

The more I tried to please them, the more pleasure they got out of humiliating me.

I never expressed any anger because I was in the habit of being a good girl. Besides, I was afraid.

My parents brought us to this country without a visa. So we lived in the constant fear of being deported. I felt that the kids in school had a right to harass me because I was living in their country without their permission.

Only when I reached high school did I realize that the way to win the hearts of Americans was not by being shy and passive. So I aggressively pursued them. I learned the English language so well that I forgot my own mother tongue, Urdu.

I got a haircut. My hair used to reach down to my hips. After the cut, it was shoulder-length. In spite of my parents' disapproval, I wore shorts when I went to the park. I started identifying myself as an American.

At home, however, I still played the 'good girl'. But, somewhere along the line, I stopped feeling the way I used to in India. I questioned the existence of Allah. I no longer wanted to marry my first cousin.

Fortunately for our family, Reagan passed the Amnesty Act and we became legal residents by the time I was a senior in high school.

'I am going get you married,' my father said before leaving for India.

Like a 'good girl', I said nothing.

In school, however, my grades were good and my high school counselor and teachers were encouraging me to apply to different universities, most of them far from Chicago. My father found a Boston University application lying around. He tore it up and threw it away.

I made friends with a guy who worked at the White Hen Pantry across the street from our apartment. He said I could use his mailbox. With the help of my high school counselor, I applied to the University of Wisconsin-Madison and got financial aid to attend. My parents, who were opposed to me going out of the state to study, did not know I was in Wisconsin until I got there.

I know other girls from my community, living in the US, who have played this passive-aggressive game.

Generally speaking, girls from our community who are born in America do not like being Indian when they are in grade school. The American media teaches them that white is beautiful and Indian is ugly.

When they reach high school and see their friends dating, they want to date too. Parents will look the other way if they catch their sons with an American girl. But they keep an eye on their daughter as soon as she reaches puberty. She is taught to fear Allah and obey her parents. Her marriage is arranged with a cousin back in Hyderabad before she graduates from high school.

Most families from our community living in the US have lots of money. They can afford to pay for their children's education. They take pride in having their daughters go to college and do well. It is becoming acceptable to let her live in dorms. However, while she is studying, she is already engaged to be married.

The girl may still break the engagement, behind her parents' back. But they will find someone else for her. The goal of the parents is to get her married as soon as she is graduated from college. They are very successful.

(Parents are not so determined to get their sons married within the community. They are also willing to let them date before marriage.) By the time the girl gets married, she has learned to accept her parents' victory.

When I say 'my community' I am referring to a specific sect of Islam. My community is a sect of Islam. (I understand there are ninety-something such sects, Sunnis being the majority. Each community believes its own religious perspective to be correct.) My community is a community of Syeds. That is, we are supposedly direct descendants of Prophet Mohamed. Prophet Mohamed had said to Fatima Bibi, 'Do not be proud that you are my daughter'. My community, however, is very proud.

Prophet Mohamed had prophesized about a certain Mehdi. The spiritual leader of my community was one of many who proclaimed to be this Mehdi. Our Mehdi, Alaisalam, was born in India about 500 years ago. He was a Turk. His followers were both Turks and Indians (perhaps some Persians too). Now we are one. One very conservative community, that is. Most of us are in Hyderabad but many of us are also in other parts of India, Pakistan, the United Arab Emirates, and the United States.

Like most cultures, the South Asian culture is largely patriarchal. As in most South Asian communities, women in my particular community do not have an identity of their own. They belong to their father before they are married and to their husband after they are married. If a man marries someone outside of the community, his wife 'belongs to us' thereafter. If a woman marries outside of the community (she would have to be very brave to make such a move), she no longer 'belongs to us'. In order not to lose women from the community, parents will have their daughter married in the community. In order not to lose women from the extended family, in many Muslim communities, parents prefer to have their daughter marry her first or second cousin.

That is why my father wanted to marry me to his elder brother's son. When I called from Wisconsin and informed him that I was going to school there, he knew he had lost. I was no longer under his control.

I feel very tempted to take the credit for my victory. So many people called me brave for going to Wisconsin to get educated, without my family's support. For a long time, I still believe that I got out of marrying my cousin because I was courageous.

In retrospect, however, I believe that I was no more courageous than other young women from my community who tried to do the same and failed. The difference was that my parents did not have the resources to control me. All of our extended family was living back in Hyderabad while my sister and I were growing up. Even if we had green cards, it would have been difficult for my parents to take us to India every summer. They could not afford such trips. They could not afford a house.

Many of our relatives who reside in the US come from landowning, highly educated families. One of my distant cousins, for example, was born in the US to parents who are both doctors. Her parents could afford to take her to India every summer. All her aunts, uncles and first cousins, slowly, moved to the US. The entire family gets together for Eid celebration at the end of Ramadan every year. She is used to going to the mall every other weekend. She has never had to take public transportation in her life. If she dares challenge her parents' desire to marry her within the community, she risks losing the love and attention of the extended family and, equally important, the material comforts of being born in an upper-middle-class family.

I never had much. Therefore, I did not have much to lose.

When I landed at UW-Madison, I felt like I was in heaven. Books, new friends, a flexible schedule, Lake Mendota, Memorial Union ice cream, no family to look over my shoulder—all provided by a red check with the University of Wisconsin-Madison logo. The 'valid' sticker on my student ID gave me access to the libraries, microlabs, recreational facilities and made me eligible to see movies at the University Theatre at a discount rate. I felt like a respectable human being.

I applied to UW-Madison because the African-American guy who worked at the White Hen Pantry had told me that UW-Madison had an excellent Physics department. Once I found myself taking classes, however, I found myself much more interested in Sociology, Psychology, Philosophy, and Women's Studies. I knew that a major in any of these subjects did not guarantee financial stability after graduation. If I did not take care of myself after graduation, who was going to take care of me?

Not my father. Not after he threw a huge engagement party for me and my cousin in Hyderabad and I broke it off.

I had a work-study grant that helped me secure a part-time job at a microcomputing facility.

As if I was not busy enough as a full-time student and part-time computer consultant, I joined the Progressive Student Union and the 'Take Back the Night' rally organizing committee. If there was anything more empowering than yelling, 'Women Unite! Take Back the Night!' with hundreds of women marching down Langdon Street, it was writing articles for Page 2 of *The Daily Cardinal*, a student newspaper.

I wrote about how sad I felt about leaving my Muslim Indian girlfriends behind. One had gotten married right out of high school because her parents believed that 'college was no place for a girl'. The other three were attending the University of Illinois, Chicago and living with their parents. My mother felt ashamed to inform my girlfriends' parents (and her own family in Hyderabad) that I was living away from home.

The process of writing, I discovered, was great therapy. The result was overnight fame. The next day, my dorm-mates stopped me in the hallway and complimented me on my writing style. In Calculus class, I saw the guy sitting next to me reading my article on Page 2 of *The Daily Cardinal*. 'It's an interesting article,' he told the guy next to him. I could not pay attention to the professor when he started lecturing.

I continued to write through my first three years at UW-Madison. But my writing lost its original simplicity and honesty. I was no longer writing for the sake of self-reflection. I was catering to an audience that saw me as 'the woman of color' on campus by writing what I thought they expected me to write. Also, progressive organizations around campus sought my participation. My ego was bloated. I attended meetings just to show my face. I did not smile back when everyone smiled and said, 'Hi, Sabah'. I could not keep track of everyone's names.

Days flew by while school was in session. Time came to a screeching halt when school closed for a holiday. Christmas was the worst time of the year. I had to choose between the deserted streets and bitter cold of Madison and my father's 'all that education is making you more stupid' and bitter cold of Chicago.

I missed Farah. She had also run away from home. I did not know where she was. She was my best friend. I could not imagine life without her. I managed to live through those suicidal days and graduated with a major in Mathematics.

Years after graduation, I am a more mature and humble person. I have become an American citizen. I voted for the first time in my life on

5 November 1996. For Ralph Nader as president. However, I am glad Clinton won instead of Dole.

My sister and I are back together. She's healthy and happy, so I am at peace. I am 26 and she is 24. We are both unmarried and not living with our parents. I do not know any other Muslim South Asian women who are living independently as we are. My closest friends are Hindu Indian-American women who are also unmarried and independent from their parents.

I respect the women from my community who, even though they have been born in the States, accepted their parents' will to arrange their marriage. Perhaps if I were in their shoes, I would have done the same thing. However, given the experiences my sister Farah and I have had, arranged marriage is not right for us.

I can see myself married to a Hispanic, Jewish-American, Hindu Indian or a man of some other race/religion/nationality. I am not desperate to get married. Therefore, if I choose someone he will be a great individual. He would have to be willing to pretend to convert to our sect of Islam for the sake of pacifying my parents and extended family.

I can also see myself remaining single for the rest of my life. As a single woman, I feel in control of my life. I can make my own decisions and have the freedom to change my mind. My sister is a perfect companion.

I have no worries and very few desires. I want to write. I want to tell my story under the guise of fiction or in straightforward essays.

When Sangeeta, the editor of this anthology, said she was interested in my writing, at first I was very excited.

I decided I was going to write my autobiography. I wrote down all the gory details about my life while I was living with my parents in Chicago.

After reading it over, I almost tore it up. What if my words hurt some Muslim fundamentalist's ears? He might decide to declare a *fatwa* on my head. As much as I am awed with Salman Rushdie's creativity, I don't envy his lifestyle after *The Satanic Verses*.

I also realized that there is no way I could disgrace my family this way. It would break my parents' hearts. Allah knows they have suffered enough ever since they came to the US. Also, I know I have played a big part in their distress. It's bad enough to do all the things I did. And then to tell the world about it!

I cannot do it.

'Why not?' my friend Raza asked.

'I don't want to disgrace my family and community,' I said.

It is important to me to tell the truth. If I can talk about my past honestly, I can let it go. There will be no desire left for revenge (against American society or my family). There will be no desire left, period. I can die.

'Once I write it down, I can let it all go,' I told him. 'That will be the end.'

'It will be the beginning,' he said.

'Beginning of what?' I asked without wanting to know.

'Beginning of a dialogue,' he said.

'With whom?' I asked pretending not to know what he was talking about.

'With your family and community,' he said.

3

A generation in transition: Gender ideology of graduate students from India at an American university

Lalita Subrahmanyan

Aditi[1] is a young woman in her 20s who completed her Bachelor's degree in India and came to the United States for graduate studies. She is bright, confident, and very optimistic about her future as a female professional. She has very strong views about gender identity, and the changing roles of women in the family. When she is asked what she thinks about marital roles, she says:

> I think the guy has got to be a little more open-minded. If he is going to have [the] old values of saying, 'No, I'm a guy. I'm not supposed to do all that,' then he will [have] problems. I don't think that will be the case though. Knowing my brother-in-law (who lives in the United States), I don't think that's the case. I mean, he helps out [at home]...

Vikram is a young man, also in his 20s, who completed a Bachelor's degree in business in India, and came to the United States for a Master's degree. He too has strong views on gender identity, and particularly the role of women in the home and outside it. When he is asked what he thinks about marital roles, he says:

> *Vikram*: At home the guy needs to help her a little bit. Or you can get some household help.

L.S.: In what way could the guy help her out? In what way would you? Suppose you had a wife who has an MBA?
Vikram: I wouldn't marry one. That's the point. Has an MBA, and who's going to spend forty to fifty hours at work. I wouldn't marry one.

Both Vikram and Aditi realize that marital roles and relationships have changed over time and, given the changing social circumstances, need to change further. But it is obvious that they are not very clear about how exactly, and to what extent, this should happen, and what the implications of such a change are in their own lives.

Hochschild, in her book, *The Second Shift*[2] has categorized three types of ideologies of marital roles that are based on the sphere—home or work—that the woman wishes to identify or be identified with, and the amount of power she wants to have—less, more, or equal—in the relationship. These ideologies are categorized as traditional, transitional, and egalitarian. Both Aditi and Vikram have an ideology of marital roles that could be clearly classified as transitional. Yet, there are subtle differences in their position within this category. Aditi's position is transitional because she concedes that household responsibilities are primarily those of the woman. Yet, unlike the generations of women before her, she feels that the practices in the home should change, and men should no longer 'come home and put their feet up on the chair with a newspaper in hand'. Men should share in the household chores, and 'treat' women as their equals. She also indicates that she is optimistic that change will not be a problem and quotes the example of her sister and brother-in-law to support her optimism.

Vikram, on the other hand, is transitional because he says he is willing to accept some societal change in which women are seeking more education and are therefore entering the workforce. But he is not willing to grant more than a very limited sanction for them. Personally, he does not want a highly qualified woman as his wife, since that means that she would spend a great deal of time away from home at work. He believes, in a somewhat biologically deterministic fashion, that women are best 'suited' to play the role of housewife and mother, but he thinks that they should not be treated as inferior on account of that. Therefore, he appears to be egalitarian in his prescription that men ought to share the responsibility at home with their wives, but when it comes to his own choices, he backs off, and is not willing to take a firm stand in creating a situation of true equality.

In this essay I examine and elaborate upon these similarities and differences between male and female graduate students from India in their perceptions of the identity and role of the Indian woman in relation to the family. I found that overall, both male and female students endorsed an ideology of patrifocality[3] by placing the ideal of preserving the family as an entity above all individual considerations. However, there were various complications and contradictions in their perception of this ideology. First, there were differences in the way each group defined the family and the woman's role within it. Second, both men and women emphasized that the family should be preserved as a stable unit, and were very critical of what they perceived as the break-up of the family in the United States. There were, however, subtle differences in the way men and women saw their roles in achieving the objective of family preservation. Patrifocality as an ideology seemed to be challenged to a greater degree, and in different ways, by women rather than by men.

My research question in this study was to find out what unmarried male and female Asian-Indian graduate students at an American university perceived as appropriate gender roles and identities for themselves and for each other. This overarching question consisted of the following sub-questions:

- What, in their opinion, is a man's and a woman's role in relation to the spouse, children, and the extended family?
- What do they think is a woman's and a man's responsibility toward paid work?
- How does their perception of the role of an Indian woman or man compare with what they perceive to be roles of their counterparts in the United States?

In order to answer the above questions, I used a qualitative research method and conducted in-depth interviews of 11 male and an equal number of female Indian graduate students at an American university. There were, at that time, more than 200 students at the University who had come from India for higher education, however, there were only 11 single women, all of whom were chosen for this study. An equal number of single male students were then chosen at random. All the students had never been married. Except for two students who had been in the US for about four years, the group that I interviewed had been in the United States for six months to one-and-a-half years. There were some differences in the group by gender in terms of their academic discipline. The 11 male students were in various branches of engineering (four), computer science (four), business (one), architecture (one), and mathematics (one); whereas the women were in engineering (two), computer science (one), business (one), architecture (one), occupational therapy (three), political science (one), and economics (one). All the students interviewed were from an urban middle- or upper-class background except one male student who was from a rural area. Both parents of all except the rural student had received at least an undergraduate college education. Seven of the males and seven females were from northern, and eight were from southern India. All except three students were Hindus, and almost all of them upper caste.

Using the qualitative research method, I conducted interviews of the students, all of which lasted at least 45 minutes. The interviews were conducted at a time and place convenient to the respondents. I showed them the tentative list of questions at the beginning and requested permission to tape the interviews. All the interviewees were told that they could switch off the tape recorder at any time. None of them exercised that option. I used broad, open-ended questions during the interview. These were interspersed with other questions for purposes of elucidation and clarification. Each of the interviews were then transcribed and coded in a manner suggested by Bogdan and Biklen.[4]

Changing gender identities in India

Research in gender relations in the Indian context is extremely difficult because of several dichotomies that complicate it. First of all, unlike Christianity, Judaism or Islam, the Hindu religion, as articulated in the ancient Vedic texts, carries a highly positive concept of the feminine principle. Most important of all, the image of the mother goddess in it is extremely powerful, and retains the idea of women as powerful, strong, and creative.[5] Such deep-rooted religious ideas naturally have various social ramifications. The social image of the mother is one of a nurturing and caring soul, but a mother, especially of sons, also wields a great deal of power within the family in decision-making, etc., and it is to her will that her son, although a patriarch, is expected to bend.[6] On the other hand, the idea of subservience and domesticity for a woman as wife is quite strong, especially in the male-dominated northern part of the country. The role of the wife, as emphasized through the epics and the mythology of the Hindus, as well as in common practice, is that of a submissive, long-suffering and self-effacing '*Pativrata Aryastree*'[7] totally devoted to her lord and master, her husband.

Another contradiction arises from the Indian philosophy of self-denial and self-restraint that is enshrined in the Hindu psyche. Both men and women, but women especially, are socialized to be able to adjust to all circumstances: they are expected to take pleasure in the giving of themselves. This philosophy, along with the notion of patrifocality, implies a special family orientation, not just toward the nuclear family, but the extended family, particularly for women. While it may avoid problems such as isolation, it often happens that the givers feel extremely suppressed! Novels and short stories in various Indian languages about traditional joint families in India are replete with descriptions of the hierarchies and power struggles among men and women depending upon their place, status, and roles.[8] The contradictions between the principles and practices of Hinduism are what make the Indian situation highly complex, and have been the subject of much research.[9]

Feminist writing in India has been divided on the issue of women's historical status primarily because of the above complications. It is suggested by some writers that the countervailing notions of women's inferiority may have been imported from Western cultures and that the traditional sex role division of labor that confined women to the home was not in itself disempowering.[10] Historian Manisha Roy's study of the contrasts between the perceptions of Indian and American women seems to support the above.[11] Promilla Kapur's 1973 study of educated, urban, middle-class Indian women provides a baseline for how notions of gender have been affected by socio-economic conditions and political changes in India. Kapur's analysis reveals that individuals— both men and women—face various problems and friction in their marriage owing to the changing role of the woman. In that sense, her study is clearly within a liberal feminist framework. She suggests that changes in attitudes of both men and women toward the role of women is the most viable solution. She also recommends what she calls changes in the work and home situation: just as in Sweden, parental leave should be given to both parents; women should be freed from repeated childbearing through family planning measures; and some organizational support, such as workplace childcare, should be provided. Sociologists Rhoda Blumberg and Leela Dwaraki's[12] longitudinal study of women revealed that while educated women wanted to pursue a career, they did not have any radically changed views about how family responsibilities could be divided. Nowhere in the earlier literature is the very basis of patriarchy challenged. It is only in Mukhopadhyay and Seymour's more recent study[13] that we see a discussion of the underlying system that causes, in the first place, the confusion in both men and women's minds within the changed socio-economic context.

Still, it is evident that unquestioned acceptance of traditional ideologies has been changing rapidly, and mixed feelings are being increasingly felt by the modern Indian woman who is torn between her cultural background, and the Western liberal ideas and education to which she is being exposed. And this is perhaps more true for the upper-middle-class women, and men, in this study who have chosen to leave their motherland and travel to the 'liberal' United States to increase their education, and perhaps eventually seek permanent residence. Compared to the prolific feminist literature in India, there has been relatively little written about notions of gender ideology among Indians living in the United States. What little there is about women, reveals one theme: again that of confusion. Confusion not merely about historical change, but confusion because of the need to reconcile the two cultural worlds: that of an 'American' and that of an 'Indian'. One thing is certain, as Jane Singh[14] states, 'While their articulations reveal global concerns and connections to homelands, these women are grounded in America; it is their home'.

Sayantani DasGupta, Shamita Das DasGupta[15] and Chandra Talpade Mohanty,[16] all of whom identify themselves as feminist activists have accepted that due to their Indian cultural background their perceptions of feminism are very different from those of white women. Sudershan Chawla,[17] a nurse, also understands that she has a very distinct cultural identity. She is 'different by choice' and it is her choice to maintain her Indianness in her clothes, behavior, and values. So she has decided to 'wear our Indian dress because of our culture, and because we are proud of it'. For all women, it takes a great deal of thinking and rethinking about their identity before they finally define themselves in terms of their gender and their ethnicity. And for some, like Amita Vasudev,[18] that has been, in her words, 'a fate worse than death'.

The participants in my study are, so to speak, at the first stage of discovering, or to be more precise, of rediscovering their identities as Indian males and females in America. And, as stated earlier, Hochschild's classification provides a convenient sounding board against which some of the complexities of the issues, as well as the differences and similarities between the perceptions of the male and female participants can be studied.

How 'family' gets defined

Of all the themes touched upon, I noticed that both men and women tend to discuss the role of the woman as worker, wife, and mother in greatest detail. This is because both groups clearly foresee more modern and less traditional relationships between Indian men and women, but they do not wish to sacrifice the stability of the traditional family structure at any cost; and the role of the woman is perceived as vital in achieving this goal.

These sentiments are highly reflective of one of the features of patrifocality as Mukhopadhyay and Seymour define it:[19]

> (Patrifocality is) an emphasis on the importance of family generally, and the extended family specifically, regardless of household composition; and on the larger kinship groups and sub-castes (jatis) in which they are embedded; and a concomitant emphasis on the subordination of individual goals and interests to the welfare of the larger family and kin group.

The group of young men and women in this study differed significantly from the above in the way they defined 'family'. Both men and women referred to only a nuclear family consisting of spouse and children. Stability of the family was discussed mainly in terms of how it would affect children. Only old and aging parents who needed care were included in the definition.

But there was an interesting difference between males and females in the way they included parents in the 'family'. Male students saw themselves as responsible for their aging parents and expected their wives to cooperate with them. One of them even said: 'In my case, my parents will stay with me, I am the only son. . . . Well, if she is not going to be able to get along with my parents, I don't think I am going to marry her, that's straight. . . .'

Female students, on the other hand, clearly saw not only their responsibility toward their in-laws, but to their own parents as well. 'A woman should be a good daughter and look after her parents,' one of them said. In fact some of them even said that they expected their husbands to be willing to share with them the responsibility of their parents, just as they were willing to fulfill their duties toward their parents-in-law. 'Like, if he would expect me to take care of his parents and keep good relations with his brothers and sisters, I think that I would expect him to take care of my parents and be responsible towards them also.' In this respect the women clearly see a more egalitarian relationship with their spouses. They see themselves as equal to the men, and capable of, as well as expecting to, wield as much power in the household. They also see daughters as having a role in looking after their own parents. This is contrary to the existing patriarchal structure in India in which sons and daughters-in-law are expected to look after aging parents.

But family, for these students, does not include the extended family and kinship relationships as in the traditional idea of the Hindu joint family. Moreover, the patrifocal view that sons are responsible for the continuity and well-being of the family while daughters are expected to shift their allegiance to their conjugal family seems to be taken for granted by almost all the males, whereas it is questioned by the females.

Now, given all these role expectations of women, as ideal wives, mothers, and daughters, how did the students then see men and women as equal? There were several contradictions in their views on equality.

'Women and men are equal'

Both male and female students agreed wholeheartedly that, in theory, women are equal to men in every respect, and should be thus treated: a human rights perspective. But, women identified themselves as individuals who should be independent and self-confident; whereas the male students saw ideal women as being more connected to men, to their children, and to the rest of the family, of course admittedly equal to them.

For example, one of the women emphasized the need for a woman to be 'herself':

I feel a woman has an individuality, she should pursue (a career). It's not that you are Mrs. X, you are somebody. Tomorrow, if I got married, I wouldn't want to be called Mrs. X, I would want people to say, 'She is Vandana, she is Vandana by herself'. Your personality shouldn't be dependent on somebody else. . . .

But the men thought a little differently. At the beginning of this essay, Vikram was quoted as saying that he would not marry a highly qualified professional woman, and that his wife would be responsible for the family and children. And yet, he said that he saw her as an equal. Kamal, a male student in mathematics, who expressed traditional views by stating that a woman is 'most suited' to look after the home and children—and by that he meant that it was more natural for women to be caring and nurturing—was, however, quick to point out that this did not mean she was inferior in any way. According to him: 'What it boils down to is... that... to see her as an equal partner. Treat her as an equal partner.'

Again, several males, but all females saw financial independence as being very important for women. All the females felt that financial independence was the key to self-confidence and empowerment. Some of the males, however, who vehemently stressed the woman's role as mother, and who strongly believed that their spouses would not or should not work full-time outside the home, did not emphasize financial independence because of the inherent contradiction. But there were others who felt very strongly that women should not depend upon a man financially. They agreed that if this was to be the case, women would have to work outside the home. In other words, women were expected to contribute financially to the household, and yet they would also be responsible for the stability of the family and the children. A tall order of the 'milch cow', as sociologist Suma Chitnis describes the situation of educated middle-class women.[20]

It seemed as if the contradictions inherent in their perceptions were completely lost on them. The men stated that women were equal to them, but when it came to the issue of caring for the old, or the young, women were expected to look after their in-laws, and it did not strike the men that they could do the same. And both men and women could not reconcile how financial independence could be achieved except through paid employment; and how the question of the family stability could be resolved if women got into the workforce in large numbers. And yet, the issue of how the parents (and of course, children) would be taken care of when both spouses had paid employment was a source of serious concern to both males and females in their discussion of the woman's role as worker. This we explore in the next section.

'Women should have a career'

All the women interviewed had come to the United States to acquire either a Master's or a doctoral degree. In fact, most of the female participants in this study were in very non-traditional fields such as engineering, computer science, architecture, and business. It would thus be reasonable to expect that they intended to pursue a career in that discipline. And all of them said that they did. All except one of them also said that they wished to get married and raise a family. For instance, during a conversation about careers, one of them said very determinedly: 'I will tell him: "Look, I have studied so much, so I am not going to sit at home, sit all the time and do cleaning and all simply..."'

In fact, they expressed in several different ways that the woman must satisfy not only her personal economic need through a career, but she must realize her intellectual potential. In India, this perception is not new. According to Promilla Kapur,[21] several studies in the 1960s and 1970s, including hers, suggest that Indian women would like to have a career for various social and psychological reasons: to use their talent, to achieve a position, or have status as an individual, etc. In this respect, the participants in this study sounded very much like the students that Seymour refers to in her research.[22] Unlike the participants in Seymour's study however, the women in this study found it hard to reconcile the two strong feelings they had: the importance of a career to a woman's sense of self, and the problem of keeping a family together if both partners were employed outside the home. Both men and women realized that there would be problems of adjustment, but the solutions that the men put forth were more traditional ones, based upon the assumption that women are best suited for, and therefore should be responsible for the family, and that their careers should definitely take second place. Women were more reluctant to make such a presumption.

Women realized that they were likely to face several problems at work. Kala, the mechanical engineer, was sure that she would have the greatest difficulties. The first one was of access.

> The first difficulty is finding a good, decent job.... The last time I attended campus interviews, I was much better academically than all the boys but I [did not get a position] because I was a girl. But not all companies are like that. One of my friends got [a job] in this company. Certain companies do [hire] girls. There were three hundred boys who appeared for the same interview, and she was the only girl selected.

Second, there was a problem with the job itself.

> When I was working in [the] R and D shop, I used to work a lot on the shop floor and I used to operate the bending machines and all that

stuff. That is quite hard to do. It was mechanically hand-operated. And I used to do that. First of all they [my male co-workers] used to think, 'My, she's trying to prove something. She wants to show off.' When I didn't do something they used to tell me, 'You think [that because] you are a girl [you need not] do your job, that you can use *that* as an excuse'.

So it was a 'if you do, you're damned, if you don't do, you're damned' situation. The women also recognized that they were likely to face problems because in spite of their place in the workforce, society still expected them to be the primary homemaker. Malashree, the only participant who was in her early 30s, and who had been employed in India before she came to the US to pursue a doctoral degree was extremely realistic when she said:

> Women clerks (in India) have told me in the past that if their husband falls sick, they are expected to stay home; [if their] child falls sick they are expected to stay home; [if their] mother-in-law falls sick, they are expected to stay home.... It's only when *they* fall sick, they frankly and laughingly admit, that they can come to the office. [And they'd rather do that] because otherwise their mother-in-law will expect them to work at home.... So they come [to the office], put up their legs and not do too much work.... [This is possible] especially if they have an understanding boss!

Therefore, it seemed clear to them that it was necessary for women to have paid employment. Yet, given the various complications and problems that could arise, they could not envisage clearly how the conflicts would be resolved.

Solutions?

Overall it seemed, however, that the men were less confused than the women, and offered solutions to this conflict based upon more traditional views of gender roles. First of all, men felt, quite unequivocally, that a stable marriage could only be a traditionally 'arranged' one, meaning a marriage that had been arranged by the parents and family of the bride and bridegroom, rather than one in which the partners had chosen each other through dating or other means. They believed that in an 'arranged marriage', both partners have fewer expectations of each other, both partners are not as 'modern' as those who choose their own spouses, and therefore such a marriage is less likely to end in a divorce. It seemed that the men were more concerned that the marriage should not break up, they did not really think about the quality of the marriage. These were some of the responses:

> *Kamal (M)*: So you can probably live with anyone, and who your parents choose is not going to be someone very terrible to live with . . . .
> *Rohit (M)*: I am more or less going toward the opinion that hey, I like arranged marriages.
> *Arjun (M)*: I think arranged marriages work out better at least in terms of durability. Very simply, because I think there is less expectation (between the partners).

Ironically, the solution women saw to the issue of keeping families together was the opposite to the one men had seen: the 'love' or 'self arranged marriage', rather than an 'arranged' marriage. Thus, the women were more eager than men to have the choice of a marriage partner. They were also more concerned with the quality of the marriage. They felt that such a choice would help them find a man who would be more understanding of their needs, and that this marriage was more likely to last than an 'arranged' marriage.

> *Sujata*: I don't think I would jump into a marriage without making sure that at least some compatibility [of ideas regarding gender] was there.

A few of the males, who were more liberal than the ones quoted above, had stated that they would share the household responsibilities with their partners. Many of them, however, still took it for granted that the woman should be the one to adjust herself to the changing circumstances—even give up her paid employment, if necessary.

For instance, Sivaram expressed it in terms of the mother's role in the family and hinted that perhaps the woman should not consider paid employment when her children are young.

> . . . the mother's role is extremely important in the family, definitely extremely important. It's a sort of moderator. . . . For example, a woman's career might be very important to her, at one stage it might. . . be quite harmful for the interest of the family. She might tend to neglect the family. At least in the initial years. . . . In later years, probably it's quite all right for her to work. . . .

Vikram, the young man we met at the very start of this essay, carried this argument even further when he categorically stated that he would not marry a professional because she would need to put in a great deal of work outside the home and would neglect the family.

The women's responses were more complex. Perhaps they had not thought about these matters at length before this. Perhaps they had not realized how complicated these issues could be.

Some of them said that they did not see any real problems. One of them said, '*Dekha jaayegaa* (we shall see).' Aditi, who we met earlier, was very optimistic that there would be no real problem: that the men would 'help' them at home, and share the work on an equal basis. Others hoped that problems would be resolved over time since Indian women have only entered paid employment in large numbers since the 1960s. Even Leela, the only one among the female participants who had mentioned the need for women to be feminists and support each other, felt that essentially it was a matter of time.

L.S.: Could you tell me what you think about resolving the problem?
Leela: Well, I think men will accept it in time.... It's just a question of time, of letting [women have] these rights, and I think that roles will just get [adjusted, and the problems] resolved over time.... And [these problems are] not something that [are] going to last, because I think that men and women need each other, they have to co-exist, they have to marry, they have to have families...

Some of the women seemed to have surrendered themselves to the situation when they said that they would like to pursue only part-time employment since the family is of prime importance to them, even though they would have a career. Two of the females interviewed said that they would work only part-time outside the home and thus be able to combine the roles of homemaker and worker easily. How difficult this is likely to be, given the status of part-time professionals, especially women, is not something of which these women seem to be greatly aware. They did however, indicate that they felt there would be greater opportunities to do this in the United States than there would have been in India. In that sense they were probably correct.

They realized however, that it was by far a more complex situation since they would have trouble resolving the conflict between their several responsibilities. They seemed torn between their need to 'realize their potential' by using their education in a career on the one hand, and keeping a functional family together, especially for the sake of children, on the other. Their confusion showed itself in their comments on the ability of women to be 'Super-Moms'. Jyoti, who was in her 20s, pointed out how this was going to be really difficult but Malashree, in her 30s, seemed to think that women had to, and somehow would be able to do it.

Jyoti: It's something like the 'Super-Mom' thing. You're trying to be **the best mother**, you're trying to be **the best wife**, and you're trying to be **the best worker**... which is not really possible. If you've got to finish some work, if you've taken [on] loads of work, and then you begin to ignore your family, it is not right, you've got to tell yourself, 'I've got to stop here'.
Malashree: ... I think women are very powerful. That given the chance, I'm sure they can rise up to the challenge, and fulfill both roles. It is tough for them... and I always think that it is weighted against them because they have to perform these roles.... There's no way out.

And of course, many of the women realized that ultimately **they** would need to compromise and adjust. This seems to be a typical reaction. According to Chitnis,[23] Westerners seem to be compelled to pursue conflict to a logical resolution often through confrontation and categorical choice. In contrast, the Indian culture places greater value on compromise. Thus, she says, Indian women tend to consider compromise positively, and view it as the most acceptable accommodation of conflicting obligations, of pressures satisfactorily resolved. And yet, these women found this obligation very stressful, even stifling. Listen to what Kala and Rehana said:

L.S.: What do you think are a man's and a woman's responsibilities regarding their work?
Rehana: I guess you have to give yourself one hundred percent to both, family and work, but that's not possible. So you have to compromise somewhere. I wouldn't really know.... I feel that work comes before family, but perhaps [that's how] I feel now because I don't have a family. I may change.... I can't influence anybody but myself. I can't tell a friend, 'Don't do the housework, let your husband help you.' So it will just affect me and the way I live.... Which is bad, I guess. I wouldn't be able to compromise. [She laughs, embarrassed.] If I had to look after the house day after day after day, I would rebel,

which would probably lead to ugly scenes, I'm sure. I don't know, I like being independent...

When Kala, the mechanical engineer, began to talk about getting married and making adjustments with her husband, she reluctantly agreed that the woman should place her family above herself.

L.S.: And just suppose he does not change, what will you do then?
Kala: Then maybe it will end up in divorce or anything, I'm not bothered. It's his problem.... But I'm sure then that people are going to hold me to it, meaning I will be responsible. They will say, 'She's the girl, she was having fun out[side] the home, so her husband divorced her.' I'm sure about that also.... But... you can't do anything about it.... But maybe I'm such a chicken sometimes that for my family pride, for my parents, I might change, not [for the sake of and] because I love my husband. I might quit my job or something...

Thus the students' perceptions of women's roles show significant variation and confusion. To some extent the study substantiates anthropologist Mies'[24] conclusion that the social ideal of woman has not undergone any radical change in India, but has only been polished up and thus made modern. That might be true, but women have different perceptions and in many instances these ideas conflict with what men think. However, neither in the males nor in the females did I see any consciousness of collective ways to change attitudes at a societal level. For instance, feminism was seen as a negative.

L.S.: Have any of your ideas changed?
Jyoti: I don't think so. I had the same ideas in India. I felt very strongly about and I still feel very strongly about.... I'm not a feminist, don't get me wrong. I feel that people discriminate against women even today, which is terrible, we're as good as men.
L.S.: You said, 'I'm not a feminist, don't get me wrong'. Can you elaborate on that?
Jyoti: Eh... it's like these feminists are totally into freedom for women etc. I don't feel that women are not free, but there are bits and pieces of discrimination that occur even today in jobs etc. I'm not totally opposed to men, like I hate men or something like that. I respect men, they are good too. It's just that we have rights too, they have to be fulfilled, we have needs too.

Second, although all the students unilaterally criticized mainstream American society for being very 'individualistic' as they called it. However, they did not express a sense of a global social consciousness of gender inequality or the motivation to do something about it.

'The American society is highly individualistic'

All of the students interviewed were highly critical of what they perceived about the American family. Their perceptions were mainly based upon the stereotypes they had heard about, television, and a few interactions with university students. They expressed serious concern about the break up of the family in America, and the high divorce rates, and attributed this to what they called a philosophy of individualism. This comment captures the essence of their criticism, a criticism that sounds highly ethnocentric, and that is obviously based on a very partial and perhaps biased image of the American family: 'Here even the husband has to knock on the door of his wife's room, because even she is keeping something private from her husband. They run their own finances, nobody really bothers.'

Yet, I found their criticism of the so-called individualism in American society very interesting. None of the students, except three, had said anything spontaneously about their own social or political duties and responsibilities and those of other men and women. Only one of them talked about service to others and another mentioned that all human beings have a duty toward the environment. Among the women, only one said that women should support each other. Others were quite blasé and said that they did not feel any responsibility toward the society.

> *Kamal*: I don't know what a man's responsibilities towards society are.... I don't care about it also.
> *Ramesh*: I don't know, I haven't even thought about it. I'm very self-centered, you know. I am only looking at my goals and my happiness. I haven't really given any thought to what I should do for the benefit of society.

To me therefore, their perceptions of individualism in American society seemed almost facetious. It seems that they are just as individualistic as the Americans they criticize, only their unit of individualism is the family: spouse, children, and sometimes, parents.

Conclusions and implications for future research

The participants of this study do not have, as I anticipated, perceptions and attitudes toward gender that are radically different from those held by Indian society at large. However, there are subtle differences between the ways in which the males view gender identities as compared with the females. And, given that these women have all chosen to pursue educational degrees in a foreign country, they are, in a sense, a very progressive group, and so their views are not surprising. To summarize, both male and female students emphasize that men and women are inherently equal, but there is a special need to maintain the family as a stable unit. In addition, they are highly critical of the mainstream society in the United States in which the break-up of the family is in their view, a very grave problem.

'An American wife or husband wouldn't mind getting a divorce, but it is a religious, social treasure, that Indian families would not do that,' said one of them, dramatically idealizing the Indian situation, not realizing that divorce rates in India are also rising. However, there are clear differences in the way men and women perceive the need to hold the family together, and the ways in which that goal can be accomplished. The women seem far more confused between their desire to realize their personal potential by pursuing a career and their perception that the woman's role as worker might jeopardize the stability of the family structure. Men seem to have traditional solutions and see fewer problems. Some of them, the liberals, are willing to pitch in with their share of household work and childcare, but there are others who prefer to exercise the choices that really only males have: they say they will have an 'arranged' marriage, and they will marry a woman who does not have a career, or they prefer that their spouse not pursue a career until the children are much older.

The women's solutions are tentative. They would, like the women in Blumberg and Dwaraki's study,[25] like to pursue a career. And having availed of the opportunity of higher education in the United States, they certainly do not wish to treat it as a parking lot en route to getting married. In this, they are quite different from the group that Indian researchers, Rehana Jhabvala and Pratima Sinha[26] encountered in the 1970s in a college at the undergraduate level whom they interviewed about their educational aspirations. In that study, many of the students said that they go to college mainly to acquire new and better qualifications in order to get a better husband. At the same time, the participants in this study seem willing to give up their liberal, modern views on the altar of family stability.

Unlike the males, they want to have a choice of marital partner as they hope that this will help resolve the conflict. The question of choice in marriage is becoming very important to the Indian woman. It surfaced very strongly as a reaction to Madhu Kishwar's article in *Manushi*[27] in which she defended the traditional system of arranged marriages as being capable of giving greater support to women, and being able to avert the severity of domestic abuse as is seen in the West, especially the United States. She received and subsequently published numerous letters written in disagreement with her views by women who say that they believe strongly in 'love' marriages, or as they call it, 'marriages of choice'. Then again, the women in this study hope there is no real problem, and that problems will be resolved over time. Some of them are even willing to give up full-time careers and pursue part-time ones. But they are confused, and fully aware that they are going to be unfair to their own sense of self if they do that.

The implications of this study are important for several reasons. First, the women in this group are clearly posing a greater challenge to patrifocality, however mild that might be. This is not surprising and parallels some of the other studies conducted in India in which women, more than men, have expressed more liberal views on the role of the woman.[28]

Part of this confusion over identities and roles can be attributed to contradictions in the Hindu image of the woman that I discussed earlier. The women here wish to challenge the idea of patrifocality, yet they wish to retain the image of the woman as mother and as the one who holds the family together through her influence on her children, especially sons. And yet, that is just the role that is most threatened by their need to express themselves through education and career. Hence the confusion.

A further complication that occurs in terms of this group of students is the fact that they are in the United States, and in most cases plan to get married and stay in this country. In fact, as far as I know, at least three to four of the women have married or started jobs and are still in this country. As I stated before, they are in the beginning stages of rethinking their identities as Indian in the United States, and these are some of their first confusions. It would be extremely interesting to see how they deal with these issues over a period of time in this country.

What are the implications of the gender differential in perceptions for this group? The large number of organizations that have been established in the United States for battered Indian women, and the rising statistics on divorce among South Asians suggests that the family structure is weakening considerably, and that women and children are most affected, emotionally and otherwise by it. What are the conflicts that have surfaced from the differences I found in my participants? That is what I came to the South Asian Women's Conference to find out! It seems that not much formal research exists in this area. I once had the opportunity to listen to a very interesting analysis of the problem from two speakers who are themselves organizers of a group in New Jersey that provides support to Asian women in abusive relationships. They had a very interesting analysis linking abuse to patriarchy in the context of the Indian nuclear family here in the United States. Their data showed that it is not the mother-in-law who is the villain of the piece (as is often claimed by sociologists and lay persons in India), because the in-laws are often not here at all, but that the man is just as much or even more abusive. I have also seen the contrasts between the views of Indians on two electronic networks, the news group Soc.culture.India, a predominantly male group, and SAWNET, an electronic-mail network of women from South Asia. Issues of gender are truly volatile, and there are clearly several differences between the way men and women see them. Also, the yawning gap between Indian traditionalism, as articulated by the males, and modernity, as expressed by the females becomes so clear, it is frightening!

One important thing to remember is that this is merely a study of perceptions, of opinions expressed, which may be altogether different from actual behavior. In this respect, a longitudinal study like that of Blumberg and Dwaraki[29] would be extremely revealing, if conducted as a case study. It would be very interesting to see how this group of students translates the ideas they express into their own lives after marriage. Another issue raised is that of the long-term care of parents. Many of the men in this study were very vocal that they would like to look after their parents in their old age. Many of the students, especially men, said that they plan to work here for a few years and then go back to India. Seeing the ethnocentrism evident in their responses one would be inclined to believe that they do indeed wish to return to their families and parents. Research on the extent of brain-drain from India to the United States however, tells a different story, and not many students who say that they will return to their home country actually do so. How, then, do these students plan to look after their parents? Is there a trend for Indian immigrants to bring their parents here to the United

States? And if so, how do they 'look after' them? Most of the wives of the professional immigrants may be employed outside the home, how are the two roles managed? Do the men actually marry women who are not pursuing a career? But once they come to this country and see the opportunities, don't the women begin to pursue a career? What happens then? These are all not only interesting sociological questions, but have tremendous implications for the status of women and policy for a pluralistic society. These questions raise innumerable possibilities for further research.

✦ Notes and References

1. All names are fictitious to protect the identity of the participants.
2. Arlie Russel Hochschild with Anne MacHugan, *The Second Shift* (New York, Viking Penguin Inc., 1989).
3. Patrifocality, as defined by anthropologists Carol Mukhopadhyay and Susan Seymour 'Introduction and Theoretical Overview'. In Carol C. Mukhopadhyay and Susan Seymour (eds), Women, Education, and Family Structure in India (San Francisco, CA, Westview Press, 1994) is an ideology characterized by an emphasis on the importance of family in general, and the extended family specifically. A more detailed definition is given on page 64.
4. R.C. Bogdan and S.K. Biklen, *Qualitative Research for Education* (Boston, Allyn and Bacon Inc., 1982).
5. Tara Ali Baig, *India's Woman Power* (New Delhi, S. Chand and Co., 1976).
6. Suma Chitnis, 'Feminism in India', *Canadian Woman Studies* 6(1), 1984, 41–47.
7. These words in the Sanskrit language, literally mean: An Aryan woman who is devoted to her husband.
8. Some of the popular novels are Rajam Krishnan, *Lamps in the Whirlpool* (Translated from Tamil original by Uma Narayanan and Prema Seetharam, Madras, Macmillan India Ltd., 1995); Choodamani Raghavan, *Yamini* (Madras, Macmillan India Ltd., 1996); Gangadhar Gadgil, *The Woman and Other Stories* (New Delhi, Sterling Publishers Ltd., 1992); Lakshmi Holmstrom, *The Inner Courtyard: Stories by Indian Women* (London, Virago Press Ltd., 1990).
9. One of the most recent articles on this subject that I have read is Thomas Coburn's ('Experiencing the Goddess: Notes on a Text, Gender and Society'. *Manushi* 80, Jan.-Feb., 1994, 2–10) analysis of the tradition of the mother goddess in the Hindu religion in the context of the social status of women featured in *Manushi*.
10. Baig. See n. 5.
11. Manisha Roy, 'The Concepts of "Feminity" and "Liberation" in the Context of Changing Sex Roles: Women in Modern India and America'. In Rehana Ghadially (ed.), *Women in Indian Society* (New Delhi, Sage Publications, 1988).
12. Rhoda Blumberg and Leela Dwaraki, *India's Educated Women: Options and Constraints* (Delhi, Hindustan Publishing Corporation, 1980).
13. Mukhopadhyay and Seymour. See n. 3.

14. Jane Singh, 'Foreword'. In Women of South Asian Descent Collective (ed.), *Our Feet Walk the Sky: Women of South Asian Diaspora* (San Francisco, Women of South Asian Descent Collective, 1994).

15. Sayantani DasGupta and Shamita Das DasGupta, 'Journeys: Reclaiming South Asian Feminism'. In Women of South Asian Descent Collective, 123–31. See n. 14.

16. Chandra Talpade Mohanty, 'Defining Geneologies: Feminist Reflections on Being South Asian in North America'. In Women of South Asian Descent Collective, 351–58. See n. 14.

17. Sudershan Chawla, 'Different by Choice'. In Joann Faung Jean Lee (ed.), *Asian Americans* (New York, The New Press, 1992), 118–20.

18. Amita Vasudev, 'Author Biographies'. In Women of South Asian Descent Collective, 371. See n. 14.

19. Mukhopadhyay and Seymour. See n. 3.

20. Suma Chitnis, 'Education of Women in India'. In Gail P. Kelly (ed.), *Handbook on Women's Education* (New York, Greenwood Press, 1989).

21. Promilla Kapur, *Love, Marriage, and Sex* (Delhi, Vikas Publishing House Pvt. Ltd., 1973).

22. Susan Seymour, 'College Women's Aspirations: A Challenge to the Patrifocal Family System?' In Mukhopadhyay and Seymour. See n. 3.

23. Chitnis. See n. 6.

24. Maria Mies, *Indian Women and Patriarchy* (New Delhi, Concept Publishing Co., 1980).

25. Blumberg and Dwaraki. See n. 12.

26. Rehana Jhabvala and Pratima Sinha, 'Between School and Marriage: A Delhi Sample'. In Devaki Jain (ed.), *Indian Women* (New Delhi, Publications Division, Ministry of Information and Broadcasting, Government of India, 1975).

27. Madhu Kishwar, 'Love and Marriage', *Manushi* 80, 1994, 11–19.

28. V.V. Prakasa Rao and V. Nandini Rao, 'Sex-role Attitudes of College Students in India'. In Ghadially. See n. 11.

29. Blumberg and Dwaraki. See n. 12.

4

Fragments of a hybrid's discourse

Lubna Chaudhry

My brother Salman has two death anniversaries. He died on 19 March
1994 at 6:00 in the morning in an accident near Islamabad in Pakistan.
Salman died on 18 March 1994 at 7:00 in the evening in Davis, California.
These days I am fearful of the mornings because something in one of
them took him to a different realm. These days I am fearful of the
evenings too, because that's when I felt him die. I did not consciously
know—I did not know until the next day, but that was the first evening
when the darkening sky took me some place else. A part of me traveled
with my brother.

Life and death... night and day... my brother, myself... even as I
question borders, I perpetuate them, reinforce them, for I have no words
to capture the complexity, the essence of my hybridity... I am alive but
experiencing death... I was in Davis and Islamabad that day in 1994... I
am my brother and I am myself...

What am I doing talking about my brother's death in the context
of a supposedly academic paper? There is this nagging voice at the
back of my mind even as I am writing. 'Well, breaking down the wall
between my personal and academic selves, of course,' I tell myself firmly.
Yet for someone who is committed to the dissolution of the self/other
dichotomy I am too conscious of the fact that my audience might not
want to cross these borders with me. Are others then just others? Are
the boundaries of my self real? Or maybe the boundaries of other
peoples' selves are real and mine are not. When you go across national
and cultural borders you lose your own...

Excerpt from class presentation, 8 May 1992

The real me! I am all of what they say of me, but I am not really any of those! Really? Essentially? What am I? Am I something, one thing?

No one bothers to get to know the real me here in this country...I am a budding South Asian academic, a Third World feminist, an acculturated Pakistani, a Muslim woman who has thrown her veil away, a non-native speaker of English who speaks the language intelligibly but not... Lubna? Lubna, no I am not Lubna, Lubna is a pretty name of Slavik origin, meaning 'beloved'...

When I am at home, no one sees the real me too... I am my parent's misfortune, a fallen woman, a Westernized individual, a heretic, an infertile womb, a drifter... one of a hundred Lubnas... such a common name out there...

My unsubstantive, fleeting, ephemeral, everchanging I trapped in words and clothes...

As a child I was quite disconcerted when I realized that when I switched languages I seemed to switch personalities... I was someone else when I spoke English, and another person when I spoke Urdu... Punjabi took me to another mode of thought altogether... Crazy? Schizophrenic? I don't know, for my I in English is incapable of taking decisions on its own...

There are no clothes that are 'me'... I become my clothes... In a frock, a full skirt I feel girlish—feminine, attractive, giggly, frivolous, unhesitant about projecting my dumb side, a little flirtatious, but rather shy... In my Shalwar Kamiz, I am womanly—responsible, mature, conscious of the burden of my sex, achingly aware of cultural, societal boundaries, dignified, in control, cool and collected... In jeans I am free of sex, at least the female sex—I can run, laugh loudly, talk crudely, push my friends around, not care how I look, look a man into the eye, shout angrily...

When I first came to the US I just wore clothes I brought from home... no money to buy new things... some dresses and skirts, a pair of jeans, but mostly Shalwar Kamizes... the other Pakistanis thought I was a good girl until... well, it was sacrilegious that I behaved like that although I wore a Shalwar Kamiz!... After raving about my Shalwar suit Molly told me that I seemed very conscious of my identity as a Pakistani... after that day, I feel I am leaving my Pakistani identity at home if I wear something else...

A Shalwar Kamiz... 'the barriers are up again,' says one of my American men friends when he sees me in one... for some it creates distance, for others it presents a challenge... 'I told my friend here I got to talk to that girl in the extraordinary costume.'

A costume?? Something I used to find the most comfortable attire is now too exotic to wear everyday... except in my room... I slip into one every time I have a migraine...

A clear case of postmodern fragmentation, some of my theoretical friends would say. The context determines who you are. I am well aware of the 'decentered status of my self'. I understand notions about the multiplicity of subject positions. And I agree, I have my postmodern days.

As I go down to get some coffee and read, the cover of a popular newsmagazine catches my attention.

Hitting back at terrorists: Clinton strikes Saddam; The FBI busts an Islamic ring[1]

'Who is the terrorist?' I ask myself angrily. 'Clinton or Saddam?' My identity as a frantic, studious graduate student in a US university is displaced by 'someone who believes in justice, equality, and human rights', I tell myself firmly.

'But aren't you reacting as a Muslim?' The critical ethnographer part of me that studies even myself inquires softly. 'You are identifying with these people, although you shrug off any claims to be a practising Muslim, aren't you?'

Later in the evening, in the midst of a heated 'intellectual' debate, one of my friends says to me, only half-jokingly, 'You are so Islamic in your behavior! Man, what intensity!'

'What is a Muslim?' asks Bilgrami,[2] when he feels like one for five minutes. I echo his query. Is the fact that I totally comprehend why people were ready to kill Rushdie when he wrote *The Satanic Verses* make me one? Or do I merely feel for/like Muslims because all the Muslims I know are 'non-fundamentalists' and I don't like it when they are bracketed with the likes of Saddam Hussain? And how do I reconcile my identification with Muslims in certain contexts with my role as a 'deconstructor' of religious thought? I must confess I also enjoy most manifestations of Rushdie's creativity.

Given this fragmentation, then, how can I explain my yearning, my desire to be whole, to affirm all my identities? In the words of Gabriel:[3]

We have never acknowledged either the birth or the death of the subject. Ours has been an ongoing search for the unseparated subject. In other words, the metaphor for the West is the human cycle (birth, life, death); the metaphor for non-Western cultures is unity/oneness/totality, etc. The former lends itself well to narrative—it is a narrative; the latter isn't, except in fragments and anecdotes—a paradox! To us this search, perhaps for a partial totality, enforces and continues meaning, thereby allowing us to inhabit in the domain of memory.

Traveling cultures, multiculturalism, hyphenated identities, are trendy topics in the humanities and social sciences. The study of cultural borderlands is to be privileged over cultural patterns.[4] A huge amount of literature and time is being devoted to the celebration of border cultures. Cultural hybrids, those who straddle more than one culture, are the inhabitants of the third space,[5] engaged 'in the creation of yet another culture, a new story to explain in the world and our participation in it, a new value system with the images and symbols that connect us to each other and to the planet'.[6]

The 'cultures' under scrutiny are geographically and ethnically diverse. Yet, most of them have one thing in common. They are non-Western[7] cultures. Identities are being ruptured, tradition is being challenged because of imperialistic imperatives. Cultural borderlands are being created out of a necessity to survive.

The border experience, for the most part, is rather one way. The presence of the South and the East might have redefined the physical features of the West,[8] but the West has not been redefined in terms of ideologies and beliefs. The dominant ideologies/ideology impact immigrant/minority lifestyle. The question is, to what extent does immigrant lifestyle, their 'culture' influence dominant ideologies?

Journal entry: 4 March 1993

Brian, a good friend of mine, is writing a paper for a seminar... he predicts a 'post-ethnic', 'post-gender age.'

'Brian!' I shout at him. 'Post in whose terms? All women become men...'

'Look, Lubna,' he interrupts, 'I just feel people should do away with a stress on biological differences, and use other salient common experiences as bases of political action.'

'Brian, my skin color and the reaction it elicits is salient enough for me. You wouldn't understand...'

'Lubna, you can think in quite white masculinist terms. I saw that in the class last quarter. You were the one who got the A+ for your impeccable logic, not me. I don't understand your obsession with your foreignness.'

And this from a man who told me that my notion of not sleeping with friends is foreign to him...

Too assimilated...

('she wears blue jeans!' 'she is more American than the British! she is so friendly!' 'she talks in class!' 'she has learned a lot about women's rights ever since she moved to the country!')

Not assimilated enough...

('she doesn't think getting drunk is fun!' 'she reads too much into sex!' 'she is codependent—she needs counseling because she has her brother living with her' 'she spends too much time with other women, even though she is not a lesbian!')

Always in a marked position... Whatever I do or say... either exotic or weird... I resist, sometimes consciously, sometimes unknowingly... but the foreign culture is affecting my psyche... nothing I do is irrelevant, it is either a reaction or an action of conformity... sometimes I go out of my way not to resist... I want to be open... beyond culture... I go dancing in nightclubs... go to bars to drink... but some things I just cannot do... what have they changed for me? They tell me it's my choice, I came to this country... academia is brainwashing me into Westernization anyway, why am I fighting it?...

'Pakistan is the 51st state of the US, anyway. I am just state-hopping!'... just a different sort of imperialism! wherever I go you mold me... you think by wearing a nose ring, by appropriating my art forms, trying to listen to my music, I influence you?... I would really feel I influenced you if next time I talk to you you don't look at your watch...

Journal entry: 12 March 1993

'Why bother about what's from your culture and what's not? Just do what you like...'

'I like certain things in my culture... I like the way we finish one thing before going on to another... I like to love my family... I want to look after my parents in their old age... I like visiting friends and relatives and having long pointless conversations before getting down to business... I like to fall in love so that I go beyond my self without being made to feel I am

actually trying to get back to my mother's womb or something. . . I like dressing up everyday even if I am a starving student.'
　　'So do what you want. . .'
　　'. . . but some things I cannot. . . I have to work on ten things simultaneously in grad school. . . I don't want to be lonely, so I try to accommodate to my friends' lifestyles. . . now I even seem to be forgetting what I used to like back home. . .'

The issue is not just the maintenance of 'culture' for those who 'used to have it'. In order to have a truly multicultural society the power differential has to be leveled out. This supposed accommodation to the non-Westerners would actually not just be a concession to their needs, but would signify a giant step in the direction of integrating those facets of different cultures that best satisfy the human condition. But again this cannot be achieved if the 'human condition' and that what is best for it is determined by the hegemonic groups. An intercultural dialogue which is not repressive is the prerequisite for this culture that goes beyond culture.

Memory becomes a site of resistance for those who are oppressed in a context where there is a power imbalance. By virtue of their ability to identify with yet alienate themselves from the different spaces they inhabit, hybrids can 'yoke together unlikely traditions of thought'[9] and contribute to the setting up of 'new structures of authority, new political initiatives'.[10] They can strategically mobilize and deploy the various discourses that they have internalized in different contexts, and herein lies their agency.

Through my consciousness of my agency as a 'hybrid' I can undertake projects of cultural translation in different contexts whereby I execute certain behaviors (physical, linguistic, or otherwise) in temporal and spatial realms which have hitherto been atypical contexts for these actions. A striking example of such an action is a fellow hybrid's recent move towards covering her hair. Although the use of the *hijab* (veil) predates Islam, in the initial stages of the spread of Islam it became a strategy consciously adopted by women to protect themselves from unwanted advances. It was 'as defined by a Medina in a state of civil war a recognition of the street as a space where *zina* (fornication) is permitted.'[11] My friend's adoption of the *hijab* in the context of a university in the US is perceived by her (and others who understand) as a strategic, creative response to what she terms as the undue emphasis on sexuality in her present environment.

My ethnographic work with Pakistani Muslim immigrant women in the US has provided me with numerous examples whereby these hybrids seek to empower themselves by confronting power structures through everyday practices[12] that can be seen as acts of creative resistance. These behaviors are enacted in so-called dominant as well as home culture contexts. As a result, cultural identities are being continually reconstituted. My analysis of the identity formation processes is grounded in theories of oppositional consciousness.[13] These theories refer to the 'grace, flexibility, and strength' developed by women of color as a response to oppressive conditions which enables them 'to confidently commit to a well-defined structure of identity for one hour, day, week, month, year', and 'to self consciously transform that identity according to the requisites of another oppositional ideological tactic if readings of power formations require it'.[14]

Excerpt from field-notes, 8 February 1994

Aisha,[15] one of the participants in my dissertation study with Pakistani Muslim women in the US, was spending the night at my place, because she wanted to use my computer. She had a paper due the next day. She did turn on the computer, but kept getting up to make herself tea, make me a late night snack, join me on my mattress to tell me what 'a perfect older sister' I was, or flip through my books to see 'if they were as boring as their titles'. Then we started talking. We discussed the implications of test-tube babies for traditional mothering roles a bit—that was the topic of the assignment. But then we moved on to other issues like why Aisha had changed her mind about becoming a lawyer. 'Hah! Data!' The ethnographer realized. As we conversed I could not resist taking notes.

'Why don't you just tape-record what we are saying? It will be easier for you. You look tired,' suggested my solicitous collaborator. I proceeded to make the necessary arrangements, while Aisha continued to explicate her career plans.

Aisha had always had a hard time in the courses the career counselor had told her would help her get admitted to law school. She had, however, not wavered in her determination. She wanted to make her mother happy. During the winter break she had realized the extent of her parents' financial strain. This had prompted her to revise the plans of her academic future. She would wait to go to either graduate or professional school. Her priority was to graduate as soon as possible with her BA, and get a job in the field of advertising. This would be against her politics, but she did not know how else she would make enough money to support her parents and her brother. She also wondered if she should postpone her trip to Bosnia, and just go to summer school in order to graduate faster. That way she would neither have to work an extra job in the spring quarter nor borrow the five hundred dollars her mother had promised to save for her.

'You know how I personally feel about you going to Bosnia. I know you want to help out at the camps with the Muslim children, but it scares me a lot. I don't want you to be exposed to any danger. But I am not sure you should spend twelve months of the year in school,' I responded as I finally pressed the 'record' button.

'Well. I could take the courses you teach, and get all 'A's,' she said cheekily. I decided to let that remark go by, and asked her if she had discussed the matter with her mother.

'Well, yeah. But it always turns into this discussion about marriage!' She rolled her eyes, threw out her hands as if in despair, and giggled. Then she said more seriously, 'I understand my mom's concern better now. My father is not worried. You know, it's the parents' farz [responsibility] to get their children married. My mom says if it remains up to my father, he will do nothing. So I want to keep marriage in mind. But who do I marry?'

'Well, what about your various love objects? Do they qualify as prospective mates? Just don't even think of that Arshad guy though. He is not good enough for you,' I was indeed 'a perfect older sister'.

'Oh no! Don't worry! I don't think I will ever marry someone I have a crush on. They go away in six months or less.' She reassured me. 'But then I don't want to marry those weirdos who come with rishtas even when they don't know me. Did I tell you about what happened at Christmas?' She launched into a tale of yet another rejected suitor.

'So you see this person sees me twice. . . yes, just twice,' she held up two fingers to stress her point, 'and he decides to propose to me. His whole family comes over. And my mom says I have to meet them. We even have to cook dinner for them. I don't understand. How come he claims to be in love with me? We haven't said a word to each other!'

'Well, Aisha, this is pretty common in Pakistan. People do tend to do this. . . ' I tried to interject my authoritative comment about the Pakistani courtship scene, but Aisha was committed to her monologue.

'I guess I am too American. Hah! But then you know I did not even like his family. They did not pray, although it was a Friday. I can't be part of a family who don't try to be good Muslims.'

This was too much for me. 'Aisha, do you realize you are being contradictory? You are too American to understand the poor guy's motives, but *then you condemn his family for not strictly following Islam. Make up your mind!'*

'Yeah,' she said thoughtfully, 'That is interesting. Now I kind of understand this whole multiple hyphenated identity stuff. In some ways I am more of a Muslim American than a Pakistani Muslim. What a thought though!' She shuddered. Then with a glint in her eyes she said, 'I know! I know! Things are not that simple, as someone I know is going to say in a sec. But come on, you have to admit I am the perfect hybrid, the perfect specimen for your study!'

Somehow Aisha did turn in a paper on time.

Here I want to introduce a note of caution. I do not see hybridity as a utopian state. As Behdad[16] points out, post-colonial travel may privilege some, and oppress others. Factors such as differences in class backgrounds in the home country, educational background, religious sect, socioeconomic status background in the US, all contribute to an uneven differential access to power.

The problematic of resistance is crucial to my own present role/roles as a woman from a Third World country involved in academic pursuits in a university in the First World's center of imperialism. I am committed to projects that challenge hegemonic modes, yet I am acutely aware of my complicity with the power and domination of the institutions with which I am affiliated.

Journal entry: 22 May 1995

'I am tired of this back-stabbing, this attacking. I am white and I am American, and this is all I know. It is so difficult,' The student, one of 25 who were enrolled in my Women, Nationalism, Colonialism course, looked as if she was about to cry. 'Here we go again,' I mentally wrung my hands, 'At least she is not crying like Anna in the summer,' I consoled myself.

'I understand your pain, Jennifer, and I feel for you. I am also grateful to you for bringing up how you feel in class. Maybe now other people who have similar concerns will feel free to talk about them with me. Haunani is very firm in her stand about Hawai'ian sovereignty and she has grounds for it. And hers is a frontal assault, not back-stabbing. That is why it is so hard to take. I know it is easier said than done, but don't take it personally. It is a matter of what one collectivity did to another, what one people did to another. I feel for you personally, and I wish I could take your pain away. But colonization happened, and is happening. It exists. I cannot deny that.

*I suggest you should get together with other people after class to talk about
these issues. We need to finish talking about* From a Native Daughter,' *I
resolutely looked away from her eyes and opened my book.*

*I later boasted about the way I handled the situation to Jeffrey, Jane,
Clare, and David. After all I had not spent the whole period holding her
and wiping her tears the way I had with Anna in the summer when she
told her story about how an African-American student in high school had
snubbed her.*

*Of course I will not tell anyone about how guilty I felt for the rest of the
week and was extra nice to Jennifer. Is it because I am a giving, caring
teacher, or am I afraid that she will write me a bad evaluation at the end
of the quarter?*

Why am I presenting my ideas in this paper that will ultimately be
published in the US? Or rather, why am I being allowed to present my
ideas in this paper that will be ultimately published in the United States?

I get a chance to 'voice' my opinions. It's a cathartic act, I suppose. A
Third World oppressed female graduate student given the opportunity
to protest against injustice. Or am I exoticizing myself in order to get
some recognition? After all, I am a different perspective, an alternative
voice.

What exactly does it mean when the Symbolic[17] momentarily ac-
knowledges the Semiotic, when patriarchy, imperialism allows femininity, the colonized to speak? When the margin speaks, it is appropriated
by the center. It is no longer the margin. The Semiotic becomes the
Symbolic, yet serving the imperialist's purpose not the colonized's, who
in one sense goes through a process of recolonization. His/her voice is
a 'valid' standpoint for reality. Yet the imperialist's way is always the
reference. Anything else is a deviance.

It is the paradox of my existence that I need the validation of my
masters. In my own country I need a Ph.D. from a Western institution to
compete in the job market and to get someone to listen to my voice. My
'empowerment' in that context derives from the credentials bestowed
on me by the most powerful in the world.

Crossing a border to get to the other side is not the same as eliminating
borders. My getting a permit to work in the US or attaining a prestigious
position in Pakistan is not going to change the oppressive consequences
and realities of colonialism and imperialism. My participation in a
project that claims to question borders such as the publication of this
anthology is doing nothing significant to eradicate them.

Even as I start questioning my border-crossing, I tell myself not to be so pessimistic. I remind myself that power relations are not homogeneous, that there are spaces where resistance can be enacted, that the center can be corroded from within. ('A face-saving,' the persistent pessimist in me asks, 'or do you really believe this?')

'It ain't where you're from, it's where you're at...' is part of the title of one of the papers[18] I reviewed for my qualifying exam question on the politics of identity. I agree with Gilroy that creative resistance within a specific context can be effective only if a hybrid is fully cognizant of the multiple power relations operating in that particular time and space. Both the 'politics of fulfilment' and the 'politics of transfiguration'[19] have to be anchored in the hybrid's realization of the 'historical and cultural reality circumscribed by the diasporan experience',[20] that is, the cultural domination of Western Eurocentrism, and the experience of exploitation, appropriation, slavery, inequality, and racism that it has entailed.

I assert, even if I risk the charge of essentialism, that 'where you're from' is as significant as 'where you're at' when it comes to resisting centers of power. A hybrid, as I said earlier, draws from various cultural resources, and this array of choices bestows on her an agency denied to others. If I forget where I am from, I am limiting my reservoir of choices. It's where I am that shapes my consciousness and subsequent resistance, but it is only if I can draw from where I'm from that I can assert my agency.

But then can I forget where I am from? And why should I? The West is in me. I cannot deny my so-called Western identity. But I also cannot afford to forget. Where I am from has contributed to the construction of my selves. It will contribute to the construction of my children's selves even if they never go there. Moreover, my memories of that 'imaginary homeland'[21] are part of me. Losing these memories or not affirming my identity which derives from that homeland is like letting a part of me die. These days I am frightened that I will forget my brother, that I will really let him die. My attachment (or whatever word that best expresses my intense feelings) towards my 'home culture', no matter how fractured, ruptured this culture may be, gives rise to the same kind of fear.

I need to move beyond dichotomies. I need to create a language that will integrate the various facets of my resistance. Such a language will neither privilege where I am at, nor will it privilege where I am from. The borders between where I am and where I am from are fluid, ever-changing, not clearly demarcated. I carry multiple realities within myself and these realities, and associated memories become salient at different times, in different spaces. My 'imaginary homeland' is not so imaginary to me always, and the material reality around me sometimes just fades away. At times these worlds even merge.

Journal entry: 7 December 1992

A couple of nights ago I had that dream again, at least a variation of that same dream. I am in Lahore with my family, in my parents' home, content but very sad at the same time... very sad, knowing the contentment is temporary... it won't last long... I just cannot stay... it is inevitable that I leave... I have to leave... I am thinking in my dream... I hope my flight will be confirmed... I don't want to be stuck here... I don't want to leave them... I have to leave them... I scream at Salman, my little brother who has taken on the responsibility to get the confirmation... I look at my father, 'I have to get there by next week... do something...' I woke up tense and angry, yet I was upset when I realized I was not at home... I was in my bed in California...

✦ Notes and References

1. This quote has been taken from the cover of *Time*, weekly newsmagazine, Vol. 142, No. 1, dated 5 July 1993.
2. A. Bilgrami, 'What is a Muslim? Fundamental Commitment and Cultural Identity'. *Critical Inquiry* 18 (Summer), 1992, 821–42.
3. T. Gabriel, 'Thesis on Memory and Identity: The Search for the Origins of the River Nile'. *Emergences* 1, 1989, 131–38.
4. R. Rosaldo, *Culture and Truth: The Remaking of Social Analysis* (Boston, Beacon Press, 1989).
5. H. Bhabha, 'The Third Space: Interview with Homi Bhabha'. In J. Rutherford (ed.), *Identity* (London, Lawrence Wishart, 1990), 206–21.
6. G. Anzaldua, *Borderlands/La Frontera: The New Mestiza* (San Francisco, Aunt Lute Books, 1987).
7. I am well aware of the problematic use of the term 'non-Western'. I am using it, though, because alternative terms like 'non-European', 'indigenous', etc. are misleading and limiting in other ways.
8. G. Gomez-Pena, 'The Multicultural Paradigm'. *High Performance* 12, 1989, 18–27.
9. Bhabha, 212. See n. 5.
10. Bhabha, 211. See n. 5.
11. F. Mernissi, *The Veil and the Male Elite: A Feminist Interpretation of Women's Rights in Islam* (New York, Addison-Wesley Publishing Company, Inc., 1991), 183.

12. M. de Certeau, *The Practice of Everyday life* (Berkeley, University of California Press, 1984).
13. C. Sandoval, 'US Third World Feminism: The Theory and Method of Oppositional Consciousness in the Postmodern World'. *Genders* 10, 1991, 1–24.
14. Sandoval, 15. See n. 13.
15. This is a pseudonym chosen by the research participant.
16. A. Behdad, 'Traveling to Teach: Post-colonial Critics in the American Academy'. In C. McCarthy and W. Crishaw (eds), *Race, Identity, and Representation in Education* (New York and London, Routledge, 1993), 40–49.
17. My usage of the Symbolic versus Semiotic dichotomy is based on a reading of Kristeva's 'Revolution in Poetic Language' (T. Moi, *The Kristeva Reader* [New York, Columbia University Press, 1986]). The Symbolic refers to the realm of language, and the Semiotic refers to that which cannot be represented through language. The Symbolic is created by and for the Law of the Father. The Semiotic falls out of the jurisdiction of this Law, because it is connected to the Maternal, the phases of life before language.
18. P. Gilroy, 'It Ain't where you're from, It's where you're at...: The Dialectics of Diasporic Identification'. *Third Text* 13, 1990/91, 3–16.
19. Gilroy, 11. See n. 18. According to him, 'politics of fulfillment' refers to the struggle for the satisfaction of desires as inscribed within contemporary societal structures, whereas the 'politics of transfiguration' refers to the striving for a future where oppressive power hierarchies would be eradicated, giving birth to a community with new values and new solidarities.
20. G. Tawadros, 'Beyond the Boundary: The Work of Three Black Women Artists in Britain'. *Third Text* 8, 1989, 138.
21. S. Rushdie, *Imaginary Homelands* (London, Pantheon Books, 1991).

5

From Starbucks to a *sangeet*: Whether at a trendy Western spot or traditional Eastern gathering, South Asian women are dealing with the same issues every moment of their lives

R. Kamna Narain

Author's note: *The following story may seem like fiction, but the only elements that are not real are the names of characters and settings of the story. Each character represents a real woman, and each woman is a voice which represents true feelings that many South Asian women have about pressures relating to marriage.*

Part one: Starbucks Cafe

'I don't care what the circumstances are, 20 is just no age to start thinking about marriage.' Avantika defiantly raised the tall glass of iced mocha to her lips as if to toast her own declaration.

We were discussing my cousin Sonam, who was about to begin her third year of college and was already on 'the marriage market'. Although Sonam was four years younger than me, it was silently accepted that I would choose my own life partner at a time which was appropriate for me. Why I was given this right, which I knew many women my age envied, was never specifically stated. I have always been very independent minded and vocal, which may be why my family assumed that I would choose my own husband just as I chose my own career path. Another reason could be that I have a visual disability, thus, people obviously realize that along with a 'good Indian boy', I also need someone who understands and accepts me and my limitations.

Sonam, on the other hand, was used to having the entire family discuss her marriage. Her photos had been sent to a few interested parties and she had even 'been shown' to two prospective in-laws. Personally, I thought that much of this may have to do with her looks. Let's face it, South Asian elders never like to see a pretty face go to waste, and Sonam was definitely *bahu* (daughter-in-law) extraordinaire material—gorgeous, docile, always smiling, and talented in domestic ways. There was also the notion that 'good boys don't just fall out of the sky when you need them.' In other words, the search had to begin now in order for Sonam, or should we say, her family, to find a suitable boy by age 22: the age by which most South Asian women have graduated from college and are thus deemed to be ready for the next phase in their life—marriage.

Realistically, I knew that my cousin was being encouraged to marry at a relatively young age because of family circumstances. Her widowed mother was planning to settle in India in a few years, which meant that Sonam could either become completely independent or settle down. While independence had its own glamour, Sonam didn't think settling down was such a bad idea.

'It's not like I can't finish school or pursue a career after I'm married,' she said to me once. 'I don't want to be married right at this moment, but, I wouldn't mind settling down in a couple of years. My best friend is 20 and engaged, and she doesn't feel trapped or anything.'

To no avail, I tried explaining Sonam's perspective to Avantika, who balked at the idea. This didn't surprise me. At 25, Avantika shuddered at the whole concept of marriage. She valued her freedom and felt that there were many more things to accomplish in life before she settled down—like furthering her career in marketing communications.

'Look Kamna, it's not like I'm against marriage,' Avantika explained. 'I just think that 26 or 27 is the ideal age to get married. By then you've done everything and can spend a couple of quality years with your husband before you have kids.'

'There's no ideal age for marriage,' Mona jumped in. She had been looking through a colleague's paper and could no longer resist the topic of discussion. 'Marriage is a patriarchal society's way of maintaining control over women. I don't know what the alternative to marriage would be, but there must be something.' She raised her voice as she concluded her statement, as the noise in Starbucks Cafe was increasing with the late afternoon rush.

'Wow, that's exactly what I think,' Avantika said with wide eyes. 'I've never articulated it that way though.'

'What do you expect from an assistant professor?' I teased.

'That too at a research university,' Mona added in an exaggerated tone.

'Seriously though Mona,' I began. 'You obviously didn't think marriage was that bad when you were 23, since you went ahead and tried it. Or was that just because you were still in Pakistan and didn't know what else to do?' My erudite friend had divorced at 25, right after she immigrated to America, and five years later, seemingly viewed the institution of marriage in a negative light. It wasn't that Mona had a tragic or traumatic experience during her marriage. Basically, after they married, her husband was no longer willing to move to America, where Mona was pursuing graduate studies, so they filed for divorce. Over the years, Mona had come to believe that there were so many more things she could do, primarily in her career, when she was not bound by the ties of wedlock. Any mystery or romantic notions which marriage had held at one time were absent now as Mona had already 'been through it' and now found the idea rather unappealing.

'Well, everybody else in Pakistan was getting married at my age, so it was kind of like succumbing to peer pressure. I was conforming to society by doing what a "good daughter" was expected to do, and that's get married so that your parents know you are settled.'

'You should've just said no,' Avantika pointed her half-filled glass to Mona as if reprimanding a teenager.

'Oh come on you guys, marriage can't be that bad. I mean, if anything, you'll have a date every Friday night.' I thought they were both being a little harsh, though I realized that they had their reasons for shuddering at the thought of marriage. Mona had already tried it and it hadn't worked out. As she put it, she valued her independence too much and was 'married to her career' now.

Avantika's opposition had evolved over the past couple of years. She did want to get married eventually, but the fact that she was being pressured by her parents to tie the knot as soon as possible, was suffocating her. The pressure had been on since she was 21, and she was actually getting used to the day-to-day nagging, realizing that, since she still lived with her parents, it just came with the territory.

'I have a cousin who got married when she was 23 and she's totally happy now. She's working on her master's degree and her husband seems to adore her.' I could think of half-a-dozen other examples of friends who had married by their mid-20s and were perfectly content with their lives. My cousin's marriage was arranged, but other friends of mine had 'love marriages' which were fully supported by their families. Many South Asian parents living in the United States, like my own, were open to the idea of their daughters dating and finding their own mates. Although, if she didn't find someone by age 24, Mom and Dad would gladly step in and arrange for her to meet some 'nice boys'. The bottom line was, the girl needed to be married by age 25 or 26, while males could wait until their early 30s, as that was the pre-existing norm of our culture, which, obviously, not many were willing to change.

This was Avantika's situation. Her mother strongly believed that if her daughter was not married by the time she was 26, there would be no 'good boys' (i.e., educated, from a good family, good looking, successful, stable, etc.) left. Since Avantika's parents did not completely approve of her boyfriend, her mom had begun putting matrimonial ads in the local Indian paper. Avantika did not want to defy her parents' wishes, and thus conceded to this (reluctantly) and explained her position to her boyfriend. In the past year, she had made contact with half-a-dozen eligible bachelors, unfortunately, meeting no one to her liking. Avantika understood where her mom was coming from—she had to think about two other daughters, one of whom was already 21, and she could not afford to 'lose' so much time on her eldest daughter. Understandably though, all the pressure did get irritating after a while. Avantika was sure that if she did not have parental pressure, she would want to get married in a couple of years, but right now, the idea only conjured up feelings of resentment.

'I know that there are happily married people out there Kamna,' Avantika's tone was exasperated. 'Half my friends are married, and they think that I should bite the bullet as well. But if you were hearing about marriage constantly, you'd get sick of it too. I think I'd rather be like Mona here, blissfully independent.'

'Don't let her fool you,' I said. 'Mona is as romantic as the rest of us, and would get married if Prince Charming drove up in a black Porsche and pulled out an offer for a meaningful relationship.'

'Of course,' Mona said matter-of-factly, taking the last sip of her expresso. 'Kamna, if you think marriage is such a blessing, why aren't you getting engaged?'

'She's afraid she'll have to cook everyday.' Pavan chimed as she pulled up a chair and set her Latte down on the square table. Pavan and I had been friends since college and she was visiting from the east coast, where she had recently graduated from medical school.

'I can't argue with you,' I said looking down at my mug of mocha. 'Don't you guys think there's a myth that all South Asian women have to turn into their mothers when they get married? You know, do the whole "cooking-cleaning-raising kids-maintain a social life in the Indian community-and then maybe have a job too" routine.'

'It's not a myth,' Pavan assured. 'I know women who learn how to cook as soon as they get engaged. I also know girls who are being versed in domestic ways so that they are more marriageable.'

'Marriage does seem like kind of a big job,' Avantika said almost sadly. 'From what I see in my family and among my friends, and even in movies, the woman is *always* making sacrifices and giving more in a marriage. For example, she has "become" a part of her husband's family and adapted to their ways of living, while nothing much changes for the husband. I feel like I'm going to have to give 110 percent of myself and spend time taking care of my husband and his family.'

'It makes me laugh when I'm sick and my mother laments that if I had a husband he would be taking care of me. Talk about unrealistic, not to mention, indirect pressure,' Mona rolled her eyes which enhanced her animated expression.

'Your mom still puts pressure on you?' Avantika asked.

'Of course. Just because you turn 30 and have a Ph.D. doesn't mean that you'll escape parental pressures. It's just subtle things here and there. My mom tells my sister that she thinks I'm not happy. She doesn't directly say anything to me anymore. I guess my parents know that I tried it, and have had relationships with other men, but it just wasn't worth it. My dad is more interested in my career. It's my mom who thinks I need both.'

'Me too.' Avantika was relieved to see that she wasn't the only person in the world who was currently dealing with indirect pressure. 'My dad thinks I should just forget about marriage for a couple of years and get my MBA.'

'Grad school, in fact, education in general, is a great way to avoid marriage,' Pavan interjected with a cheeky smile. 'In the Punjabi [Sikh] culture, girls who don't want to get married at 18 go to college so that they don't have to deal with it until they are 21. I don't know why Sikh girls seem to get married at such an early age. Maybe it has something to do with the fact that our religion is so young and people still want to preserve tradition and culture, which is defined by the religion.'

'Is that why you went to med school, to avoid marriage?' Mona asked.

'No. I've been pretty independent all my life. I was the first girl in my family to go to college and my family knows that they can't force me to do anything.' At 26, Pavan did not have to deal with the same pressures many other women her age encountered, primarily because of her career choice and her liberal-minded mother's support. 'Of course, there are always little hints from the extended family, "Oh *beti* (daughter), it would be so nice to visit two people instead of one," blah, blah, blah.'

We all giggled at the ridiculous familiarity of Pavan's comment. It seemed that the South Asian community was overly interested in the private lives of its youth, especially the females. Their keen interest in itself was a form of indirect pressure. When growing up in such a culture, one simply became accustomed to it, ignoring it when necessary, and laughing it off at other times. At the same time, although we laughed about it now, we all knew how easy it was to reach a 'boiling point' as well; when the pressure became unbearable and we felt that our lives were being controlled by the standards of society.

'Well ladies, I must get going,' I stood up and pushed the wooden chair in.

'Have fun at the *sangeet* (bridal shower),' Pavan smiled.

'She will,' Avantika grimaced sarcastically. 'Nobody will be asking her when her turn is.'

'Kamna, do you realize how lucky you are?' Mona questioned.

'Yea, I do. It's bad enough worrying about men. But I guess having the entire world asking you when you're getting hitched with one is worse.' I waved goodbye to my friends and weaved through tables. As I made my way out of the cafe, I thought about what an interesting scenario I had left. Four professional women, each advancing in their own respective careers, were sitting in a very Western atmosphere, yet their topic of discussion was something that only South Asian women could truly relate to. It just goes to show that you can take the girl out of the country, but you can't take her away from the pressures of the culture.

Part two: Ladies' sangeet and mehndi

'Imagining what your own might be like?' I sat down next to Nisha, who seemed a million miles away from the festivities of the ladies' *sangeet* and *mehndi* (ceremony in which henna is applied to the bride's hands and feet).

'Kind of,' Nisha smiled shyly. Her sober demeanor was what, according to my mother, made Nisha a girl that any family would be lucky to have as a *bahu*. It was only a matter of time before Nisha would adorn some lucky family crown. She had just turned 23, and although she was still an occupational therapy student, her family felt it was time for her to get married. 'Rita is lucky though, she's marrying someone she has dated and who is from here.'

I understood the weak tone of Nisha's voice. In about six months she would be taking a trip to India with her family—the goal of the vacation was to find a husband for Nisha. They had raised their daughter with traditional Indian values and did not see any reason why she would not get along with a boy from India. Her parents were open to their eldest daughter finding someone on her own, but no one special had come into Nisha's life yet, and time was ticking away. Her cousins had been married in their early 20s, and nobody felt that things should be any different for Nisha. Along with pressures from her immediate and extended family in America, relatives in India were constantly asking her parents what was taking so long. It was mainly for her parents' sake, that Nisha had agreed to marry whoever they approved of. What I admired the most, was that Nisha did all this begrudgingly.

Although she vehemently opposed the idea a couple of years ago, Nisha had come to accept the fact that she was destined to get married, or at least engaged, within the next year or so. Her attitude reminded me a lot of my cousin Sonam's. Both of them had heard so much about the issue since they were teenagers, that they had become conditioned to accept it. Yet, neither of them was bitter, which was probably healthy. 'Moving out isn't a realistic choice for me as my parents will not let me since the college I attend is local,' Nisha had told me once. 'I'm just going to make the best of it.'

'Yea, Rita is lucky,' I said, looking at the 27-year-old radiant bride-to-be as she sat in the center of the room while some of the older ladies sang traditional wedding songs and the younger girls danced. 'But she deserves it. She had so much pressure to get married, especially from her mom.'

I recalled Rita telling me stories about how her mother was obsessed with marriage. Ever since Rita was in college, and even as she pursued a career as a banking professional, Rita said that her family could talk about nothing other than marriage. 'What really hurt,' Rita once confided, 'was that they didn't care about any other aspect of my life. It was like I wasn't worth anything if I wasn't married.' At one point, Rita's entire perception of marriage was altered and she hated the thought of it. 'When everyone tells you to do one thing, you almost want to do the opposite.' Her mother had even placed a matrimonial ad in the local paper, without Rita's knowledge. Fortunately, for Rita, she met a guy on her own and was now going to be his wife.

'Nisha, do you think that South Asian parents are in such a rush to get their daughters married because they feel like they have to answer to society? You know, be able to tell their friends and family that their daughter is getting married in a timely manner and at the appropriate age.'

'Maybe, but I also think that they really believe that their daughter's happiness lies in getting her settled as quickly as possible and finding the "home" she will spend the rest of her life in. Everything else seems to follow. Like education. My dad is all for education, but he doesn't see why I can't do it after I'm married. After all, my cousins did it.'

Rita walked towards us and I smiled up at her. 'Your mother sure looks happy.' She just laughed as she headed upstairs to change so that the *mehndi* could be applied on her.

'God I'm tired!' Sangeeta practically fell on the floor next to me. She had been dancing for the past hour. She was extremely energetic and light on her feet. No one would guess that she had just finished her masters degree in philosophy. 'Can you believe how many people are here?'

'That's what Indian weddings are all about,' I said, winking at Nisha. 'The extent of hoopla you have is directly related to how successful the wedding is overall.'

'You don't need to remind me of that.' Sangeeta gulped down ice water. 'My sister just got married, and there was enough hoopla to leave a sour taste in my mouth. That's one of the reasons I don't want to get married.'

'Why?' Nisha exclaimed. 'Don't you want your wedding to be memorable?'

'Sure, but there are limits, especially when you're living in this country. I saw what my parents had to go through, both financially and emotionally. Believe me, it's not worth it.'

'That's no reason to not get married, just have a small ceremony,' I suggested.

'My mom has already said that they can't afford to throw the wedding of the century for me. But that's only part of it. I really just don't feel like this is the right time for me to settle down. There are too many things I still want to do.'

'Don't get married until you are willing to share everything with your partner. Your life is not your own after marriage. When you know you do want to share everything with someone, that means you're ready.' Rita chirped the words as I replaced a hair pin in her braid.

'Thanks for the advice Rita. Now go get painted with henna,' Sangeeta playfully tugged at her braid.

'Are your parents pressuring you to get married?' Nisha resumed the conversation with Sangeeta.

'They'd like for me to get married. But considering I'm 26, they're not pushing it as badly as you'd think they would. I think the fact that my sister got married at 27 might be why they are not too worried, or maybe it's just that they know how stubborn I am. In fact, my married friends are the ones who are just obnoxious about the subject, constantly hinting and trying to set me up. My poor parents are just waiting for me to find someone or say "Okay I'm ready, go ahead and find someone for me." Anyway, I think that my mom wouldn't be too surprised if I never got married. She'd probably be sad that she couldn't tell her friends that I was settled down.'

Nisha and I exchanged knowing glances. Maybe it was society our parents were out to please after all. The older ladies kept singing and I settled back against a throw pillow, realizing the same things I had realized earlier when leaving Starbucks—I was rather lucky to not experience any direct pressures to get married. My mother was not obsessed with marriage, like Avantika's or Rita's. And I didn't feel like I had no choice but to settle down, like Nisha or Sonam.

As I surveyed the room and every ounce of excitement which filled it, I concluded that marriage itself was not a bad thing, it was the pressure to enter into it before one is ready, which clouds our perception of it. It's the fact that we are made to feel that we are not worth anything without a husband that makes us cynical. Despite our accomplishments in our professional, academic, and family life, we are still viewed as incomplete if we are not married. It seemed a shame that many South Asian women were robbed of the excitement and happiness which is supposed to accompany marriage, because they are forced to enter it prematurely. Not all South Asian women were as lucky as Rita and not many were as accommodating as Nisha or Sonam. I couldn't imagine Avantika or Sangeeta, or even myself for that matter, basking in the joy of our wedding if it happened at a time when we were not prepared to take this serious step. After all, we were meant to walk down the path of life, not run. The road from Starbucks Cafe to a *sangeet*, the bridge between Western society and Eastern culture, may seem long, but it's actually only a short sprint.

Epilogue & analysis

This publication went to press approximately one year after interviews were conducted and these stories were written. Much can change in one year. See for yourself.

Avantika married the summer after she was interviewed. Ironically, she was being equally pressured by her boyfriend to make a decision about marriage as his family was pressuring him to get married (he's approaching 30). Avantika married her boyfriend, and although her parents were not thrilled with the idea at first, the wedding was nevertheless a grand affair. As for Avantika herself, once she got engaged her negative attitude about marriage lessened each day. She was very excited about moving into her own place and the wedding itself.

Sonam got into a serious relationship right after she was interviewed. While this lessened marriage pressure in general, she was now being pressured to marry this specific guy. Her mother wants to know if he will marry her or not, and if he doesn't, the plan is to arrange Sonam's marriage after she graduates from college. She, of course, wants to marry her boyfriend.

Mona is still single and her attitude towards marriage hasn't changed much. According to her, 'it's just a piece of paper'. She is, however, in a significant relationship and her family is happy that she has finally found someone. She and her significant other considered living together, but as he is rather conservative, Mona feels that he will probably want to get married, and she is open to the idea.

Pavan also remains single but she is now feeling great pressure from her family to get married. Even her mother brings up the topic in subtle ways. Pavan believes that much of the reason for this is that her male cousins who are younger than her have gotten married or engaged, thus, the issue inevitably arises for her as well. Pavan still refuses to have an arranged marriage. She says that if she marries someone, it will be someone she has found and chosen.

Nisha was married in December as planned. However, her marriage was arranged with a man who was already settled in the United States and they went back to India for the ceremony four months after they were introduced to each other. Nisha has found marriage to be a good experience and is happy with her husband.

Rita also got married the summer after she was interviewed. She is quite content and is busy planning a delayed honeymoon.

Sangeeta is feeling great pressure to get married. Her mother has said that she must be married within a year, and Sangeeta feels that she has no choice in the matter. She still is not thrilled about the idea of marriage and says that she is scared that she is not ready for marriage and everything it encompasses.

Given their initial interviews and what has happened since, it seems that South Asian women can't really escape the pressures of marriage. Yet the pressure does not just come from parents; extended family, significant others, and friends can all add pressure in their own way. And the fact of the matter is, that this occurs in all cultures and societies. People always seem to be interested in marriage and the topic inevitably comes up, particularly after a woman is settled in her career.

In South Asian cultures though, women end up succumbing to this pressure more often. The question is, are they talked into it or do they marry against their will? Women like Avantika, Nisha, and Rita may have needed a little convincing at first, however, once they warmed up to the idea of marriage, it became more of a positive experience. Sangeeta, Mona, and Pavan cannot even imagine getting excited about a marriage that they are not 100 percent in favor of.

No matter what a woman's frame of mind, the recurring theme with the women in this chapter, as well as most other South Asian women, is that marriage is perceived as a very significant and serious institution. While most other cultures would agree, South Asian cultures take it one step further, thus, many women associate marriage with added responsibility and a loss of independence and freedom, and that too, at a young age. Their male counterparts, on the other hand, do not face these same pressures until later in life and the responsibility which is highlighted for them is financial, there is no implied emotional sacrifice or loss of independence.

Why South Asian women feel this way needs to be fully explored and examined. The reasons are varied and may range from their female role models, media images of South Asian women or values they were brought up with. In the meantime, every South Asian woman should realize that they are not alone. Many other women are also facing pressure to get married. Furthermore, South Asian society needs to understand the ramifications of the pressure which it directly or indirectly places on its women.

Part II

Redefining Family

6

The management of desire: Sexuality and marriage for young South Asian women in America

Karen Leonard

Paging through *India West*, a South Asian ethnic newspaper published in California, one recent photograph struck me as most unusual: I was looking into the eyes of a happy young bride, her address a California one, seated next to her groom. The contrast with the literally hundreds of photographs of Indian and Pakistani brides I have seen was striking: this girl looked straight into the camera and her smile was direct and dazzlingly broad.[1] Typically, however, South Asian brides, on video or in photo albums, look down modestly, and often they are partially covered with a veil of one sort or another. But the second[2] and later generations of South Asians in America are culturally different from their parents, and sexuality and marriage are crucial sites for self-assertion and resistance, although that resistance may be hidden and not openly expressed.

This chapter begins to explore issues of sexuality and marriage for young South Asians in America, that is, for young adults of primarily Indian and Pakistani background who were born, brought up, or educated in the United States. The exploration is not based upon systematic interviewing but upon a close reading of the South Asian ethnic press and knowledge of a few cases of somewhat impulsive and often secret marriages made by young South Asian American women, cases which have come to my attention in the course of studying and teaching

South Asian history and culture over the last three decades. These secret marriages are undoubtedly quite dramatic, certainly atypical examples of self-assertion and resistance, but they should not be thought of as marginal to the experience of South Asian Americans. Everywhere I have talked about these secret marriages, young people in the audience have come up and told me of other such cases known to them. Statistically, such marriages may be a small proportion of second generation South Asian marriages, but their symbolic impact gives them more than statistical importance. Furthermore, these secret marriages only carry to an extreme the strategy most commonly employed by young people to deal with their differences with their parents: *non-disclosure*. The same kinds of generational tensions characterize other post-1965 Asian immigrant communities,[3] but comparative studies ascertaining the similarities and differences with respect to issues of sexuality and marriage remain to be undertaken.

Second generation South Asian Americans participate in American culture in all its contemporary diversity and intensity. They are very different from their parents, and the differences are evident in many ways. Topics for discussion at the 1994 South Asian Youth Conference at UCLA included Interracial Marriage, South Asians and Hip Hop Culture, Homosexuality, Premarital Sex, and Violence Against Women, as well as Identity Formation, Discrimination in Corporate America, and Racism. A recent full-page ad for the Northern California Youth Awards Night printed a conspicuously placed dress code announcing that no jeans, sneakers, or jackets with gang symbols would be allowed. Only a few years ago, perhaps even now, it is hard to imagine this announcement would be needed. *India West* (an ethnic newspaper published on the west coast) has a 'youth page' with young Indian American writers, and it recently ran columns on gay and lesbian issues and on unmarried young couples living together before marriage. Its counterpart, the *Pakistan Link*, had a 'youth column' written by an older man and actually focused on families, but it has recently changed that and begun publishing columns by young people, though the topics are more traditional ones.[4]

With respect to that very important life event, marriage, the generational differences become magnified, sometimes assuming crisis proportions. Immigrant parents come from South Asian contexts in which arranged marriages have been the norm, valued for the protection and security afforded by family (not individual) selection and support systems. Caste endogamy, and/or marriage within some other kind of group (sectarian, kinship, regional), ensured that the young people shared similar cultural backgrounds and lifestyles, minimizing sources of difference between them. Immigrant parents are accustomed to extended family and caste or caste-like group involvement in marriage networks and remain attuned to those groups for approval and status. They also see the high divorce rate in Western 'love marriage' societies and feel that arranged marriages are the better alternative.

Because of widespread parental opposition to dating and 'love-marriages', the children of South Asian immigrants are usually put into an either/or situation. They must trust their parents to arrange their marriages, or they must trust themselves. It is my argument here that when they do trust themselves and act upon their own wishes, they sometimes elect to keep the marriage secret. They are reluctant to make public the betrayal of their parents' trust, to show that they have made their own decision in a matter so crucial to each generation's sense of self. (Perhaps it is not their own parents whose reaction they fear, but that of the wider family, in the US and/or South Asia, so this fear may be on behalf of their parents as well as themselves. But this possibility, the weight given to the extended family or marriage network by immigrant parents and their children as they make decisions in the US, falls outside the scope of this paper and awaits further investigation.)

The impulsive and/or secret marriages being made in America by some young South Asian women which I will discuss, direct our attention to the generational and contextual differences within the South Asian American communities. What is the thinking of the young woman who enters into such a marriage, often suddenly and with a non-South Asian man?[5] Why does she keep it a secret from her parents? These marriages clearly present opportunities to the young women, or they would not be entering into them. Just as clearly, these marriages present problems to the South Asian parents, or they would not be concealed from them. Young women are acting to secure the husbands they desire, and only afterward are they trying to reconcile their conflicting family responsibilities.

I am hypothesizing that these marriages represent serious, considered attempts to reconcile sexual desire, emotional commitment, and responsibility to one's family. They also represent resistance, in relation to a strategy of power—I am treating parental arrangement of marriages analytically as a strategy of power, since in the US context, that is the central interpretation given to it by the young people. However, they are not offering overt confrontational resistance, but rather resistance which is subordinated and compartmentalized. It is the kind of resistance which 'transforms the way in which they [the young people] are subject to someone else [their parents]', which transforms 'the manner in which they come to be tied to their own identities through self-knowledge', and 'serves to reshape subjects by untying or untidying that relationship [to the parents]'.[6]

Dominant cultural influences in American society teach the children of South Asian immigrant families that parental love is to be honored, but that sometimes parental power can be resisted. The young people learn to admire individual freedom, particularly with respect to the choice of one's own spouse. Recent movies about young people of South Asian ancestry being raised in the West highlight these generational tensions. The sensitive documentary, *Do You Take This Man: Pakistani Arranged Marriages*, has a mother emphatically telling her daughter that love for one's parents means trusting their choice of one's spouse. If the daughter insists on choosing her own spouse, her mother says, she is rejecting parental love, not trusting her parents. Another film, the acclaimed *Bhaji on the Beach*, features an interracial love relationship kept secret by the girl from her parents. In the latter film, the viewer's primary empathy is with the young South Asian woman, but viewers are also drawn to sympathize with the girl's lover and his father and with the young woman's parents. The film carefully contextualizes the different perspectives of those involved.[7]

Recent research by South Asian Americans shows that family bonds are placed above individual choice in parental teachings about gender roles. Chemba Raghavan[8] discusses the way first generation Indian immigrant mothers communicate 'proper' gender roles by retellings of the Sita myth, stressing the devotion and faithfulness of Ram's wife Sita despite the many trials and tribulations she undergoes in the Ramayana epic. She shows that the significant theme for the mothers is 'the embedding of Sita in a socio-familial relationship, not in a personal contractual scheme'. The daughters are being raised in a dominant American culture which values individual independence, yet the first generation South Asian mothers are trying to teach them to place social-familial aspects of female identity foremost. The necessity of staying within family lines or boundaries is their message. Similarly, Sangeeta Gupta,[9] a second generation Indian American, understands the traditional arranged marriage, with no impute from the young people involved, as a system to control young women and keep them within parentally ordained boundaries. In the conclusion of her article, she questions the lack of the young peoples' participation in this decision-making process which is crucial to their future.

Turning now to the several marriages that have come to my attention and that provoked this exploratory essay, the young women are bright, attractive, and confident members of the North American society in which they have been largely raised or educated. In the course of their schooling or work, these young women met men, the majority of them Euro-American men, whom they enthusiastically dated and then rather quickly married. Yet at the same time, they continued to relate to their parents as dutiful daughters, striving to maintain a close and undiminished relationship, albeit one in which the husband played little or no part. While they confided in woman friends, their own sisters and both South Asian and Euro-American friends, they usually did not turn to male siblings or friends, and they have been largely uninterested or unsuccessful in forming close relationships with their new in-laws. This presents, of course, something of a problem to the husbands and their families, the families into which these women have married.

The following brief accounts cannot be as specific as I would like, partly because my own knowledge is incomplete. These cases sometimes have come to my attention from the young women involved but also from their mothers-in-law and women friends, and one must protect identities. I am all too aware of the limitations of this suggestive set of accounts, but I hope they will stimulate more systematic research exploring the thinking of, and the effects on, the men and women involved in such marriages.

In some of these cases of impulsive and secret marriages, geographic distance clearly played a role in maintaining the secrecy. Typically in such cases, a young South Asian woman came to the US for higher education, fell in love with a fellow student, and moved immediately to a sexual relationship and engagement or marriage. One woman became romantically involved with a European fellow student but knew too little about birth control; she became pregnant almost at once and therefore got married. She finally told her parents of the marriage but not of the baby until several years afterward, since the birth date would have revealed the motivation for the marriage. In another case, the young woman conscientiously avoided having sex with the Euro-American colleague with whom she fell in love but immediately made a commitment to marry him and eventually did. In the meantime, after a few years, her parents sent a succession of potential spouses for her inspection in America and were increasingly frustrated by her refusal to consider them seriously and choose among them. Another young woman had a succession of Euro-American lovers, but she insisted upon an immediate engagement to each one in turn. She was not living with or near her parents and told them nothing of these engagements. She finally eloped to Las Vegas, and later revealed this to her parents.

In two other cases, again of young women away from their parents for higher education, the management of desire involved delayed or partial informing of the parents. In one, a flirtation almost immediately became an engagement, and a local relative was informed of it months afterward and only because the couple had determined to get married shortly. In yet another case of sudden infatuation upon arrival for study in the US, a student from India and one from Pakistan married each other only a few weeks after meeting. Here the outcome was different, since this couple eventually did tell both sets of parents back in South Asia, precipitating family crises in both families and leading to a lengthy separation and traumatic divorce for the young couple. (This last case was complicated by the crossing of national and religious borders and the intervention of international visa regulations as well.)

In two other cases, young South Asian women who grew up in America entered into secret marriages while simultaneously fulfilling familial responsibilities locally. One woman was strongly attracted to a Euro-American co-worker. They got engaged and informed her parents of the engagement, but the parents' reaction was so negative that the young couple took no further public step. However, they got married secretly and began living together. Despite his conversion to her religion, her sister's presence at their wedding, and a phone answering machine message making it clear that they were sharing an apartment, over three years have gone by and this young woman still has not told her parents, although she visits them nearly every weekend. She explains this by referring to the distress already caused by the engagement and by her mother's heart condition, but in the meantime the husband has become uncertain of her commitment. The husband's family also has great difficulty understanding the situation (and one thinks of the similar position of the West Indian lover's father in *Bhaji on the Beach*). In yet another case (and one about which I unfortunately know very little), a young woman married a Euro-American, became pregnant, and allowed her mother-in-law to host a baby shower for her. But she had not told her own parents of the marriage, and the day after the baby shower she got an abortion and then proceeded to file for a divorce.

In both these last two cases of rather extended and somewhat problematic deception, the women, after being married for some time, spoke to their husbands about divorcing and then remarrying with their parents' full knowledge and participation. They saw this as a possible solution to the dilemma they had created by marrying secretly. In both cases, the husbands were apprehensive about such a scenario. Yet it seems that the young women were questioning, not the marriages, but the ways in which they had gone about marrying. Each woman was taking the husband's commitment for granted and seeking to gain the consent and commitment of her parents. The women wanted a win-win situation, the support of their new and old families.

Two things strike one in considering these cases. First, there is the certainty with which the young women moved to make immediate and strong commitments to the men, through sexual relationships, engagements, and/or marriages. Driven by a powerful knowledge of themselves and what they wanted, they acted to gain it (and, in the cases best known to me, their marriage choices seem to have been good ones). Second, one is struck by their near unanimity in choosing to delay or avoid telling their parents of their involvements. Probably they knew their parents and their apprehensions were (or are) well-founded. But to delay the disclosure is surely a short-term solution, postponing the problem of reconciling one's parents to one's choice without forfeiting their love and attachment.

The generational problem here of non-communication or non-disclosure is conceived of differently by the generations. The first generation immigrants from South Asia are greatly concerned about 'the youth problem'. Many conference sessions, public talks, and private conversations are devoted to worrying about the children of South Asian descent being raised in the US. Some concern comes from religious leaders and organizations, both Hindu and Muslim, but even then the focus seems to be on control of sexuality and marriage, not on the problem of communication between parents and young adults. In a recent North American edition of *Hinduism Today*, the publisher, a Shaivite *sanyasi* or Swami, discussed the threat to Hindu families represented by marriages not arranged by the parents, marriages most often with non-Hindus in the US. Stating that 80 percent of the young Hindu women in Texas are marrying outside of Indian tradition, the Swami blamed parents for not arranging marriages soon enough, for permitting their children to pursue personal fulfillment rather than fulfillment of duty.[10] In *Pakistan Link*, a medical doctor from Pakistan wrote from an

Islamic perspective, opposing dating on the grounds that it inevitably led to having sex or to date rape.[11] This view of dating as inevitably involving sex also prevailed among the parents in a two-generation survey of post-1965 Indian immigrants carried out in 1990.[12] Thus the parental emphasis is on external control of sexuality by prevention of heterosexual contact or parental screening of companions, and there is no parental confidence in self-control of sexuality by the young people themselves.[13]

The second generation sees the social landscape very differently. While the experience of growing up in America has not been a uniform one, most youngsters of South Asian descent go through a cycle of early identification with American culture and then, later, identification with South Asian culture.[14] Even after they become more interested in their heritage, these young people do not necessarily see themselves as part of a larger community of South Asians or Indo-Americans. But, as a young South Asian woman writer asserts, what they do have in common with other Indo-Americans is their parents, 'parents who are overinvolved, overworried, overprotective. Parents who have an opinion on every minor life decision, who make demands, impose guilt, withhold approval'. She writes:[15]

> We entered the world the axis around which our parents' lives revolved, their source of fulfillment, their contract with the future... as children of immigrants, the promise we fulfill is our parents' own promise, long-deferred and transmuted now into the stuff of American dreams (and nightmares). So we must become respectable, make money, buy a house, bear children.... My parents' love supports me and enfolds me, but sometimes also weighs me down... still I carry the burden of their unhappiness.

She writes of becoming interested in her Indian heritage, but

> as this Indian fire flickered and grew—it shed light on my American self, too.... I see that I am in love with the complexity of the American culture I grew up in, and cherish my easy familiarity with it... that I love to defend it against detractors, revel in its excesses... that after attending many Indian dinner parties... I long to be with American friends, because with them I relax and return to myself.

The young people realize that it is the young women of South Asian background, not the young men, who are of most concern to the

parental generation. The reasons for this have to do with the patrilineal, patriarchal cultures from which the South Asian immigrants
come,[16] and in the case of Muslims with a strict religious prohibition
on Muslim women marrying non-Muslims. As a young Indian Muslim
woman wrote, 'in my culture, it's O.K. for a man to marry outside our
Muslim community, go away to college, stay out at night, do whatever
he pleases. A girl, on the other hand, must learn to cook, not say what's
on her mind, and repress sexual desires. . . . Moslem boys brought up
in America integrate much faster into American society than Muslim
girls.'[17] And in a 'Focus on Youth' feature in *India West*, a young Hindu
woman made a similar point, citing a father who stated that daughters
can get pregnant so they are controlled much more strictly than sons,
since it is they who can damage the family's reputation. This writer
asserted that it was time to face up to the issue of sex in her Indo-
American generation, and she quoted a Hindu woman doctor who said
that 40 percent of her Indo-American patients are sexually active. The
writer and the doctor both termed the refusal of parents to accept this
possibility as 'extreme denial'.[18]

Since both Hindus and Muslims have been mentioned above, one
might comment that parental concern about South Asian youth crosses
all religious boundaries. At a Sikh parent-youth dialogue in Michigan in
1996, the parents were concerned with transmission of Punjabi culture
and the Sikh religion, while the youth were interested in the issues posed
by American culture, particularly issues of dating and marriage. The
youth talked about how hard it was to meet eligible Sikh youth—they
set up university events 'organized around feminism or whatever, but
parents don't let their kids go to these events,' one said. Parental equation of dating with intended marriage made it difficult to do things
with Sikh friends of the opposite sex too, because 'uncles' from India
would immediately be calling up to inquire when they should be planning a trip to the US for the wedding![19] And the publications of the US
Parsi or Zoroastrian association, FEZANA, and the various Sri Lankan
and Nepalese associational presses, also reflect concern with the second
generation's marriages.[20]

Both the dangers of raising girls in America and the double standards
are constantly emphasized in the South Asian ethnic press. During
Women's History Month in 1993, a series had a finale focused on this. A
young woman said that 'one of the healthy aspects of living in America
is that you are taught to question and you are taught to think. In India
you don't question your parents, while in the American culture you do.'

Another testified that while parents get changed by America more the longer they are here, the generational clash is strongest on the issue of marriage. 'Parents have frozen some vision of the India they grew up in which necessarily does not exist today at all in terms of today's youth.' A third young woman, commenting on how young Indo-American women deal with the pressure for an arranged marriage, said 'A lot of kids just do things and [do] not tell their parents.'[21]

The passages above all converge on the issue of non-disclosure, not telling one's parents about the significant choices one is making in life. Priya Agarwal's discussion of social issues for second generation Indo-Americans opens with a quote from a young man who dated a girl for four years without telling his parents anything about the relationship. Even more tellingly, more than half the young people in her survey preferred to date without telling their parents.[22] In a recent ethnic press column on dating, a young man, while saying that guys have it easier than girls, cited a male friend of his who had not told his parents about a girlfriend of three years standing. 'If he tells his parents, his relationship is basically over. Yet, on the other hand, going against his parents is something he does not want to do. It goes against everything he believes in.' In the same column, a young woman testified that while most of her friends date, 'their parents do not come into play until the relationship is serious. . . . Indian parents have difficulty grasping the concept of a boyfriend-girlfriend relationship. . . many Indian parents tend to overanalyze or underestimate the seriousness of their daughter's relationships. . . . I must give credit to Indian parents for being so concerned with their daughter's well being. However, there is a limit. I don't believe in overprotective parenting.' She advocated simply bringing a boyfriend into the home and confronting one's parents with the fact of an existing relationship.[23] Since dating is not disclosed, second generation South Asian young women cannot turn to parents for help when they become the victims of date violence, an issue publicized by a South Asian women's referral service for domestic violence.[24]

Some young women are marrying before undertaking the difficult task of confronting their parents; one can only guess at the enormity of the risk they feel they would be taking. They have gained the husband they want, but they do not want to lose their families as a consequence. Perhaps these young women too are being overprotective, fearful of hurting the parents whom they value so highly. This was certainly a factor in the one case of a secret marriage best known to me, where the poor health of the mother was given as the chief reason to withhold the fact of the marriage.

The concept of 'culture' as a bounded and portable thing which one brings along to a new country and seeks to 'transmit' without corruption is the major problem here.[25] Parents are thinking of their children as culturally South Asian, heirs to an identity which is an extension in space and time of 'a prior natural identity rooted in locality and community.'[26] The children, however, think of themselves as negotiating and inventing their own identities in the American setting. While the parents see their own 'failure' to 'transmit' cultural identity and values to their children, the children locate themselves firmly in the American social landscape, and they are engaged in building new conceptions of ethnic and national identities in the US.[27]

Clearly, the management of desire, of sexuality and marriage, is an area of crucial negotiation for second generation South Asians, perhaps the most significant of the areas in which they resist and reformulate the identities imposed by their elders. They may have come to critical assessments of their parents' own marriages, or they may have observed the failures of some arranged marriages among their friends (and divorces are taking place nowadays when marriages do not work out, both in South Asia and in the US). The relationship between South Asian young people and their immigrant parents has become a contested one, but usually not overtly so. Despite considerable mutual love and respect, members of the second generation no longer fully trust their parents to make crucial decisions for them. They do not, however, want to break the relationship, but they make it untidy by controlling and limiting what their parents learn of their feelings and activities. They trust in themselves as agents, as makers of their own destinies, while at the same time maintaining the relationship with their parents as best as they can.

✦ *Notes and References*

1. *India West*, 18 March 1994, 84.
2. I am using second generation to include not only those born in the United States to immigrant parents but also those largely brought up in the US, those whom others sometimes term the 1.5 generation.
3. For the experiences of the small number of South Asian immigrants before the 1960s with respect to marriage, see Karen Isaksen Leonard, *Making Ethnic Choices:*

California's Punjabi Mexican Americans (Philadelphia, Temple University Press, 1992). Asian immigration was curtailed by discriminatory laws in 1917 and 1924 and opened up again only in the late 1960s after the passage of the 1965 Immigration Act.

4. For the 1994 conference, see the publicity flyer; for the Youth Awards Night, *India West*, 12 August 1994, 71; for the *India West* columns, 1 and 29 March 1996 issues; for *Pakistan Link*, 1994–96 issues.

5. I have no statistical data on this, but my impression is that secrecy is more often chosen because the partner is non-South Asian; parents are thought to be less accepting of this alternative. See Joan Massell Soncini ('Indians and Pakistanis Who Choose to Marry Interculturally'. Paper prescribed at the National Asian Indian American Conference, Rutgers University, 13 April 1997) on cross cultural marriages by Indians and Pakistanis.

6. See Jim Ferguson and Akhil Gupta 'Introduction'. In Jim Ferguson and Akhil Gupta, *Culture, Power, Place: Explorations in Critical Anthropology* (Durham, NC, Duke University Press, 1997). They develop Foucault's definition of resistance as an experience that transforms the identity of subjects.

7. Elise Fried, *Do You Take This Man: Pakistani Arranged Marriages* (Flying Fish Productions, 1989), and Gurinder Chadha, *Bhaji on the Beach* (90 minutes, 1994), are films which feature the second generation/first generation tensions in the areas of sexuality and marriage.

8. Chemba Raghavan, 'The Role of Myth in the Communication of Parental Beliefs about Gender: Is Sita Relevant?' Paper presented at South Asian Women's Conference, Los Angeles, CA, 1994.

9. Sangeeta Gupta, 'Indo American Women and Divorce'. Paper presented at South Asian Women's Conference, Los Angeles, CA, 1994.

10. Satguru Sivaya Subramuniyaswami, *Hinduism Today*, June 1993, 2.

11. Dr Shahid Athar calls for an Islamic perspective on America's problems, which he lists as abortion, teenage pregnancy, alcohol and drugs, homosexuality, AIDS, right to life [sic], poverty, and child and wife abuse (Dr Shahid Athar, Column in *Pakistan Link*, 20 May 1994, 44).

12. Priya Agarwal, *Passage from India: Post 1965 Indian Immigrants and Their Children* (Palos Verdes, California, Yuvati Publications, 1991), 48–49.

13. Thanks to a reader of this paper for making this point explicit.

14. Those who came earlier, before Indian immigrant culture really developed in the US, may have even more pronounced differences with their parents than the more recent immigrants. That is my impression from personal experience and from research produced over the last 10 years in my undergraduate field research class at the University of California, Irvine.

15. Gauri Bhat, 'Tending the Flame: Thoughts on Being Indian-American'. In *COSAW* (Committee on South Asian Women) *Bulletin* 7(3–4), 1992, 1–6.

16. See Karen Leonard, 'Ethnic Identity and Gender: South Asians in the United States'. In Milton Israel and N.K. Wagle (eds), *Ethnicity, Identity, Migration* (Toronto, Center for South Asian Studies, University of Toronto, 1993), 165–80.

17. Saba, 'Reflections of a Young Feminist', *COSAW Bulletin* 7(3–4), 1992, 8.

18. See Smriti Aggarwal, *India West*, 30 July 1993, 62. Should South Asian parents read Michael Moffat's 1989 book (*Coming of Age in New Jersey* [New Brunswick,

Rutgers University Press, 1989]) on American college students in the late 1970s and 1980s, particularly the chapters on sex and sex in college, they might be even more fearful—he gives a picture of the multiple functions of the college years for American young people which is familiar to those of us who teach in colleges and universities.

19. I have written about the second generation of Sikhs in the US in a forthcoming book, N. Gerald Barrier and Pashaura Singh (eds), *Sikh Identity: Continuity and Change* (Columbia, MO, South Asia Press, forthcoming).

20. I am thinking of the *Sri Lanka Express* and the *Lankan Tribune*, both published from Los Angeles, California, the *Nepal News* of the America-Nepal Society, published from Torrance, California, the newsletter of the Association of Nepalis in America, published from Woodbridge, Virginia, and *FEZANA*, official publication of the Federation of Zoroastrian Associations of North America, published from Sunnyvale, California.

21. Lavina Melwani, 'Voices of a New Generation', *India West*, 26 March 1993, 49, 57–58.

22. Agarwal, 50–59 on inadequate communication between parents and children, and 48–49 for the dating quote and statistics. See n.12.

23. See Sunil Bagai and Monica Doshi in *India West*, 23 September 1994, p. 55. Sangeeta Gupta's research (this volume) also shows that parents are not told about relationships until they become 'serious'.

24. *India West*, 27 January 1995, Section C, 53.

25. Sally Falk Moore, *Social Facts and Fabrications* (New York, Cambridge University Press, 1986), 4–5; Jim Ferguson and Akhil Gupta, 'Beyond "Culture": Space, Identity, and the Politics of Difference', *Cultural Anthropology* 7(1), 1992, 6–23.

26. Ferguson and Gupta, 9. See n. 25.

27. See Stuart Hall, 'New Ethnicities'. In Michael Keith and Steve Pile (eds), *Place and the Politics of Identity* (London, Routledge, 1993)—the original and fuller version was published in the journal, *Black Film British Cinema* (London, Institute of Contemporary Arts, 1988), 27–31. See also James Clifford, 'Notes on Theory and Travel'. In James Clifford and Vivek Dhareshwar (eds), *Traveling Theory Traveling Theorists* (Santa Cruz, Center for Cultural Studies, 1989), 188. I have argued for strong gender and generational differences in identity, and for a better understanding of the historical contingencies of identity, in Karen Leonard, *Making Ethnic Choices: California's Punjabi Mexican Americans* (Philadelphia, Temple University Press, 1992); '"Flawed Transmission?" Punjabi Pioneers in California'. In Pashaura Singh (ed.), *Transmission of Punjabi Heritage to the Diaspora* (Ann Arbour, University of Michigan, 1996), 97–111; 'Second Generation Sikhs in the US: Consensus and Differences'. In Pashaura Singh and N. Gerald Barrier (eds), *Sikh Identity: Continuity and Change* (Columbia, MO, South Asia Press, forthcoming); *South Asian Americans* (Westport, CT, Greenwood Press, 1997).

7

Walking on the edge: Indian-American women speak out on dating and marriage

*Sangeeta R. Gupta**

Priya looks lovely as she circles the fire in her mother's wedding sari. Her face is serious yet radiant as she pledges herself to the man at her side—a man *she* has chosen. The picture in front of me changes as, in my mind, I see a different bride: Priya's 16-year-old mother, wearing the same red sari, taking similar vows which also bind her to a man—a complete stranger whom *her parents* chose for her according to customs observed for hundreds of years. Only one generation separates these two women, but in her mother's era, Priya's marriage, which crosses caste, religious, and regional boundaries, would probably have never taken place.

Asian-Indian parents have, for generations, screened potential marital partners for caste and social-class compatibility, regional and religious similarities, and family background.[1] Recent generations have added educational background and the groom's earning capacity as additional criteria. Individual personality traits are not emphasized as marital partners (primarily the brides) are expected to adjust to each other after the marriage ceremony. Regardless of their chronological age, young South Asians are usually not considered adults until they are married, therefore, the parental generation believes it is the best judge of poten-

*I would like to thank Georgina Dodge, Christian Ghasarian, Sapna Kumar, Valerie Matsumoto and Damon Woods for their helpful and insightful comments on earlier drafts of this paper.

tial partners for its children. By eliminating the self-selection process, traditional Asian-Indian culture is able to prohibit male–female interaction before marriage. This is in direct contrast to mainstream American culture that stresses individuality and believes that each person should find self-fulfillment by selecting a partner who satisfies his/her specific needs. Consequently, ample premarital interaction becomes necessary.

With one foot in each culture, and facing these constraints, how do Indian-Americans negotiate what has become a virtual marital minefield? This chapter will explore how Indian-American women in their 20s and 30s are weaving conflicting marital traditions into a new pattern, one they can live with.[2] Their responses will be compared to other ethnic immigrant groups, with an emphasis on other Asian communities, to situate their experiences. Although this research resulted in a plethora of information for both sexes, this chapter will focus on the process that Indian-American women are undergoing as they negotiate a bicultural identity. These women compare and contrast the gender roles they have observed in their parental homes with their expectations of their own relationships. They state their opinions regarding dating criteria and parentally arranged[3] versus self-arranged marriages and the taboo subject of divorce which is still an uncomfortable issue for this community.

History and immigration overview

The first wave of Asian-Indian immigration consisted of several thousand primarily Punjabi Sikh farmers who settled on the west coast of the United States between 1900 and 1910. For more than half-a-century, Asians in general, faced various discriminatory laws that prevented immigration, family reunification and the acquisition of US citizenship.[4] In 1965, under revised immigration laws, a 'second wave' of Asian-Indians were admitted. This second group was significantly different as the new laws gave preference to highly skilled and professional immigrants. One decade later, approximately 100,000 engineers, physicians, scientists, professors and business people, along with their dependents, had entered the US.[5] This trend continued and by 1985, more than 500,000 Asian-Indians had migrated to the United States—10 percent of all Asian immigrants.[6]

When compared to the Punjabi Sikhs and other earlier immigrants who were primarily from rural backgrounds, the second wave of

Asian-Indians, urban, English-speaking professionals, had a vastly different experience. Their skills and educational background provided the tools necessary for a relatively smooth transition into their new home which in turn enabled them to quickly build a secure financial foundation. With their economic base established, Asian-Indians were able to focus their energy on creating ways to maintain and pass on their concepts of Indian 'tradition' and 'culture' to their children, the second generation. The terms 'tradition' and 'culture' are problematic as their meanings fluctuate not only between societies, but also within an individual society. However, for the purpose of this chapter, tradition will be defined as the 'handing down of information, beliefs, or customs from one generation to another'. Culture will be defined as 'constituting the way of life of an entire society...[including] codes of manners, dress, language, rituals, norms of behavior, and systems of beliefs'.[7]

The changing face of 'culture' and 'tradition'

Asian-Indians and Indian-Americans face a double bind in the United States. On the one hand, there is the mainstream emphasis on individuality, while on the other, there is often tremendous pressure from the Asian-Indian communities to conform to their traditional ideals. They face the social censure of their ethnic communities that are often more vigilant than Indians in India in maintaining their cultural heritage. While their peers in India are influenced by Western culture, immigrant Indians who came to the US in the 1960s and 1970s attempt to recreate and maintain the India of their childhood within their new communities. They are, in effect, existing in a 'time capsule'. They are trying to preserve social values that were present in India when they were growing up, forgetting that India itself has changed. The India in the memory of the first generation is dramatically different from the reality of India as the 21st century approaches.

By living in this time capsule, the parental generation puts a great deal of pressure on second generation women to maintain expected ideals of behavior, now often outdated in urban India. This static view of culture and tradition which is being handed down to the second generation is simply the first generation's *perception* of Indian tradition and culture. In reality, tradition changes and responds to its environment. Therefore, it is a fluid not a static process. Changing traditions and evolving concepts of culture in the last few decades have created an India and a United States that are dramatically different from what was experienced by the parental generation when they lived in India and after they immigrated. Thus, the second generation faces different, yet complex, challenges as they reconcile the culture their parents are passing on to them with the current experiences and realities of their birth country in order to find their own unique niche.

This juggling act is one that immigrants of all ethnic groups attempt. Donna Gabacci contends that the second generation of both European and Asian immigrants are, 'heavily influenced by parental values and power' and face 'particularly complex choices. . . because cultural change and structural assimilation proceed at different rates'.[8] In attempting to bring together two divergent cultures, children of immigrants often feel they are 'walking on the edge' of several worlds. By trying to balance both world-views, they create a space in which they attempt to find a self-identity. Second generation Americans of European and Asian descent blend the old and the new in ways that make sense in their individual lives. Ethnicity, like tradition and culture, is not a concept that is just passed on from one generation to the next, rather it is 'something dynamic. . . [and it is] a matter of becoming as well as of being'.[9] Therefore, the development of an ethnic identity is a continuous lifelong process. This process is one that many Asian-Indian parents, like other immigrant parents, have a difficult time understanding. They believe that not only is one simply 'born Asian-Indian' but also that it is a homogeneous identity. Furthermore, the parental generation does not take into consideration that their children are both Asian-Indian and American and will express both these identities.

Although Asian-Indians do not form ethnic enclaves, there are places where they have formed pseudo-ethnic communities (Little Indias). These places, where Asian-Indian immigrants are numerous, are always in a flux and constantly adjusting to the changing ideology of individual members. In fact, as historian Valerie Matsumoto states in her study among California-based Japanese-Americans, 'newcomers have the opportunity to influence their own culture, shaped by their concepts of tradition and the demands of the new environment'.[10] Yet, changes are often met with hostility as immigrants cling to the familiar. One of the major battlefields of resistance is the traditional structure of the family and all that this structure stands for: established gender roles (usually more restrictive for women); social mores; and perhaps the most volatile of all, courtship and marital traditions.

Immigrant groups attempt to hold on to their culture through the most basic unit of society: the family. Traditional family structure, for most societies, is patriarchal and has the established corresponding gender roles. Immigrant groups also have another thing in common. They all believe that *their* family structure is the most appropriate and most stable. Studying the effect of immigration on Asian family dynamics is not an easy task as previous studies on family structure and ethnicity in the US have not considered the vast variety of people of color. Matsumoto states that ethnic community studies have been based 'on a biracial model' which has focused on European-Americans and African-Americans. For the most part, people of color are nowhere to be found. Their voices need to be heard as their experiences have also been woven into the tapestry of American identity.[11]

A few recent studies focusing on Asian immigrant families found striking similarities among the various sub-groups. In fact, when sociologist Harry H.L. Kitano describes the structure of Japanese and Japanese-American families as possessing a 'strong solidarity, mutual helpfulness and a patriarchal structure', he could just as easily be characterizing Asian-Indian and Indian-American families.[12] Matsumoto's observations that the traditional Japanese family possesses an emphasis on 'filial piety, respect for age and authority, and a preference for male children' also could have been written about Asian-Indians.[13] The traditional Asian family structure described above is, however, under siege and some of that pressure comes from the process of migration as evidenced by Nazli Kibria's study of immigrant Vietnamese-American families. These immigrants believed that 'migration had enhanced intergenerational tensions [due to the] growing cultural schisms between the generations as well as a decline in the power and authority of family elders'.[14] Thus, some of the intergenerational tension can be traced to changing family dynamics. The second generation is struggling to find a middle ground between what they feel are the outdated perceptions of their elders and the rapidly changing environment they have grown up in. The traditions and cultures this group eventually retains will depend on many individual factors. Of the two sexes, it appears that women are the most affected by the changes. They are re-evaluating the traditional gender roles their mothers observed on one hand, and on the other, trying to balance them with the increasing opportunities for women in today's world. Most Indian-American women are walking a tightrope between two cultures as they attempt to create a niche for themselves that incorporates the values of their Asian-Indian heritage with those of mainstream America.

Changing roles for women in a new land

Many immigrant groups believe that their traditional family structures provide a sense of stability in a new land and that their particular structure is the most appropriate one. According to Kibria, the
Vietnamese-American population envisions their family structure not
only as something unique to them, but also considers it to be the basis
of their ethnic identity. Their traditional family is the glue that holds
them together and provides security in a new and complex environment. Therefore, for many immigrants, its organization is jealously
guarded and they are resistant to change.

In my study, the overwhelming majority of the respondents described
a two-parent family with traditional female and male gender roles. It
appears that these gender roles were maintained even though the majority of the mothers worked outside the home. This pattern is not
surprising nor is it limited to Asian-Indian families. The division of
labor according to traditional gender roles, reminiscent of the mainstream American nuclear family of the 1950s and 1960s, is in fact, still
the norm in the United States.[15] According to a 1993 Families and
Work Institute study, 'a traditional division of labor still holds, even
in today's two-career households'.[16] Therefore, even though women, in
general, have joined the workforce in unprecedented numbers, they are
still handling household responsibilities the same way their mothers and
grandmothers did—by doing most of them! According to the respondents in my study, the same situation exists in many first generation
Asian-Indian households.

The fathers of the respondents, still seen primarily as breadwinners,
assumed responsibility for paying bills and doing household repairs and
yard work. Their mothers handled the traditionally female household
jobs: cooking; dishes; laundry; and decisions regarding social interactions. This is despite the fact that the majority of the mothers are
employed outside the home as professionals[17] and, therefore, are also
contributing, sometimes substantially, if not equally, to the family income. By taking on the majority of household responsibilities and working outside the home, these women are clearly experiencing what Arlie
Hochschild refers to as the 'second shift'.[18] The household chores are
not the only thing still divided in the same old way. When asked
whom they would turn to for financial and relationship concerns, 67
percent of the respondents stated they would approach their fathers
for financial advice while 72 percent would consult their mothers on

relationships. Thus, traditional Asian-Indian and US mainstream gender roles, the father handling the technical/financial aspect of the family
and the mother handling the emotional/nurturing issues, continue to
be the norm.

This division of labor, expected among first generation women and
men, is not limited to any one population but transcends national and
cultural boundaries. However, it appears that some changes are being
incorporated into the family structure. In a study conducted among
Indian-Canadian women by Josephine Naidoo and J. Campbell Davis,
it appears that these first generation women—like their second generation daughters—are combining traditional and contemporary values.
The Indian-Canadian study defines 'values, beliefs, and customs' passed
down for generations and resistant to change as 'traditional'. In contrast,
contemporary values are those existing in the mainstream culture.[19]
The Encyclopedia of Sociology defines a modern individual as someone 'who is open to new experiences... [has shifted]... allegiances from
traditional figures of authority (parents, priests),... abandon[ed] passiv-
ity and fatalism in the face of life's difficulties... [and is]... ambitious
for themselves and their children to achieve high educational and occupational goals'.[20] These definitions act as a window into the lives of
Asian-Indian immigrant women who are not firmly and completely
entrenched in either camp. Naidoo and Campbell Davis state that
Indian-Canadian women, while adhering to traditional beliefs regarding family and marriage, express contemporary beliefs when discussing
their 'careers outside the home' and what they wish for their daughters'
future.[21] To summarize, these 'women seem to want the best of both
worlds... they desire a greater range of freedom outside the home... but
they continue to ground their identity in the family'.[22]

The phrase 'we have the best of both worlds' echoes a sentiment that
is common in the Asian immigrant culture, in fact, those very words are
often used. Asian-Indian immigrant women, like other Asian women,
are combining traditional and contemporary values to create a way of
being which facilitates their individual growth and aspirations within
the basic family structure. This is a Herculean task as the traditional
Asian-Indian woman is not encouraged to develop herself as a separate
individual. Rather, she is praised when her self-identity is connected to
and defined by the societal and cultural norms of a patriarchal familial
structure.[23] Specifically, a woman's identity is often defined and contained within the parameters of her social relationships to men. This
was true even in ancient India as evidenced by the Hindu legal code, the

Laws of Manu, which state that in childhood a woman is under the rule of her father, in adulthood, under her husband and in old age, under her son. It should be noted that these expectations are also present in other patriarchal cultures, for example, the 'three submissions' expected of Vietnamese women or the 'Three Obediences' set forth for Chinese women. According to Confucian tenets, a 'woman was ordered to obey first her father, then her husband, and finally her eldest son'.[24]

Given these constraints, opportunities for a woman to express herself as an individual separate from her familial roles and obligations have been limited. When these expectations are carried to the new homeland and there is an attempt to transmit them to the next generation, the women do not always cooperate. Furthermore, gender roles have changed in the last few decades in many parts of the world. Increased educational and economic opportunities and changing social norms have altered women's attitudes regarding the traditional family structure and their place within it. This situation has created a feeling of unease and rebellion in Indian-American women of all ages. In speaking to these women, it is clear that they are searching for individual fulfillment. With their mothers and other older female role models undergoing a transformation of self, there can be little surprise that second generation daughters are negotiating a similar identity minefield. One-on-one conversations with women in their mid-20s to 30s reveal feelings of confusion and unrest regarding their role in society. Their bicultural identity and changing roles for women are creating a conflict for these women as they re-evaluate the gender roles they observed in their parental homes. The desire for change is evident when I examine, in a later section of this chapter, the gender role expectations that these young women have for their own marital relationships. In fact, changing gender roles have affected the level of autonomy that women desire in every aspect of their lives. However, this trend is particularly evident as young women re-evaluate interpersonal relationships—one of the most troubled areas of immigrant family life.

Dating—an intergenerational conflict

The traditional arranged marriage structure is no longer an option for these women as they are increasingly demanding more input in the selection of their spouses. How much participation they demand and what they are actually granted varies from individual to individual and from family to family. Coming from a generation who did not date and who, for the most part, had arranged marriages, parents are resisting, in varying degrees, their daughters' desire to date and choose their own partners. Inexperienced and confused, parents and their daughters are attempting to grapple with issues ranging from dating etiquette to premarital sex—issues that mainstream America began to resolve several generations ago when dating became prevalent in the 1920s. In *Homeward Bound: American Families in the Cold War Era*, Elaine Tyler May concludes that peer-enforced dating rituals were established in the nation's high schools as 'enrollments increased in the 1930s and 1940s [and] dating became nearly universal among teenagers'.[25] Dating is, however, not an established nor recognized part of the Asian-Indian culture and has only recently become an issue in their immigrant communities.

As the second generation of the post-1965 immigrants reach marriageable age, their attempt to 'update' the traditional arranged marriage structure with new patterns of courtship has led to an intergenerational conflict. In fact, dating is the number one cause of conflict and stress between parents and their adult children in Asian-Indian communities according to the results of a recent study conducted in conjunction with the School of Public Heath at UCLA.[26] This conflict is not limited to Asian-Indian families in the United States. Indian-Canadian studies also reveal that first generation women are stressed when their children date and that 'free choice marriage based on romantic love' caused intergenerational conflict.[27] However, the desire for individual mate selection versus familial choice is growing, even in traditional patriarchal societies. Despite parental disapproval, the majority of Indian-American women in this study have been or are currently involved in dating relationships. These women are making a conscious choice to resist the restrictions on their interactions with members of the opposite sex. They are choosing a different path than the one their mothers walked—a path that includes marrying a man they have selected for themselves. The factors propelling this trend include: higher educational levels for women; an inclination to delay marriage until they are older; an urban lifestyle; and the process of industrialization.[28] Interestingly enough, these same factors are not producing the same results in India according to a 1996 *India Today*–MARG survey conducted in Mumbai, Calcutta, Hyderabad and Lucknow. Eighty-one percent of the respondents reported that they had an arranged marriage while the other 19 percent reported a 'love marriage'. Fifty percent of the respondents in arranged marriages stated that they preferred this type of marriage as their parents knew what was best for them, while 20 percent wanted a spouse of a similar social standing and 18 percent wanted parental support in the event of any marital difficulties.[29]

Research on dating and self-selection marriages is scarce for Asian-American groups as dating is not the traditional norm for establishing and/or maintaining interpersonal relationships within these communities. However, the few studies conducted indicate conflict surrounding these issues among not only Asian-Americans, but also in other ethnic immigrant groups. For example, Nazli Kibria discovered that among Vietnamese-Americans, 'conflicts with family elders often revolved around dating'.[30] Similar results are documented in George Sanchez's work with Mexican-American women. Sanchez states that 'young Chicanas living in East Los Angeles with their parents increasingly challenged the elders' notions of dating and courtship, even while they maintained a deferential attitude toward them in other areas'.[31] Like the young Chicanas, second generation Indian-American women are not rejecting the idea of parental input. They simply want to increase their own participation in the entire process—from beginning to end. These women feel this is important because their goal is to change the structure of the Asian-Indian marriage itself. Like millions of women around the world, they are not willing to settle for someone simply because he will be a good provider or comes from an acceptable family background. They want companionship, friendship and intimacy; they want someone who will treat them as a partner and they want romance.

Their mothers, who married and spent their wedding night with a stranger, were told that love comes after the wedding ceremony. The second generation women in my study want to chose a partner they are attracted to and feel they are compatible with. While their parents have a list of qualifications they want to use in selecting a son-in-law; these young women want to add their own criteria to the screening process. They have definite ideas about the qualities they feel are necessary or important in potential partners and it is not caste or the regional origin so dear to their parents.

The ideal man

Asian-Indian arranged marriages have traditionally been based on similarities of caste and class, region and language, and religion. In India, the majority of the population still socializes only within their specific caste designation. With approximately one million individuals of Asian-Indian descent scattered throughout the United States, one wonders if the second generation is adhering to traditional caste restrictions when they choose a partner. This section examines whether overall Indian origin is considered in the selection criteria and more specifically, what is, if any, the importance of caste, regional affiliations, and ability to speak a specific language. Respondents were asked to answer these questions for both their dating partners and men they would consider as potential marital partners in order to see if the criteria changed. In other words, was overall Asian-Indian origin, caste, regional affiliations or the ability to speak a specific language more, less, or equally as important if the desired end was marriage rather than dating? This section will also examine what specific personality traits and characteristics the women respondents are looking for in their version of the 'ideal man'.

Among the participants in this study, 40 percent of the women were open to dating a non-Indian-American. However, only 26 percent would be willing to marry one. When asked why they would prefer to marry an Indian-American, the women state: 'I need someone who can share and appreciate my cultural and religious beliefs' and 'Marrying a non-Indian would mean hell—undergoing criticism for the rest of our lives from family and outsiders'. In contrast, the women who are willing to consider non-Indian partners for marriage comment: 'If I fall in love with a non-Indian, we'll see what happens' and 'I would marry *anyone* for true love'.

Interestingly, caste, regional origin, and language were not important considerations for these women. Ninety-seven percent of the women respondents state that caste is not important; 94 percent state that regional origin is not a criteria and 84 percent state that having the ability to speak a particular regional language is not important in a dating partner. Regarding their marital partners, caste, regional origin, and the ability to speak a specific language were not a consideration for 94, 78 and 74 percent, respectively, of the women. The women did state, however, that the caste and regional origin of the prospective partner were important criteria for their parents and many expressed apprehension about introducing a man from a different caste or region to their parents. Although women in the Asian-Indian culture, like many women world-wide, are considered the 'bearers of tradition', the respondents in this study are not excessively concerned about specific ethnic characteristics when selecting their partners. However, 74 percent did express a desire to marry within the larger Indian-American community. The desire to have endogamous marriages is not unique to the Asian-Indian culture or even the larger Asian-American community. In fact, a preference to marry within one's ethnic group is present in most communities. A nationwide study, *Sex in America*, recently conducted by the University of Chicago revealed that '90% of the couples [who responded] are of the same race or ethnicity'.[32] The preference to marry within one's own ethnic group is also illustrated in Kibria's research: '... most young, adult Vietnamese Americans, both male and female, did not favor marrying a non-Vietnamese person, because of cultural differences'.[33] Kibria states that it was the 'anticipation of family disapproval of marriage to non-Vietnamese persons' that encouraged the younger generation to stay within their ethnic group.[34] The Mexican-American community exhibits similar marriage patterns as illustrated in George Sanchez's intergenerational study. He discovered that 'almost 83 percent of the marriages involving Mexican immigrants in a sample of 1,214 marriages took place within the Mexican/Chicano community'.[35] Therefore, in regard to the ethnicity of marital partners, the data from the Indian-American population is consistent with research conducted among other ethnic populations as well as the mainstream US population. Furthermore, the data in this study reveals that general Asian-Indian origin, rather than specific regional origin or caste, is the most important criteria.

In addition to the traits mentioned above, the women expressed a strong propensity for certain personality types or other characteristics when evaluating a prospective partner. Respondents to the questionnaire for this study were asked to rank thirteen personality and descriptive traits as mandatory, very important, somewhat important and not important in regard to a dating and marriage partner. Interestingly, these women listed the exact same criteria in the same order of importance for both dating and marriage partners. Kindness, rated the highest by women, was followed by integrity, intelligence, communication skills, and formal education.

When the respondents were asked for any additional criteria they would use to select a marriage partner, they replied: 'North Indian', 'Hindu', 'good moral standards', 'strong believer in equal rights', 'must not have strong pre-conceived notions as to a woman's place', 'he has to respect me and my views', and lastly, 'he must respect my ambitions and understand me'. Although the first few comments echo what their parents would most likely say, the comments regarding equality for women and treating them as partners are certainly new additions to the list. These women are clearly rewriting the criteria used by their parents. Another trait listed as 'very important' to 'mandatory' for both dating and marriage partners was the ability to communicate effectively. This is not surprising in today's era. Communication has become an increasingly vital skill as relationships change from the limited interaction between spouses inherent in the extended family system to ones where the members of the smaller nuclear family increasingly look to each other for companionship and the emphasis is on the husband and wife as partners. Asian-Indian parents, attempting to hang on to their various cultures are not readily acknowledging that these changes are taking place or if they do accept it, they are minimizing the impact. Open communication is also important between parents and their daughters, especially when premarital sexuality, another potential minefield, is the topic.

Sexuality—an Asian-Indian parent's nightmare

If knowing that their daughters are dating is stressful for parents, hiding the fact is equally stressful for the second generation. In addition to the subterfuge required to maintain a secret relationship, these young women are cut off from any potential guidance as they cannot openly discuss various issues of dating with their families. Therefore, their reference points may be other, equally confused, Indian-Americans or members of the mainstream population. Following the lead of the mainstream population can cause internal as well as increased intergenerational conflict due to cultural differences between the two population groups. These differences can be pronounced when dealing with premarital sexual relationships. For example, consensus among the second generation is that relationships proceed at a slower pace with dating partners from the Indian-American communities as sexual involvement is not a casual 'next-step'. Rather, it generally implies an understanding that this relationship will lead to marriage.

With Indian-American partners, there is also greater and earlier family involvement than with a mainstream American dating partner. Informal group discussions[36] with married and single Indian-Americans in their mid-to-late 20s provided some interesting insights regarding the role of families. For example, these groups revealed that holding hands with an Indian-American partner in front of either set of parents indicates a more serious relationship than if the partner is a non-Indian-American. They acknowledge the existence and acceptance of a different set of unspoken relationship 'rules' if their partner is of Asian-Indian origin. It should be mentioned that these 'rules' have not been solidified, are still being actively negotiated, and although subjective, there does appear to be a basic consensus.

Along with their reluctance to allow their children to date and often even to discuss the subject, Asian-Indian parents seem even more disinclined to consider that their children may be sexually active and therefore, this subject is avoided. This 'gag' rule, of course, does not translate to sexual abstinence in the second generation. Regardless of the silence on this issue, which many of the second generation also contribute to, 24 percent of the female respondents revealed that they have been or are currently sexually active. As this sexual experience is contained to the group over 20 years of age, it could correspond to relationships formed while in college and away from strict parental control. The sexual partners of this group are a mixture of Indian-Americans and mainstream Americans. Interestingly, the ethnicity of the dating partners did not determine whether Indian-Americans were sexually active. The number of sexual partners reported are limited to one to two partners, even for women in their late 20s. This again indicates that casual sex is not an option for these Indian-American women, rather, sexual intimacy is limited to committed and monogamous relationships. However, it also indicates that for approximately one out of every four women, sexual intimacy is an integral part of a relationship. It should be noted that these numbers are probably underreported. Many Indian-American women are reluctant to disclose these details as they are fearful of gossip and the negative stereotypes associated with female sexuality that are still prevalent in the communities. Data from the *Sex in America* study indicates that 71 percent of Asians have had one to four sexual partners after turning 18 while 55 percent of 'white' Americans have had a similar number. When analyzed by gender, 67 percent of women and 41 percent of men have had one to four partners after the age of 18. The rest of the population has had more than four sexual partners. Therefore, the Indian-American women, if utilizing the numbers actually reported in my study, have had fewer sexual partners.[37]

It is clear from the data in my study that Indian-American women are moving towards relationships based on specific personality traits and desired characteristics while retaining some traditional ones their parents consider important, primarily that of a partner of Asian-Indian origin.

Yet, as these desired relationships involve extended interaction between the sexes, they are leading to conflict with first generation parents. Despite this, young Indian-Americans are pushing, in varying degrees, for greater autonomy in this area. With the second generation increasingly wanting to make their own decisions regarding marital partners, is the traditional Asian-Indian arranged marriage system a thing of the past? It is—at least as far as the 'traditional' aspect of little or no input from the individuals about to be married is concerned. However, the second generation is willing to consider an 'updated version' in which they can actively participate.

The price of deception

'If I had my way,' Anita states as she twists the small diamond ring on her left hand, 'I would wait a couple of years before we get married. But my parents are in such a hurry.' Nineteen-year-old Anita emigrated with her parents less than a decade ago and has just finished her first year of college. Our conversation began innocently enough with my asking her how she had met her fiancé. Her story, seemingly unique to her, echoes the stories I have heard from dozens of Indian-American women. 'We secretly dated for a year,' she slowly tells me and then continues to describe a year lived on pins and needles and filled with deception, for which she still feels guilty. Her then-boyfriend was introduced as her brother's friend so that he would be welcome in her home and her parents would have a chance to get to know him and hopefully approve. Her stories of group get-togethers, secret dinners and other stolen moments were all-too-familiar and yet, were also stories of resistance. Outwardly docile and submissive, the 'proper' Asian-Indian daughter, she was quietly waging a battle to resist her parents' rigid ideas and their plans of an arranged marriage for their only daughter. Yet, what price did she pay for this resistance? Her guilt is still evident as she struggles to justify her actions.

Matters apparently came to a head when one of their secret dinners was discovered and the small Asian-Indian community in her hometown was ablaze with gossip. She sighs as she recalls her mother in tears and her father avoiding her for days afterwards. She felt as if she had disgraced her family. Now unmasked, the boyfriend, accompanied by his parents, came to 'officially' meet her parents who pushed for an engagement to diffuse the gossip and save the family honor. This story, which is reinforced in Asian-Indian movies, is often repeated across the United States. Anita is now safely 'settled'; an elaborate engagement followed by a wedding ceremony has given her parents' public stamp of approval. But I cannot help wondering if the relationship would have developed to this stage if she could have pursued it openly and without the constant pressure. Clandestine meetings may be romantic and add excitement, however, when discovered, the repercussions are usually swift and predictable. Parents place pressure on the young couple to justify their actions and feelings through a formalized agreement to marry. Yet, how many of these relationships have the ingredient necessary for a successful union? And how many would have eventually faded if the secrecy surrounding them was removed? As casual dating is not acceptable to these communities, the majority of Indian-Americans state that they will not openly acknowledge their dating relationship in the preliminary stages. Their involvement is made public only when it has been established as a serious committed relationship. Some of these statements are also age-sensitive. Individuals in their late 20s and beyond appear to be willing to discuss certain aspects of dating more openly. However, these conversations are more general in nature and do not reveal individual personal experiences.

In addition to the stress involved in developing and implementing a strategy to maintain these secret relationships, there are also other drawbacks to the deception. As a result of being cut off from parental access and advice, some young Indian-American women are also struggling with emotionally and physically abusive relationships. In a recent *India West*[38] article, a few of these women revealed how a lack of parental guidance made them vulnerable to abusive and exploitative situations. They were unable to discuss their unease over specific situations with their parents and sometimes even their friends. For the vast majority of second generation Indian-Americans, these concerns are hidden from their parents who may not approve of their daughters dating in the first place. The parents who do allow their daughters to date are in the minority and out of these, the majority do not approve of multiple relationships, which are commonplace and almost expected in mainstream America. These radically different viewpoints position young Indian-Americans with one foot in each culture as they attempt to grapple with the inherent complexities of interpersonal relationships.

When the relationship is or becomes known to the parents, there is pressure that it should eventually result in marriage, the quicker the better. Due to this urgency, women are under constant pressure to get married. Also, behaviors that might trigger concern in a more experienced individual may be overlooked. Thus, by restricting their daughters, Indian-American parents may be exposing them to dangerous relationship problems. The traditional arranged marriage system places women in the US at even higher risk as the limited interaction with a potential partner can mask behavior problems which may be more difficult to hide in an interactive relationship. However, it is not for this reason alone that women want to renegotiate the arranged marriage system and bring it into the 21st century.

Arranged marriages in the 21st century

The Nisei (second generation Japanese-Americans) in Valerie Matsumoto's multi-generational study were influenced by 'mainstream middle-class values of love and marriage [and they]... moved away from the pattern of arranged marriage'.[39] A similar movement is taking place among the second generation of Indian-Americans who advocate increased intergenerational communication as they push for greater participation in the selection of their future spouses. The participants in this study are opposed to the limited, if any, involvement expected of the bride and groom in traditionally arranged Asian-Indian marriages. However, as stated earlier, they are open to an updated version of this system. Ninety-four percent of the women surveyed are willing to be introduced to prospective spouses *if* they are able to establish some of the screening criteria and have considerable interaction before *they* make a decision. In one-on-one discussions regarding this modified version of the arranged marriage, the participants explain their willingness to be introduced to potential partners as similar to being set up by friends. In reality, this may not be the case. Potential spouses have already been screened by the extended family and sometimes family friends before introductions take place. Thus, rejection at this point may involve more repercussions than a simple set-up by friends. Consequently, there is considerable pressure not only to participate in the process but also not to reject 'too many' potential partners, especially for women. However, there is, at present, no clear-cut definition of what constitutes 'too many' rejections.

If the arranged marriage system is, in fact, being restructured into more of an introduction service with the women stating that they want to participate in the process, how much participation do they want prior to reaching a decision? Ninety-eight percent state that they would need to have a dating relationship before they would be willing to marry someone they have been introduced to. The women further stated that they would want to date this individual for an average of 15 months before they would agree to a marriage. Thus, they are viewing the traditional arranged marriage system as more of an introduction service with potential partners engaging in a semi-Western-style dating relationship before they make up their *own* minds. However, parents seem to have a difficult time understanding why this decision takes so long. When *they* were married, they, *if* their opinion was asked at all, were expected to decide within a few minutes of meeting the prospective partner.

At this time it is unclear how much progress has been made towards more consensual or semi-arranged marriages. In this updated version of the system, I would argue that individuals are still coerced, but the impression is given that they are doing it of their own free will in that they are allowed to choose a partner. What is clear is the constant, sometimes unrelenting, pressure surrounding the entire marital process that women are reporting. I would also argue that the subordinate status of women in the Asian-Indian culture does not allow them to participate in this selection process at the same level as men. Even today's professional women are often viewed as a liability and they enter the marriage market at a disadvantage simply because they are women. However, the women themselves do not intend to perpetuate their subordinate status when they are married. The communities may often view them as second-class citizens, but they see themselves as full partners in their marital relationships.

The new marriage—reality or fiction?

The single respondents of this study have definite thoughts above their future relationships. Overall, the data suggests that the younger generation of Indian-Americans is moving toward increasingly egalitarian relationships and that the majority of women expect to work full-time, with careers. Although women observed that their parents engaged in a traditional sexual division of labor, they want and expect a more egalitarian arrangement for themselves. Indian-American women almost unanimously state that they expect their future spouses' involvement in household tasks to be comparable to their own. This viewpoint is one that is shared by recent generations as discussed in Elaine Tyler May's study of American families. Polls conducted within the last 20 years indicate most single women believe that, after marriage, both partners would work and be jointly responsible for child care and household responsibilities.[40] Yet as Hochschild's *Second Shift* demonstrates, this does not happen in reality and 'domestic gender roles [have] remained resistant to change'.[41]

The young single Indian-Americans in this study echo the respondents from the 1970s poll when they state that they expect to divide household responsibilities equally. I would argue that as these respondents are single, they are projecting into the future and describing an ideal situation. Future Indian-American couples can expect to encounter the same issues currently faced by millions of two-career families in the United States and in India. Sudha Sethu Balagopal's research on two-career Indian-American households (in this volume) indicates that women are carrying a larger portion of the household responsibilities than their husbands. While a direct correlation cannot be drawn as these women are first generation immigrants (although younger than the parental generation) brought up with more traditional gender roles, some trends can be established. These women, like many Indian-American women, tend to be educated and in well-paying professions and many can afford some domestic help. This cuts down on part of the 'second shift' without relying on the husband's participation. Also, the women who speak up about needing help are the ones most likely to get it. A few of Sethu Balagopal's case studies were based on women who felt it was their 'duty' to do everything and they would not or could not discuss a more equitable division of labor with their husbands. Therefore, it appears, that in these cases, it was the woman's lack of power, perceived or real, which doomed her to the 'second shift'. However, as the younger generation is already expecting egalitarian relationships, they may be one step ahead and, therefore, able to negotiate these issues from a stronger position.

Until death do us part?

The younger generation recognizes that marriage is a compromise and like their parents, they respect the sanctity of the relationship. Yet, at the same time, they expect a level of fulfillment which takes the marital relationship to a different level. They also recognize that individuals and circumstances change and have accordingly adopted a different attitude toward divorce. Currently, Asian-Indian culture views divorce as a somewhat acceptable solution to relationships involving physical abuse or other extreme situations. Even under these circumstances, divorce is still a social taboo and, therefore, only to be undertaken as a last resort. Furthermore, there is not an established infrastructure in India which facilitates the process of divorce and makes it a viable option. Although divorce rates are rising as women gain greater levels of economic independence, the current social climate is continuing to make divorce an unpleasant alternative. The first generation of Asian-Indian immigrants have continued this belief system and often view divorcees with reservation and suspicion. As in most patriarchal systems, it is the woman who bears the brunt of the negative associations attached to divorce. The divorced man is able to remarry with much less difficulty and social stigma. The matrimonial ads in Indian-American newspapers bear witness to the importance of being the 'victim' in a divorce action with the ever-present statement 'innocently divorced'.

This view of divorce is one which is not shared by the young respondents in this study and clearly the concept of divorce has changed dramatically within one generation. However, a deeper look indicates that, whereas the second generation may be more willing to leave an unhappy marriage, divorce is still a taboo with regard to remarriage, especially if the divorcee has children.

Ninety-four percent of the women believe that divorce is an option to an unhappy marriage. Furthermore, 45 percent believe that mutual incompatibility is adequate reason for a divorce while 45 percent cite refusal to have children as grounds for ending the marriage. This is quite a contrast from the parental generation which believes that divorce is an acceptable option only in extreme cases. The following comments were typical of the responses when asked if divorce was an option: 'Definitely. Why stay in an unhappy marriage' and 'Yes, marriage is no reason to live in misery'.

The strong change in attitude toward divorce is indicative of the change in the belief system regarding marriage in general. Marriage is increasingly seen as an interaction primarily between the two individuals involved rather than as a familial one. This viewpoint is not limited to the Indian-American communities and is found in other Asian-American groups. In Kibria's study of Vietnamese-American families, she concluded that 'the involvement of the family in the marriage decisions of young adults was far more superficial and symbolic in quality than it has been in Vietnam'.[42] Matsumoto also observed these changes in the Japanese-American community. She concluded that there is a second and third 'generational shift in the meaning of marriage and family, from an alliance concerned primarily with obligation and survival to a union centered on the concept of individual happiness'.[43] Therefore, marriage is increasingly viewed in terms of companionship rather than as a social structure which supports patriarchal constructs of the extended family, still prevalent in India.

In response to questions as to whether they would date or marry someone who was divorced and a second set which asked if they would date or marry a divorced individual with children, the majority of respondents still reflected some traditional views. While some would consider dating or possibly marrying a divorced individual, the vast majority will not date or marry a divorced individual with children. I would argue that these views reflect a transitional view of divorce. Whereas an unhappy marriage is not something they will suffer in, divorce is still constructed within a theoretical framework. Numerous members of the younger generation know someone of their age group who is divorced. However, they are viewed as the unlucky minority. The numbers are still small enough that these divorced individuals are viewed as an anomaly and, therefore, divorce is often not within their immediate realm of experience. For the most part, this younger generation is still in the courtship phase of their interpersonal relationships. I would argue that as this generation ages and the rate of divorce increases, remarriage will be a more common occurrence and, therefore, dating or marrying a divorcee will be more frequent and ordinary simply because there will be more divorced individuals. Currently, the divorced population of young adults is so small that, whereas it is increasingly an acceptable option, there is no open discussion of what it means to be divorced or the process itself. Therefore, there is still a strong stigma of perceived failure as well as a lack of understanding. Divorce is more of a topic of gossip rather than a reason for empathy.

Although the respondents felt that divorce was an acceptable option, they believed that, in general, people needed to work harder to make their marriages work. Some of the comments were, 'Two people should not live together if they are unhappy. However, divorce should always be a last resort' and 'If talking or counseling did not work, divorce would have to be considered'. It should be noted that respondents specifically mentioned using professional marital counseling to avoid divorce. This is a definite shift from the first generation Asian-Indians who, like other Asian groups, have negative feelings about involving outsiders in private 'family matters'.

Conclusions

Indian-American women, while expressing a desire to date and marry men of Indian origin, also mentioned that these men can be sexist and that they often attempt to confine women to antiquated roles. The old gender roles clash when they are combined with additional expectations that women also have the ability to function within the mainstream American culture. Numerous female respondents, after completing the questionnaire, spoke of the frustration of trying to balance two divergent views regarding women. On the one hand, there is the submissive, obedient and demure role expected of a 'proper' Asian-Indian 'girl' and on the other, the independent and assertive qualities necessary to achieve success as a 'woman' in a very competitive Western culture. They also spoke of Indian-American men in their late 20s who prefer women who are 20–22 years old as they are not as 'outspoken' nor do they express their needs and expectations as clearly. These women believe that these men preferred young girls to mature women whose personalities are stronger and more developed. This viewpoint was confirmed by several men who openly state that younger women (20–22) did not expect as much in a relationship and are 'easier to impress'.

In on-the-spot informal interviews conducted after the questionnaires were filled out, the male participants also spoke at length regarding their feelings about the women in their communities. Their comments confirm the complexity of the struggle Indian-American women face in their interpersonal relationships as they attempt to negotiate between two cultures. Some men expressed the view that Indian-American women are 'too assertive', 'too independent', 'too outspoken', 'too demanding', and not 'Asian-Indian' enough. When asked to expand on this concept of not being 'Asian-Indian' enough, they state that Indian-American women, in attempting to be equal members of society, were losing the 'femininity' that separates them from mainstream American women. They believe that Indian-American women should be more demure and a little more helpless. One participant specifically stated, 'I like making all the decisions.' These Indian-American men appear uncomfortable with women who directly and clearly state their expectations in the relationship. They state that they want independent women who will be equal partners, yet ask them to maintain the softness and malleability of a more submissive and, therefore, unequal partner. These comments may be more of a gender role conflict rather than a purely cultural one. In other words, these viewpoints are not simply a result of the men being Asian-Indian in origin—sexism transcends cultural boundaries and is not limited to a particular ethnic group. It should also be noted that many of the Indian-American men expressed their ease with strong, assertive women and their desire for an equal partnership in every sense of the word.

A phrase often utilized by Asian-Indian communities to describe their experience in the United States is 'we have the best of both worlds'. Asian-Indian immigrant women, like other Asian women, are combining traditional and contemporary values to create a way of being which facilitates their individual growth and aspirations. This is a monumental task as the traditional Asian-Indian woman is not supposed to nor encouraged to have an individual identity. Rather, her identity is one that is usually connected to and defined by the societal and cultural norms of a patriarchal familial structure. Specifically, a woman's identity is usually defined within the parameters of her social relationships to men. This ideology continues to be instilled in the second generation of Indian-Americans. Consequently, women in their 20s and 30s reveal feelings of confusion and unease regarding their role in society and a lack of individual fulfillment. The mainstream society expects individuals to assert themselves whereas Asian-Indian communities want women to be more subservient and follow more traditional gender roles. These contradictory expectations are creating intergenerational and inter-gender conflicts within the communities.

Indian-Americans, while more progressive than their parents regarding marital relationships, are still strongly influenced by their heritage and feel that others of Asian-Indian origin would make the best marital partners as they share a common culture, language and religion. Most members of these post-1965 communities are still first and second generation Americans and, therefore, maintain a strong sense of their more conservative Asian-Indian heritage. They are often reluctant to marry outside the culture due to societal and familial pressures and more importantly, for their own sense of self-identity and a desire to maintain their heritage. They are willing to date non-Indian-Americans, however, approximately three out of four intend to marry Indian-Americans, barring the influence of cupid's arrow!

Overall, Indian-American women are more egalitarian in their outlook whereas the majority of men in the community are still in the transitional phase.[44] In terms of household responsibilities, women expect their partners to share the work required to maintain their homes. It may take this younger generation of Indian-American women instilling their concepts of equality in *their* sons before the men are also in the egalitarian stage.

Group discussions with the parental generation indicate that Asian-Indian parents have a difficult time comprehending the redefinition of boundaries that occur when their children become adults in the eyes of the mainstream American culture. Asian-Indian parents, often very involved in their children's lives, are attempting to exert control over dating and courtship. They are uncomfortable that their children may be, in the words of one mother, doing more than 'kissing a little' and feel that having several relationships prior to finally settling down reflects a low moral character. The parents, were, however, open to a dialogue and felt that these issues needed to be widely discussed within the Indian-American communities.

This is not a definitive study due to the small number of respondents. However, it does indicate that the young Indian-Americans surveyed for this study are willing to be introduced to prospective partners, want to have more participation in the selection of their spouses and are moving toward more egalitarian relationships. Further research will be needed to discover what they teach their own children in terms of gender roles, personal boundaries, and the preservation of their Asian-Indian heritage.

✦ Notes and References

1. Asian-Indian will be used to denote the first generation of immigrants. Indian-American will be utilized when discussing their American-born children who identify themselves as American and as Indian. The term Asian-Indian is used in the US census to identify individuals from India. It is also used to denote US-born natives whose parents immigrated from India by describing them as second generation Asian-Indians. However, I believe it is problematic to use this term for the second generation and not also name them as Americans. This brings up the controversy as to who has the right to name a group. Researchers may, for the sake of simplicity, use first and second generation Asian-Indian to denote these two groups, however, many of them refer to themselves as Indo-American or Indian-American. Therefore, I will use both designations in this paper.

   Asian-Indian Hindu society is divided into major caste groups. These caste groups were originally occupational and there was some mobility. Over the centuries, the major groups have subdivided into thousands of sub-castes and the system has become rigid. Although the caste system is outlawed by the Indian Constitution, is still exists in practical terms both in India and, to varying degrees, among Asian-Indians in the diaspora.

2. To research attitudes towards gender roles, heterosexual relationship experiences, marriage and divorce, an anonymous questionnaire was distributed, by mail and at meetings of South Asian groups, to approximately 1,380 Asian-Indians and Indian-Americans. Both groups, like other Asian ethnic communities, are very private regarding personal information. Therefore, a questionnaire regarding their social interactions had to be carefully formulated and the purpose explained before they were willing to complete it. However, even with an assurance of anonymity, many individuals were reluctant to complete the portion of the questionnaire that dealt with sexual experience and relationships. Only 160 (12 percent) completed questionnaires were returned. Thus, those who responded to the compete survey may be more open to answering questions regarding sexuality or other personal data and some of the resulting data may be skewed towards more progressive views, for example, the number of people who consider divorce an option to an unhappy marriage. The questionnaires were supplemented with one-on-one conversations or group discussions on these issues.

   The respondents are undergraduate and graduate students and professionals who live in California, North Carolina, Washington, Illinois and Texas. They range in age from 17 to 34-years-old with the average age being 26. All respondents were single at the time of the study and predominantly came from two-parent families where the majority of mothers worked in some capacity outside the home.

3. Parentally arranged marriages refer to marriages arranged by the parental generation with varying degrees of participation by the younger generation. Self-arranged marriages are more in the 'Western' style and consist of marriages where the parents have little or no participation in the selection process.

4. Racially based immigration laws prevented the original Asian-Indian immigrants from bringing their wives and children to the United States—thereby separating some husbands and wives for decades until the laws were revised in 1946.

5. Joan M. Jensen, *Passage from India: Asian-Indian Immigrants in North America* (New Haven, Yale University Press, 1988), 280.

6. Jensen, 282. See n. 5.

7. *Webster's New Encyclopedic Dictionary* (New York, Black Dog & Leventhal Publishers, Inc., 1993), 1100 and David Jary and Julia Jary, *The Harper Collins Dictionary of Sociology* (New York, HarperPerennial, 1991), 101.

8. Donna Gabaccia, *From the Other Side: Women, Gender, and Immigrant Life in the US 1820–1990* (Bloomington, Indiana University Press, 1994), 114.

9. George J. Sanchez, *Becoming Mexican American* (New York, Oxford University Press, 1993), 12–13.

10. Valerie J. Matsumoto, *Farming the Home Place: A Japanese American Community in California 1919–1982* (Ithaca, Cornell University Press, 1993), 8.

11. Matsumoto, 6. See n. 10.

12. Matsumoto, 33. See n. 10.

13. Matsumoto, 62. See n. 10.

14. Nazli Kibria, *Family Tightrope: The Changing Lives of Vietnamese Americans* (Princeton, Princeton University Press, 1993), 146.

15. For more information on the 1950s and 1960s US family structure, see Elaine Tyler May, *Homeward Bound: American Families in the Cold War Era* (New York, Basic Books, 1988).

16. Margery Rosen, 'Her Work vs. His Work', *Parents' Magazine*, December 1995, 119.

17. Occupations frequently listed: engineer, physician, accountant, and scientist.

18. A phrase which refers to the double burden many working women have when they work outside the home and then come back to a full shift of household responsibilities. For more information, see Arlie Hochschild with Anne MacHung, *The Second Shift* (New York, Avon Books, 1989).

19. Josephine Naidoo and J. Campbell Davis, 'Canadian South Asian Women in Transition: A Dualistic View of Life', *Journal of Comparative Family Studies, Special Issue: Family in India and North America*, XIX(2), Summer 1988, 313.

20. *The Encyclopedia of Sociology* (Connecticut, The Dushkin Publishing Group, Inc., Guildford, 1974), 190.

21. Naidoo and Davis, 321. See n. 19.

22. Norman Buchignani and Doreen M. Indira with Ram Srivastiva, *Continuous Journey: A Social History of South Asians in Canada* (Toronto, McClelland and Stewart Ltd., in association with the Multiculturalism Directorate, Department of the Secretary of State and the Canadian Government Publishing Centre, Supply and Services, Canada, 1985), 157.

23. For the purpose of this paper, patriarchy refers to a family structure which includes the following: patrilineal inheritance; an extended family with sons and daughters-in-law living with the parents and sometimes the grandparents; and the oldest male having authority over the younger males and the women.

24. Judy Jung, *Unbound Feet: A Social History of Chinese Women in San Francisco* (Los Angeles, University of California Press, 1995), 18.

25. May, 119. See n. 15.

26. Snehendu Kar, Kevin Campbell, Armando Jimenez, and Sangeeta R. Gupta, 'Invisible Americans: An Exploration of Indo-American Quality of Life', *AmerAsia*, 21(3), Winter 1995/96, 37.

27. Naidoo and Davis, 321. See n. 19.

28. Murstein, 'Mate Selection in the 1970's', *Journal of Marriage and the Family*, 42, 51.

29. Madhu Jain, 'A Search for Intimacy', *India Today*, 31 December 1996, pp. 78–85.

30. Kibria, 152. See n. 14.

31. Sanchez, 143. See n. 9.

32. Robert Michael, John Gagnon, Edward Laumann, and Gina Kolata, *Sex in America* (Boston, Little Brown, 1994), 45.

33. Kibria, 163. See n. 14.

34. Kibria, 163. See n. 14.

35. Sanchez, 138. See n. 9.

36. Seattle, WA, 3 September 1995 and Chicago, IL, 14 September 1996.

37. Michael, 101–2. See n. 32.

38. *India West*, 27 January 1995, Section C, 53.

39. Matsumoto, 13. See n. 10.

40. May, 223. See n. 15.

41. Hochschild with MacHung, 223. See n. 18.

42. Kibria, 163. See n. 14.

43. Matsumoto, 200. See n. 10.

44. Hochschild with MacHung. See n. 18.

8

The case of the brown memsahib:[1] *Issues that confront working South Asian wives and mothers*

Sudha Sethu Balagopal

India is a contradiction. One only has to read newspaper stories that speak tellingly of dowry deaths and bride-burning on one hand while extolling the abilities of Kiran Bedi, India's highest ranking police woman, on the other, to understand why it is a contradiction. In India, it is not uncommon to find women laborers carrying heavy loads to build a modern office complex in a major city; an office complex that will probably house several women engineers, managers, and executives. In a dramatic shift from their mothers' generation, today's Indian women, whether they live in India or outside, accept working outside the home as commonplace.

This chapter focuses on working South Asian wives and mothers in the United States. They are working professionals who are still trying to maintain what they consider to be the cultural standards of South Asian wives and mothers in the home. The new family with a working mother is still trying to find a balance in the tug-of-war between these two roles.

Although many things are changing in India and in the United States, the contradiction still remains. Some women are submissive and docile and play the 'typical' Indian wife. On the other hand, careers being an option for many Indian women, a new dimension has been added to their marriages. For them, a third job has entered the fray, where there used to be just two, one for the woman and one for the man. This third entrant is the woman's career.

So how does the equation balance itself? Is it one-and-a-half jobs for each person or is it one job for one person and two for the other, or is it something in-between? The combinations can be many and varied. It all hinges on whether the Indian husband accepts these changes and whether the Indian wife enforces them.

The past few decades have seen a revolution in the job market as an increasing number of women entered the workforce. The situation is complicated as many of these women had small children at home. The stresses and strains brought on by the working mom are many. As more mothers step into the workforce, are the traditional gender roles changing and if so, how?

Technological and economic leapfrogging has perhaps left behind the accompanying sociological changes. For many Indian men who have never seen their mothers work outside the home—mothers who accepted their traditionally defined roles as mothers and wives—the changes in their own marital structures are difficult. How do their wives maintain a balance between their roles in the workplace and their roles at home? Is walking that tightrope hard, or have changes taken place both internally and externally making things easier on them?

When women stayed at home in their roles as mothers and wives and men took on the role of the provider, there were two very clear-cut jobs. For centuries women have been portrayed as the 'gentler' sex—one that needed to be taken care of. In India, tradition dictates that women behave in a certain way, arranged marriages are the norm and middle-class women rarely go out at night without an escort.

Do Indian marriages in the United States reflect the changing realities of two-career families? Has working outside the home impacted their lives at home? The six case studies chosen for this chapter provide insights into the changes that have taken place in some South Asian marriages with the advent of the working mom.

The case of the work-at-home mom, Urmila[2]

Urmila is an artist. Her home is her office. Is she a working mom? Most certainly. In fact, she is a frustrated working mom who feels her work is not being taken as seriously as it should be by her family. She wants her work to be considered just as important as the work of women that actually work outside the home in an eight-to-five situation. Her situation is particularly hard since she is always 'on-call' and cannot have a set work schedule—a situation which is both positive and negative.

'No, I wouldn't call myself a career woman. I've never thought of myself as a career woman. But I have a career. More than a career, I have a vocation, I think. You think of a career as something that takes you out of the home, for which you get money. I have a vocation. It might get me money, it might not,' she says.

Working roles

Urmila, who is in her late 30s, was a career woman for seven years. Things changed after her daughter was born because the roles changed. 'And that I would attribute to my husband. In an ideal partnership, roles have to change for both. But that doesn't usually happen. Because women are expected to do all the changing. And I did a lot of the changing,' she explains. In fact, she feels that the women themselves feel compelled to believe that they have to make all the adjustments.

'I believe I have to adjust and give her attention, because she is my child. But I do not believe I should have to do it to the extent [I did]. He could have done more. I believe I would have adjusted more anyway, simply because he is the bread earner. It's all economics you see.'

Not that she could have continued working. She feels she would have had to give up her job in any case, since her child was frequently ill. And now that her daughter is growing fairly independent, how has that affected her career plans? 'No one is going to give me a job now. That is the sad thing. I have been out of the job market for a long time now,' Urmila says.

However, had she, at the time of her child's birth, continued on a part-time basis, then in five or six years she would have been in a position to rekindle her career. Without adequate experience in the past few years she cannot be hired as an artist.

'I had to compromise on my potential, yes,' she admits. In a more fundamental sense, in marriage, you get relegated to various roles, she feels. When it should really be a partnership. 'We did not marry to have somebody put food on the table for us. We were capable of earning a living for ourselves when we got married. What I have now is entirely on my own with absolutely no encouragement. I could have reached this point in my life and not have had anything, no grants etc. Now that

I have some money for my work, [he has] a grudging sort of respect. If you are working and you love what you do, regardless of whether you get money for it or not, it has to be respected,' she feels.

As far as her professional life is concerned, when her child is at school, she works... on her job. But that is on normal days. With illnesses and a continuous stream of guests and other things, her professional life is constantly interrupted, because she is at home. So how does she handle it? By negotiating with her husband. 'We had a big talk about it. If he feels compelled to invite guests, then he has to help take care of them. I am not going to give up my work for these things. When you work from home only "you" take your work seriously and if you don't take your work seriously no one else will.'

The first time she traveled, on a fellowship, her child was three-and-a-half years old. Fortunately, her husband had time off. So he looked after her daughter for three weeks. Even though everything went off smoothly, 'when it was all over, he wanted my gratitude. And I wouldn't give it to him. It was his child [too], wasn't it?'

Roles at home

With her kind of work she cannot afford household help. 'Can't afford it on one income,' she says. So she expects help from her husband when it comes to doing household chores. How about cooking? 'It's the health thing here again. My child is allergic to a lot of things, and my husband needs a specialized diet. I'm ending up doing more than I'd like to. I keep my cooking to the minimum, however. I do it every other day. I let the house go. I've never had an inclination for housework, anyway. I do my laundry every other day. As far as the rest is concerned, if it bothers him, he can do it.' Before our child was born, everything was fifty-fifty and there was no argument about it, she explains. 'It was absolutely equitable, there was no counting. Now because of the fact that he's the one working outside, I took on more and naturally I had to.'

Who works with her daughter? She does, of course. Not just her schoolwork but extra work too, is her responsibility. Her biggest problem is the lack of time. 'I had no time. I had to fight for every little bit of time that I got,' says Urmila. She had to ask for time to work. All the things that she expected would happen automatically, did not. Things had to be explained to her husband. And, of course, such situations were not very pleasant.

'Husbands always end up saying that they are, after all, working for you, earning for you and for the child,' she says. But, 'I don't believe that, because if he weren't married he'd still be doing what he was doing. Really, he is doing it for himself.'

Urmila's only hobby is reading. So, everyday she reads for two hours. Recently, she started going to ballets and plays, without her husband, since he is not interested in these things.

'I feel that if I don't give him the responsibility, he will never learn,' she says. And, of course, every time she returns from one of her trips, the child gets sick. 'I really pay for it,' she laughs. Things are not the same in the house, the laundry is not done, the groceries are not bought and it enrages her. How does she deal with her anger? 'By taking it out on him,' she says.

Indian men in the United States have changed to a certain extent, in the sense that they do help out, she feels. But, as she points out, 'I don't want to be grateful for the crumbs.'

Equal jobs and equal roles in Radha's household

Radha has a great career. In addition, she has a husband who pitches in with all the household chores and is as involved in the raising of their son as she is. How did they achieve this equilibrium? 'I am very fortunate. Perhaps it has to do with both of us having gone to school together and having similar careers,' she mulls.

Originally from South India, 37-year-old Radha has a Bachelor's degree in Chemical Engineering from Calcutta, where she and her husband were classmates. The two came to the United States for graduate degrees and they both got jobs in 1984 at the same company. For almost 10 years they worked at their careers, consolidating their positions and reaping rich rewards. Then in 1993 their son was born and that brought about a big change in their lives. 'It has been a big adjustment for us,' she says. 'We are trying to juggle everything. Having to raise a son alone without having any family here, or the infrastructure we are used to, we are finding it very hard.'

Career and child

Radha manages a research and development facility for a large technology company and has about 220 people working for her. 'Raising a child and having a career is the toughest thing I have done in my life,' she says. The first year they had help from the grandparents. After they left, they were on their own and the reality of the situation hit home. They went through six nannies in the first eight months. 'I wanted him to grow up in the home and not in a daycare situation,' says Radha. They finally found a friend who goes to school in the evenings and hired her to take care of their son during the day. Even this arrangement puts a few restrictions on them, in the sense that one of them has to leave work on time to make sure their son is picked up before the sitter leaves for school. Sometimes Radha is ready to give up. 'It is very hard negotiating for five minutes here and five minutes there,' she says. Radha and her husband sit down every Sunday night and actually compare calendars to see how they can organize their week.

Often Radha has thought that maybe she should take a break from work. Her husband has also considered switching and starting his own business to get some flexibility in his work schedule. At present they both continue to juggle their schedules.

Uniquely equal

This marriage seems perfectly equitable. At night the husband takes care of their son, puts him to bed. Her husband even woke up at nights when he was a baby. 'I do the before-dinner bit and he does the after-dinner bit,' she elaborates.

How about her own travel? 'It's my own personal thing,' she says. 'I just don't like to do it. I know my son will be well taken care of, but I still don't like to leave him. If I didn't have a supportive husband, that is the key I think, it would be difficult. Many times I have thought of quitting. It is too much in terms of just coordinating the time and having to plan everything and negotiating for five minutes here or there. When we didn't have a child everything was different. We were like two independent people living together. I cannot go to a business meeting for example and stay for dinner. I have to make sure my husband is available to be with our son. You can't have your own schedule,' she explains.

Does it impact her work in anyway? 'I network less. I don't attend half the semi-social events I used to. Probably more than half,' says Radha talking about some of the changes she has had to make. But she does not resent it. 'As Indian women, we have a lot of attachment to our family. I will never compromise on anything for my son. Work and everything else is secondary. If my son is sick, I will not leave him with some other caregiver. Our company provides sick care and I know many other women that avail themselves of this provision.'

Her husband has never put any obstacles in the way of her career or tried to put his career before hers. In fact, she says, '...it is the other way round. He is always encouraging me.' Does economics play a role in all this? Is he making adjustments because they are equals in their jobs?

'He does not consider all this an adjustment. He enjoys being with our son. But I feel if he is taking care of my son, that's all he can do. I can cook, do the laundry and take care of my son all at the same time.' Yet, she says in terms of child rearing, they both spend equal time with their son.

Role as mom and wife

She does not think of herself as a super-mom. But, 'I think I am a better mom because I work. It is better for me to work or do something.'

Radha's husband also cooks. However, right now someone cooks for them and delivers once a week. But before they had help with the cooking, she would cook and he would clean. Simply because she likes to cook and not to clean. She likes having the food delivered. Otherwise, as soon as she returned from work, she would start cooking and her son would be hanging around waiting for her to finish. They have help to clean the house. 'I want to spend all my available time with my son.' How about other activities? They are trying to avoid anything else.

'Often, I feel guilty. Especially if one of us is sick. If I am sick, it puts double the load on my husband. If my son is sick, I feel like I have to stay home so we each have to take half a day off.' Her husband is very competent in raising their son, probably because of his upbringing, she feels. In addition to the fact that his mother has always worked outside the home, he comes from the state of Kerala on the western coast of India. Kerala has the highest literacy rate for women, is considered to be more egalitarian than the rest of India and portions of this state are more 'matriarchal' in comparison to the predominantly patriarchal structure of the rest of India.

This family seems to be perfectly well adjusted. The equilibrium between their jobs, the home and their son is well maintained. According to Radha, it could not be anything else. 'Because we both have demanding jobs and raising a child is very important for both of us.

You can't have everything unless you are both willing to pitch in. Very often we feel we don't have time for ourselves, though.'

Yet, despite all his help, having two careers is still difficult. 'It is hard...it's not all wonderful. We are exhausted all the time.' But they continue to work together.

Usha: Unequal jobs, unequal roles

Usha came to this country as a bride in an arranged marriage. Armed with an MBA from India, she was starry-eyed and idealistic, with big dreams and bigger hopes when she arrived. Being accepted into the competitive MBA programs in India was in itself a big victory. She was determined to chart a career course in the US, where she saw opportunities she had not imagined existed. But it was not to be. After marriage came the children. And her husband definitely did not think that their children should be left in someone else's care.

Compromise

And so the years went by. Now that her children are 12 and 9-years-old, she, finally, has a full-time job. 'I am an office manager for an engineering company,' she says. 'I didn't work for five years after the kids were born and after that I started working part-time and now I work full-time. I am basically a career woman and now I can say I am, because I am in a full-time job. Till now I was always very cautious. My first priority was always my children and then I started working part-time. I took a step backward because I knew they needed me more.'

How are things now that she has started a full-time job? 'It is very tough. We just go from day to day. We keep our finger's crossed that the kids will be healthy. Last week my son fell ill and we were all in a hurry to get him well, for which I felt really bad,' she says. So who stayed home when her son got sick? 'We made a compromise this time. My husband took some time off, finally, after 16 years!' It has not always been this way. Ordinarily, she would stay home with a sick child. But this time he had no choice, because she had just started a full-time job, she could not take the time off. For a man who is a workaholic and has never taken time off, that was a supreme sacrifice.

Torn between roles at home and work

Is she restricted in her career moves? 'Family always comes first, because I am an Indian woman. These are the restrictions I face. I am scared to take on more responsibility at work. What happens is, in this country, we don't have anyone else for the kids. We have no extended family or joint family and they basically depend on me for everything... food, shelter... everything,' says Usha.

Her husband helps with the kids, with things like homework. Has she ever had to travel as part of her job, and if she did would her husband take over? 'Oh no, I never take such jobs,' she laughs. But she is able to go out for business lunches, dinners or other after-work events that require her presence.

She leaves early in the morning, at 6:30 a.m. when the kids are asleep. Her husband's responsibility is to make sure the kids are ready and that they go to school. He had never done this before. Yet, 'I think it's high time I did something on my own too. My kids are little bit older now, 12 and nine, I think they can manage.'

Although she speaks with bravado, things are not that easy. She still has to worry about whether they make the bus on time. She gets up very early to make lunches for everyone. Her husband does not help with the lunches. Why? She laughs, 'He has a nervous breakdown if I ask him to do things like that!'

'However early you have to go, these are the things you have to do, because it won't be done otherwise,' she says. 'You cannot ask because it won't be done. Maybe I do too much but that's how it was for the last so many years and it is difficult to break habits you know. Like the old dog refusing to learn new tricks.' She even gets breakfast organized before she leaves, by doing things like leaving the cereal on the table. 'I just don't have the patience or the time now to teach them.'

She has a cleaning lady who comes to clean the house. Also, she has someone to do the yard. Laundry and dishes and other household jobs are still hers. Her husband's adjustment with the new job has come in the form of his sending the children off to school.

Rearing children

Usha feels she would have been better off in India. Not that her husband would have helped, but she would have had more help from outside sources. She compares herself to her sister, a professor. Her sister travels all over the world but the grandparents are there to take care of the children. For Usha, rearing the children is her job. Now that they are older, her kids help her a lot. 'I want to make sure they don't end up like one of the Indian guys we are married to!' she laughs.

Would it have been different if she was on par with her husband, in terms of a career, in terms of the money she brought in? 'Well, we basically prioritized our lives. The kids were number one. And number two, one of our careers has to have priority and I chose to have it this way, because somehow the mom has to be there for the children, right?'

Her sons are very proud of her. They think, however, that moms should stay home, that is what they have seen in their own home for a long time. They do help her but they certainly have traditional gender stereotypes embedded in their minds.

Learning to make changes

Sometimes Usha resents it. Now that she is in her 30s, she feels she has wasted time. Her career should have been her focus when she was in her 20s. 'Now, even if I want to I can't...I don't have the stamina or the motivation,' says Usha. If she had not had an arranged marriage, she feels, she would probably have been more outspoken right from the beginning. Her husband-to-be would have known who she was. In arranged marriages, she feels, there is a lot of stress, especially when you are outside India.

Do they spend time together as a couple, she and her husband? 'No, we'd like to, but we don't have the time,' she answers. Even now, she cannot let go, she feels like she should do everything and is still torn between her job and her home. Her kids still need her, she feels, in her heart. 'Whatever I do, even my job, it is related to my kids,' she says. That is why, she is home when they come home from school.

She resented the shattering of her dreams and she blamed her husband for it in the past. Now she's slowly emerging from that confusion. With her new job things are changing. Her husband and children help more, her confidence is restored. And she is learning to deal with her resentment by explaining things to her husband.

This couple is working towards an egalitarian division of household responsibilities. Usha is slowly learning to state her expectations. However, she is still dealing with her belief that she has to do everything.

Rani: Unequal jobs but equal roles

Outspoken Rani has a home in which every member has an equal role to play, the husband, the children and the wife. They all pitch in with the chores whether it is laundry, cleaning, or cooking. She does not think that it is fair to expect the wife and mother to do everything at home.

Rani, in her 50s, is a nurse who has two girls, both of whom are now in college. She worked while they were little and still does. Although it is a lot easier now that they are away from home, she has faced the same issues that the other women talked about. How did she handle it then and how does she handle it now?

'Everything has been male-oriented so automatically it's turned negative on us,' she says. 'Now we are emerging out of it.' Unfortunately women are doing it to themselves, she feels sometimes. In the way we think, in the way we subjugate ourselves. 'The way we think we need to cater to men, we think that's being a woman and we like that role. Even working women sometimes like to stay in the role. Not because the men are demanding it but because we like to make it our power base.' Maybe we are not doing it consciously, but subconsciously we like to be in control, she feels.

Rani was a professional when she got married. Then she migrated to the US and stayed home for a number of years, raising children. She went back to work after that hiatus and has been working ever since. As someone who has seen both sides of the issue, she can shed ample light on the working woman's life.

Background

For the first 11 years of her marriage, she did not work outside the home. And she thoroughly enjoyed it. She states that she made the decision to stay home. 'I made a conscious decision not to work, [after marriage] because it was, in a way, an arranged marriage and I decided that I was going to get to know this man, be free of work and all those responsibilities,' she admits.

Even then her husband was very much involved in her daily life, both in terms of child rearing, and all the household chores. He did not dictate whether she should work or not work at her career. So it was very easy to fall into a pattern. Soon, however, at the instigation of her mother, she went to graduate school.

Then they moved back to India. There was no question of her working since she was in a new situation one more time. After 11 years, India was a different world. And when she returned, she found that the women in India had moved ahead and that she had stagnated living in the US.

They moved back to the United States, however, since things did not work out in India. And at that time Rani decided that she would do things differently. They settled in, she took a refresher course, did her boards again and was back in the workforce.

Career and home

'It was not hard,' she says. 'I had to make arrangements. He had no choice, he had to work mornings and against all the feelings I had, I had to work in the evenings.' She hated every bit of it because she missed being with her children.

In her nursing position, fortunately, there was no travel. She did her housework in the mornings. And left for work at 2 or 2:30 p.m. How did she decide when and how to get back into her career? Her desire for a career and the family's financial needs motivated her actions and may have contributed to her children's acceptance of the situation.

Rani was concerned for their safety when they were little, when they were with babysitters and had to walk home from school alone. Even now she has concerns. But her career has kept going. She has progressed in her work, not as much as she would have liked to, but she is certainly progressing. Of course it helps that she has fewer restrictions on her time since she does not have little children to run home to.

Day-to-day

Rani is as much a force in the decision-making process as her husband is. Both husband and wife share the cooking. When she is away, he cooks. When the kids were younger, they worked closely with their father, cooking with him. 'To be truthful, I feel I do very little,' she laughs. In this egalitarian household, everyone pitches in. Is it because she is working? No, it was almost the same, when she did not. 'Yes, some changes were forced upon the household, when I started working because of the timings and such,' she says.

Her husband is completely self-sufficient and does everything including laundry. 'In a lot of households, we are just women who do all the work,' but not so in Rani's house. When she entertains she cooks because she takes great pride in it and she likes to do it properly, with flower arrangements and a planned menu. Her daughters have always helped as has her husband.

Super-mom?

What about the super-mom syndrome? 'Occasionally, I did get exhausted. But so did he. It was not all on my shoulders. It is his personality and a little bit of his upbringing also, I think. I make only half of what he does but it is important and it has always mattered.' She does not feel, however, that because she makes less, she has to work harder at home to make his life a little bit easier. 'I love my work and if I had to do it again, I would do the same thing. I've never felt less than the other person. That's because I am a very strong personality. My husband is not a man I can push around, but he sees the point when I make one. When [the] kids were sick, there [have been] times when he has had to take care of them. Nothing, luckily, ever happened that was serious. And we shared, he takes a day off and then I do,' says Rani. Now, she gets help once a week, to clean the house. 'He has done it, and so have I, while the children were growing up and now we need a break,' she justifies.

The family does things without her having to tell them to do so. Her daughters have grown up in a household where everyone pitches in. Tasks are not divided by gender lines. For example, it is not assumed that her husband will handle financial issues, traditionally a man's domain. In fact, Rani handled the finances for a while and then they switched. It's perfectly self-propelled. He does the investing now, taking the advice of friends who are more savvy. She concentrates on her work which gives her more satisfaction that anything else.

A stay-at-home mom does provide a certain level of stability but it can also reinforce traditional gender roles. 'But what happens when you have sons and they grow up, is that they want to marry someone like their mom and that perpetuates the system of roles,' she feels. 'I tell my friends who have sons, please don't do everything for them.'

Hard-to-break precedents in Shobha's home

As an educated woman, Shobha was perfectly capable of launching a rewarding career. However, after she got married, she chose to put her career on the back burner for a while. Torn between the family and wanting a career, she compromised for several years by doing odd jobs. Today, she is trying to re-establish herself while trying to break the precedents she herself has set.

She worked for a lecturer at Agra University for three years before she got married and came to the US. She eventually started taking a couple of classes since she could not find the kind of position she had in India. However, to complicate matters, her first child, was born soon thereafter, so she could not do much. She taught kindergarten and first grade for a couple of years—jobs that gave her flexibility—when her son was little. While her jobs did not contribute to her ultimate career goals, they gave her something to do.

Start of career

Forty-two-year-old Shobha went back to school in 1988 as a full-time student for a Master's in Education, and finished with her Ph.D. in 1992. Meanwhile, in 1991, she also had a second child, a daughter. But she was not ready to give up her education with her doctorate almost in hand. Yes, she readily agrees, because she got married and because she had children, she had to make sacrifices and, 'I wanted to,' she admits. She had a one-year-old when she completed her Ph.D. and she says that it was very difficult. In 1992 she started working in earnest as a faculty member at a local university. While her position is technically part-time, the sheer amount of work she does makes it very demanding.

What restrictions does she face? 'It is not easy to be a mom and a homemaker and also do what I am doing,' she says. Many of the problems that needed to be solved were of her own making. For example, when she started traveling she readily admits, she had her own issues to sort out. 'In fact I'd never traveled extensively before,' she says. Now, with the help of her colleagues, she is more comfortable and her family copes, although it is a lot of work for her husband. 'He has to, [do it] there is no choice,' she says. Does he like it? 'No, and so far he has not said "don't go". But there are times when we have had to talk about it,' she says. If she is late at work, she feels she has to call and tell him she is going to be late. 'Before going to work, I was always asked what is your schedule going to be. I understand, it is primarily because things have to be taken care of. My schedule is not eight-to-five you see.'

Roles at home

What happens when she is in town? 'No matter how tired I am, I still go in the kitchen and I start doing the things that I have to do. There are days when I come in at 9:30 at night because of a late class, then they manage with dinner. So far, however, I have never heard him say "just stop this 9:30 business". I am grateful, yes, because the thought is ingrained in me that this is not their job. There was a time where there was the expectation that the woman was to do a lot of housework in addition to the daily cooking... like making pickles and *papads*[3] and things. Now women have stopped doing those things and have started doing things outside the house. So, I feel since I am not doing all those extra things, at least let me make dinner. So if you get any help then you feel like you should say thank you, thank you.' She feels grateful because he is doing the kind of work in the home that traditionally men do not do.

She does most of the cooking except on the days she works late. When they entertain, she does most of the cooking also, although he assumes responsibility for some of it. But overall it is her responsibility. So does it mean that he cleans up after? 'There is no such predictability. It's "thank you" if he does it. The only predictability is in the outside work. Like mowing the lawn.'

There are days when she is exhausted. She feels that just like men like to talk about their day at work and the attendant problems, women would appreciate some conversation regarding their work day, especially if it has been a bad day.

There is no time for anything in the arena of personal development. What do they do together as husband and wife? 'There are times, we recognize we need to do things together,' she says. Then they drag each other to a movie or something, 'maybe once in three, four or five months,' she laughs.

Do her children have stereotypical roles in their minds about what a woman should do and what a man should do in terms of their roles in the home? 'There are times when I hear, "but mom that is your thing", but I'm still promoting this idea that a woman is not responsible for folding laundry all the time, is not responsible for cleaning dishes all the time... I'm training my [teenage] son and I think I am succeeding to some extent.'

When you come home from work, both partners should work together, she feels. 'That's my image of marriage.' Does she think that because she is making less than her husband, she is expected to do more? 'I don't think it can be attributed to any of those factors. It is a coaching process that has occurred over a period of time. Dinner time should be an activity done together. I don't even watch TV. I basically don't even know what's happening in the world because I'm involved in so many things,' says Shobha.

When the kids have to go for their extracurricular activities who takes them? It depends on who has more time. She gets help with the housework, in terms of having someone clean the house for her. It bothers her when her children fall sick. 'I've taken my daughter to the doctor at 10:00 at night,' she says. Does she have to drop her work and take time off? It depends on the day. 'If there is no other way... it is difficult [for him] but he has to do it. It happened last week and it was so nice of him to take time off. It would be very difficult if both of you don't recognize these things.'

Restrictions and changes

She feels she faces many restrictions. 'I've had to take a job in the city in which my husband is. I can't move. And so I restrict myself right there. And if I want to take another job here, I'm overqualified,' she says. 'What are my own problems? I would feel guilty if I didn't cook even if it is not in the agenda, I would do it for the next few days or so or to prepare for some emergency in the next few days!!!!'

Shobha is yet another of those women who did not enter the work-force right after marriage. A number of things influence her situation, the arranged marriage itself, getting to know her spouse and a new country with its different systems and at the same time, becoming a mother, without any extended family for support. And Shobha, edu-cated though she is, has herself set precedents that are difficult to break. Shobha carries a lot of guilt because she thinks she should be doing more at home. Far from resenting her husband's lack of help, she is very grateful for any little thing he does at home.

Neena's household: Trained for equal roles

Neena started her career when she was 28. She had been married for a while by then and had a three-year-old daughter. Although the roles were hard to change, this family worked on it and established a totally new pattern for themselves.

According to Neena, the stage at which you begin your career makes a difference in the pattern you set for your marriage 'It makes a difference because I started my career after seven years of marriage, so it wasn't as if I went into the marriage as a career woman. It's a function of age as well as a function of the role, I think,' she says. 'I was fairly established in my marriage and the roles were established too. So it was a matter of changing the role as well as establishing a career.'

When Neena got an offer outside the city in which they lived, her husband quit his job and followed. 'We did not have a single discussion where we were not going to do it . We were surprised by the offer. And we moved. Not many Indian men would have agreed to do it. But this was a good company [the one that made the offer], and a good job so it was a logical decision. His view of the move, making sacrifices, the perspective he takes is that as an entity it was better for us.'

'The biggest fear when I first started was... 'would I do well?' I was starting a job in a large well-known company and the people around me were good at what they did. There is an anxiety to prove yourself. Plus we were in a brand new city. No family, no support system. We did not know a single soul. We couldn't get our bearings. For the first time in her three years my daughter was going to start daycare.' These were some of the issues Neena had to contend with as she started her career.

Business travel

Neena's job requires a great deal of travel. In the beginning, she would try and pre-cook meals. She found herself trying to organize her family's lives before she left. Over time she gradually realized that she could not work herself to the bone until she left and come back from her trip and start again. 'If he did not follow my plan, I would get upset. So, over time I started doing less and I let them manage. Once I am out of the house, I mentally distance myself from the home issues,' she admits. 'Over time you try to strike a balance. I don't know to what extent that is because I am an Indian woman, I think any woman would do the same things I do.'

Her career aspirations do not take second place in her household. Does she feel perfectly justified in concentrating on her job? Does that mean that her husband accepts her doing less in the home? 'It is not as if one day I make the same amount of money and all of a sudden there is this sudden equality in the sense of division of labor,' she says. 'It has just evolved over time. It is subtle to some extent. I don't have to prove anything and I don't make any bones about the fact that my job is a whole lot more stressful than his. Still I do some things at home, more than he does. Not for him, but to validate my role as a mother, rather than as a wife. But I don't want to be viewed as this career mother who just does her job and nothing else,' she explains.

Does she have the ability to rise to her potential at work? She readily admits she has progressed. 'I can definitely make progress and I have. To get to the really top positions, you have to make a lot of sacrifices and those sacrifices are tough to make, when you are a two-career family and when you are a wife and mother,' Neena says.

Roles men play

Do we blame men unfairly, then? 'We have to give the men the opportunity to play the role we want them to play,' she feels. 'Just as we have difficulty in transitioning to different roles because of the stereotypes that are in place. Take my mother. Even now she says, "Why don't you take a part-time job because that's the right thing. Your first job is as a mom and wife". [In the US] we are far away and [this] helps to establish your own roles. If we were right in the middle of the Indian community and with family, then it would be difficult,' she thinks.

But would things have been different in India, if they lived in India? 'Then it is a different thing. The support is coming from somewhere else. The man is still playing his role, that of the breadwinner, the traditional role and doing very little around the house. What the support system does is allow the woman to have a career and sustain it,' is Neena's analysis.

Now, logically, they have divided up what comes naturally. 'There are a whole lot of things he does because my work eats up more than eight hours of my day,' she says. With her daughter's homework, she tends to do more. Now her daughter is almost completely self-sufficient, though. What happens if she gets sick? It all depends on who is in town if she is sick. He has had to take care of their daughter even when she was very little, and Neena was out of town.

What do they do for themselves? 'He takes time to play tennis. That's his thing. Whether I like it or not!' she says. They don't have much time together. 'We have become very comfortable spending very little time with each other,' she jokes.

Stereotypes

In terms of perceived roles, Neena's daughter believes that her mother does more in terms of cooking and as a caregiver. Although her daughter is now used to her mother's career, she does not want to follow in Neena's footsteps. 'My daughter has made comments a couple of times, things like "I don't want a job like yours, it would be too hard".

Does power come from economic independence? 'Gradually your confidence in your contribution grows. It's not arrogance and it's not financial independence. It's not that. It's not a question of certain jobs being less important... a lot of it is self-perception. So how are the gender roles going to change? The men in our lives have never been prepared for it... for the pseudo-traditional female roles. If they are prepared for it, they may be different. It's how you prepare people for the roles. Potentially if children today are raised in an environment where the roles are a function of what makes sense in your module as opposed to gender specifics, then their view of life may be different,' says Neena.

Do older parents play a role in all this? Most certainly, feels Neena. 'If our parents come here and start reinforcing what the role of a woman should be, all of a sudden the men start questioning their own roles!'

Was it hard for her husband to make all these adjustments, starting with her career and the kind of demands it makes on their own marriage? 'I think I can speak for my husband... if I ask him whether he's happier today or was he happier eight years ago, he'll say today. For while there may be a few things that he may have given up because of my working, [but he has also] gained a lot of big things. He has gained peace of mind. He does not have the worry of being the sole provider.'

Mom, wife and career woman

Is it hard being a mom and a wife and career woman? At 37, the wife part of it does not bother her, apart from the lifestyle change. 'You are both adults and there are benefits that accrue that you both enjoy. The mom part bothers me because no matter how much you try to balance it, you are not there for your child, for some things, so you just hope that you make the right decisions and try for some sort of balance,' she admits.

If she did not have a job that paid so well, she admits that so many adjustments would not have been made at home. Because, really, it is in her husband's interest to make this arrangement work. 'If things didn't work and I quit, it would highly impact not just my life but his life too.'

'It would be great if our husbands could be totally intuitive, totally sensitive and just rise to the occasion. But that does not happen. So part of the responsibility of training them to the role rests with us.'

The 'second shift' across cultural boundaries

The double burden that women who work outside the home carry and the shifting gender roles is a situation that crosses all boundaries. And these women often have little structural support. Ellen Goodman states that what is missing in the women's movement is the movement. 'It's 1992 and women simply feel stuck. Stuck juggling work and family. Stuck below the glass ceiling. Stuck in institutions they fought to enter but can't change. Stuck with rules they are allowed to follow or break, but not re-write.'

According to Harvey L. Ruben, M.D., over half of all two-parent families have both parents in the workforce. He feels that given these numbers it is clear that many cultural institutions, including the family unit itself, need restructuring. The term, 'working mother', itself should be banned, he feels, because, 'the so-called working mother is a full-time wife, full-time mother, and a full or part-time wage earner living in a family that hasn't noticed!'[4] For starters, Ruben believes these families should be called 'dual-career families'.

Shirley Sloan Fader has written a book for working wives, showing them how they can stop feeling overwhelmed and start enjoying life, stating that working American women are still carrying the load of the paid job and the family's childcare and housework: '... most wives will tell you they're chronically exhausted from carrying paid employment and nearly all the family work. Many admit they're also discouraged. Though modern husbands often do pitch in, it's usually not nearly enough to make a real dent in their wives' overload.'[5] One of the case studies in the book is that of Carol Smith, a mother of two young kids who works full-time. She states that she shoulders the bulk of the work at home. 'But I don't see any way around it. I value my marriage and I value my family and in order to give them everything I need to give them, it is essential I work outside of the home.' She admits, however, that she has an edge over a lot of other parents as her own parents take care of her children when she is at work. 'I am still expected to come home, do the laundry, do the dinner, get them ready for bed, do the bills, clean the house, all the homework, getting them to and from activities. I do three-quarters of the yard work.' And she says, 'This is going to sound depressing, but I honestly don't see men changing.'

Conclusions

The case studies in this chapter do not represent all South Asian women as others may have different stories to tell. However, there are certain common issues that bind these very different women together.

Four of the women in this group had an arranged marriage which may have contributed to the career paths these women undertook. The added element of getting to know and live with a new person in addition to leaving their country to come to the United States may have delayed the establishment of their careers.

A lack of time and constant fatigue were common complaints. Those with young children seem to have a more difficult time than those with older ones. And they all agree that had they been in India things would have been easier, not because the men would be different, but because they could have the support and help that is missing in this country. While this may not be an accurate perception as working women in India also struggle with similar issues, the reality is that none of these women have extended families in the US, the security of an established social network or the comfort level that comes with familiar surroundings. So in addition to the stresses and strains similar to the working mom in India, the South Asian working mother in the United States also has to deal with issues surrounding the immigrant experience.

With their hectic lifestyles, entertaining in all the households is kept at a minimum. The spouses also spend very little time with each other and hobbies are rare. Although the husbands are certainly doing more than they would have had they been in India, the women still feel that they are constantly tired.

Some of the women feel grateful that their husbands are doing so much and there is still the tendency to think that the men are doing things that are not really in their domain. Women with sons are training them to be different than their fathers. Even those who do not have sons agree that by training the boys to do all the chores in a home now, an entirely new generation of men can be created, those who are equally involved in the household. Gender stereotypes are also being conscientiously demolished by most mothers.

The majority of these women have household help. With increasingly demanding jobs and less time, certain things have become less of a priority and housecleaning seems to have fallen into this category. As expected, a woman's earning capacity is directly proportional to the power she seems to wield in terms of the kinds of adjustments she can expect at home. This is not a very conscious action on the part of the men. They just seem to adjust more. Therefore, financial contribution does seem to promote increased gender equality.

Many of the families interviewed for Arlie Hochschild's study on working women bear similarities to the South Asian women interviewed for my study. Hochschild states that the exodus of women into the economy has not been accompanied by a cultural understanding of marriage and work that would make this transition a smooth one. The workforce has changed. Women have changed. But most workplaces have remained inflexible in the face of these changes, and at home, most men have yet to really adapt. This situation makes it difficult for South Asian women who, like other immigrant women, have to find reliable daycare for their children in a culture so different from their own, struggle with issues such as job security, promotions, and, of course, the complexities within their own marriages.

So how can these families arrive at an equilibrium that is acceptable to all? 'The happiest two-job marriages I saw were between spouses who did not load the former role of housewife-mother onto the woman and did not devalue it as one would a bygone "peasant" way of life. They shared that role between them. Up until now, the woman married to the "new man" has been one of the lucky few.'[6] This situation has to change as more and more women either choose to, or, for financial reasons, have to work outside the home.

✦ Notes and References

1. The same title was used in an article published in *Femina*, a women's magazine from India, authored by Preeti Mathur and Sudha Sethu Balagopal, December 1987, 8–22.
2. All names are fictitious. Identifying information has also been changed to protect the identities of the women interviewed.

3. *Papads* are made with lentil flour. *Papad*-making is a labor-intensive and time-consuming annual affair. Stay-at-home wives undertake *papad* projects in summer and then store them for deep-frying at a later date.
4. Harvey L. Ruben, *Super Marriage* (New York, Bantam Books, Inc., 1986), 124.
5. Shirley Sloan Fader, *Wait a Minute, You Can Have It All* (New York, G.P. Putnam's Sons, 1993), 15.
6. Arlie Hochschild with Anne MacHung, *The Second Shift* (New York, Viking Penguin Inc., 1989), 278.

9

The paradoxes of the Kama Sutra and the veil: Asian-Indian women and marital sexuality

Mantosh Singh Devji

The Asian-Indian woman (henceforth referred to as Indian), lives within a complex matrix of societal and cultural biases and expectations that shape many aspects of both her public and private life, including her sexuality. The puzzle is further complicated when these traditional values must be reconciled with those of the mainstream American woman. The freedom, expression, and desires considered normal and healthy in the Western context are different from, if not diametrically opposed to, what has been traditionally ingrained in Indian women as 'proper'. Despite the fact that India is the birthplace of the world's most ancient chronicle of the sexual arts, the Kama Sutra, in practice, sex is shrouded in a veil of secrecy.

Constantly bombarded with images of sexuality by talk shows, women's magazines, advertisements, and every other form of popular entertainment, the issue becomes hard to escape. We are starting to see an adaptation of a new standard as Indian women become more assimilated and American in their sexual mores. In some cases the old puritanical standard is modified so that the feelings of morality remain intact and the guilt is minimal. There are others who toss out the sexual morality of their mothers and grandmothers and adopt a totally new morality which is at odds with their family's rules and the rules and expectations of Indian society in America itself. A sub-group that is slowly and painfully metamorphasizing as its members simultaneously try to adapt to their new culture and hang on to the propriety and socially defined sexual morality of the 'old country'. Both married and single women are now raising and facing questions of sexual preference, desire, compatibility, and satisfaction in ways that they had never previously been willing to discuss.

Not immune to the pitfalls of Western life, some Indian women are now finding themselves in the same position as many of their mainstream American contemporaries: divorced, but the standards of many of their peers within the Indian community remain unchanged. Divorce still creates a stigma and ostracism in the Indian community, leaving the divorcee isolated and vulnerable. At this point the sexual life of these women is supposed to be over, but an increasing number of women are rejecting these old standards.

Do married Indian women merely 'submit' to sex for procreation and the pleasure of their husbands? Are their expectations changing, and do Indian men have a double standard as to what is appropriate sexual expression when dealing with non-Indian women?

These are just some of the questions that the Indian community will have to come to terms with as the winds of change lift the veil of taboos and secrecy that has shrouded its sexual practices and expression for so long.

1

I should have married the man I loved but my father did not allow me to do so. He was locked into a rigid mind-set which equates stubborn, unshakable adherence to tradition with honor, integrity, and virtue. If he had to, he would punish me and himself by upholding tradition to the highest degree. I understood the unwritten laws which had been in place for hundreds, if not thousands, of years. I was born on the cusp of a time which bordered between the traditional world and the modern technological era.

Educated in Catholic convents and raised on romantic English literature and legends of Punjabi lovers like Heer Ranjha and Laila Majnu, one day I made the innocent remark at dinner that I could never marry someone that I did not love. There was sudden pin-drop silence, it was as though everyone stopped chewing and stared at me. My grandmother looked down into her plate as the breeze from the ceiling fan stirred her cream chiffon *dupatta* (veil) around her covered head. My beautiful mother, diplomatic and cautious, called for the bearer and said something distracting about the food or drinks. My father froze. His knuckles turned white as he clutched his knife and fork tightly. He shook with controlled rage as he told my mother that she had not raised me properly. It was his privilege to choose my husband. Later I told my mother that I could not think of making love to someone I did not love.

'One day you are strangers and the next you are expected to be intimate,' I said. I had horrible visions of a total stranger disrobing me.

'I have to marry someone I love, Mother, I cannot have an arranged marriage.'

I remember the rage and despair of my father as he asked, 'All the girls in this family have maintained our traditions, why is this one different?'

My own story began somewhere between the Valley of Flowers and the Gangotri Glacier, the source of the river Ganges, at an altitude of 1,600 feet in the Himalayas. I fell in love with a dashing young captain whom I will call Captain Pundit. He was a Brahmin from Banaras and my brother-in-law's best friend. We were on a hiking trip with the Bengal Sapper's Mountaineering Club.

While my newly married sister openly expressed affection for her husband, I maintained the aloof demeanor of the well-bred single Indian woman. I kept my eyes lowered when I caught Captain Pundit looking at me.

The chemistry between us was incredible, though we never said a word about it to each other. We held hands once while climbing a mountain. I remember catching my breath as I glimpsed him bathing in a mountain stream gazing towards the rising sun, or turning away from the statue of Krishna in a temple in Haridwar, the Gateway to the Gods. I also remember his magnificent eyes, ardent yet shy.

The day I was leaving he asked me to marry him. I told him my father would never agree. As expected, my father had a fit and I was forbidden from ever seeing Captain Pundit again.

I was swept off my feet some years later by another man who came into my life. He was the nephew of the prime minister of India and was being prepared to take political office. He had been educated abroad and spoke Hindi with an English accent and his stomach got 'wobbly' when he ate Indian food. He was an oddity on the Indian scene, he wore a bow tie and sneakers. I suspect in hindsight he needed a political wife, he often used to say to me, 'Darling, the masses love you!'

My father spurned the offer for my hand in marriage by the ruling family. 'They do not have a tradition of good marriages in their family,' he said.

I was determined not to lose this man who said he loved me, as I had lost Captain Pundit. I made the wrong decision of marrying him against my family's approval. We spent the first day of our marriage in a luxury hotel, 'I don't want to be tucked into bed by my mother,' he said. I remember an endless night of passion. He was experienced, I was totally innocent. He was an excellent lover, the barometer being that he gave me intense pleasure, but he lacked emotion and human warmth. He continued to see a European mistress who suddenly reappeared on the scene, would come home with the phone numbers of women he had met at parties, and when reprimanded by his mother told her that he was only married, not a slave.

When I decided to walk out of the marriage his parents begged and pleaded with me to stay, and then his mother threatened me. I was told that if I tried to leave I would die of a mysterious illness in the night. It was a blow his reputation and career could not afford.

This brief, disastrous marriage ended on the grounds of adultery, desertion, mental cruelty, and change of religion (he converted to Christianity for purposes of divorce). I left to study at the University of Pennsylvania and begin a new life.

About 20 years later, on a visit home, a friend said, 'Oh, Pundit is in town, he has just been posted to Army Headquarters.' I had mixed feelings about seeing him, but when the awaited telephone call came, my heart stood still, 'Army Headquarters, Madam. General Pundit would like to speak with you.' My shy young Captain had now become a General.

When we met, I had changed, but he was almost still the same. I was now in a white silk dress instead of the white saris I had loved. I was now a woman, not a child and most importantly I was now also an American. I walked hand in hand with him on the lawns of the army boat club as the moon came over the rippling waters of the Yamuna and the fireflies danced in the dusk.

'I never dared to touch you,' he said. 'What if I threw you down and made mad, passionate love to you?' I teased. It would have been impossible for me say anything like that 20 years earlier.

As he held me in his arms he told me that he had told Radha that we had found each other again, that we were as much in love as we were before, and that he was going to marry me.

'Who is Radha?' I asked innocently.

'Radha is my wife.'

I stood bolt upright. He looked at me, surprised.

'I thought you knew. My mother forced me to marry her when she was dying. I've never loved her, I've been a good husband and father to her daughter (from a previous marriage), but I want to spend the last years of my life with you.'

I left for America with a broken heart. I could not take a man away from his wife. I should have married my first love 20 years ago.

I was not trying to be different, I was being myself. There have been many times that I wished that I had been like my cousins, aunts, sisters, and friends, who had all, with varying degrees of trepidation, married the men that had been chosen for them in arranged marriages. They soon had mansions, servants, a host of children, and most importantly, the support of their families and communities for being good and dutiful daughters. We never discussed our sex lives, once in a while a veiled remark would surprise me and make me perk up my ears. An aunt who was supervising the cooks as they prepared the evening meal kept looking at her watch and hurrying everyone along, 'This man is a nuisance, he must have "it" all the time,' obviously referring to my uncle who kept calling her from an upstairs bedroom. Though innocent in the matters of sex at the time, I could sense his urgency and her irritation. It obviously was not something that turned her on. She was submitting to a purely physical need he had, not withstanding that it was the middle of the afternoon, and that it would be obvious to the servants and innocents like myself that something was up.

Many years later a favorite aunt asked me if American women made a lot of noise when they made love. I mumbled something about, 'I'm not sure…I don't know.' I suppose now that I lived in the United States I was an American woman to my relatives, or maybe she was asking me about 'real' American women. The women in the Jackie Collins novels that she read or the ones that she saw in Western movies. Women with voracious sexual appetites who made the women from the land of the Kama Sutra look like nuns.

I have always thought of myself as a very passionate woman for several reasons. First, we Sikhs are supposed to be hot blooded (at least that's what everyone says about the men, I don't see why it shouldn't apply to the women as well); second, Indian women are associated with a certain sensuality and eroticism, a mystique exists around the sexuality of the 'Eastern woman', we are supposed to be exceptionally adept at the art of lovemaking. This strikes me as funny. Doesn't one become adept with a great deal of practice? Virgins have to be taught the art of intimacy, and according to most reports, Indian men are notoriously poor lovers. They do not teach, cajole, woo, arouse, or practice seduction. Instead, according to a doctor's wife who lives in Phoenix, they conquer or basically use sex for personal release.

Inexperienced, childlike, or maybe childish, Indian men may turn on some horny American women, but the average Indian woman complains, 'My husband never touches me.' While refraining from making broad generalizations, this is the common complaint of many of the women I interviewed for this chapter. The 'submission' of the older generation of Indian women is no longer acceptable to younger and more modern Indian women.

The stories of the four women in this chapter are by no means a scientific study or statistical survey, but they are stories of Indian women who generally speak of mediocre sex, with the exception of one, who is breathless as she talks about her sex life.

'Lovemaking begins in the morning at breakfast. We know when we are going to make love. There are sexy little things that happen all day that lead up to hot explosive sex, after the children go to bed.'

I'm delighted to know that my ideal of a loving and passionate marriage is alive and well somewhere.

'Pardon? What do you do all day?'

'Oh well, he'll stand real close to me while I cook breakfast, he will caress me if no one is looking and the children are out playing. We both know we can't wait. The waiting makes it so much more fun.'

'He'll wait for hours until I'm ready. He will do anything to make me reach that point. I tell him sometimes, *Arty Baba*, it's okay. I'm satisfied just cuddling and kissing, but he is so patient, he will not do anything until I'm ready.'

This is Damini, whose eyes dance and whose voice quickens with excitement as she talks about her husband and her sex life. Damini's happiness is in deep contrast to Rani's dissatisfaction and sorrow about her marriage to a man from San Francisco.

Rani speaks nostalgically about the young husband she lost to a sudden heart attack in India, and whose present marriage to an Indian in America is full of the squabbles of a second family and grown children. She loves romantic songs and music parties with other Indians, where the evening is spent singing songs of lost love, yearning for the beloved, old Urdu *ghazals* (love songs) which are quintessentially full of romantic agony.

Then there is the beautiful Monika, a former beauty queen, worldly and tough. Her hazel eyes hold a challenge as she walks through the world with a certain cool insolence.

'When I walk into a room, believe me, people notice.'

Her marriage ended in Europe where her husband worked for a major international corporation and where she worked as a senior executive in the hospitality industry and owned her own successful boutique.

'I felt so rejected and betrayed that I went wild,' she explains with a certain amount of regret. 'I had to reassure myself that I was attractive. I flirted outrageously with everyone. I had men from the CEOs of major corporations to my husband's closest friends interested in me. All I needed to do was give them a signal. Some came right out and asked me out, others said that if I ever needed anything they would be there for me. The implications were more sexual than anything else.'

'Didn't you offend the wives?'

'I didn't care, all I wanted to do was to put him down,' she says defiantly. Then she adds thoughtfully, 'I was very careful to include the wives in everything. I would entertain beautifully, my parties were famous. I was hurting so badly myself, I only wanted to punish him for the years of accumulated abuse and hurt,' she says, referring to a relationship that consisted of put-downs, indifference, and rough drunken sex.

Today she lives in Chicago and is trying to make it big in international trading. She claims that her focus is finance, not romance or sex. When her ex-husband comes into town they occasionally get together. The physical attraction may still be there but there is no love or respect.

'He is still trying to use, control, and put me down like he did before, hoping that I'll fall on my face. He hints at getting together again, but I don't want that,' she says adamantly. 'But I do dream of being a family again.'

The last story is that of Savi. Coming from a prominent North Indian family, she was engaged at 16-and-a-half and married at 17. Her first marriage to an army man ended in divorce. She remembers that marriage basically as, 'sleepwalking'.

'I was numb, it was as though I was standing outside myself and watching everything with detachment. I begged my parents not to marry me off so early, to at least let me finish college, but my mother cried and said, "that's what Father wants". We were raised with the idea that you could never do anything that would hurt or upset Father...or something terrible would happen. He would either get sick or get very angry.'

'For years I didn't tell anyone how unhappy I was. He told me that he had this terrible urge to be with other women. I asked him to get it out of his system but he never completely did so. He told me that I and our child were like a millstone around his neck and he wanted me to leave. He hit me once. I summoned all my strength and hit him back so hard that he was stunned. I told him that if he ever touched me again I would kill him.'

During these strained years, when her family would not hear of a divorce, a ray of light entered Savi's sad life. She met Peter, a diplomat, at a party in New Delhi.

'Western men are so thoughtful. They compliment you, bring you flowers, and make you feel cherished. I never expected to make love to him, it surprised him too. I had never known love to be so sublime. I had nothing to compare it to until then. We just fit! Indian men have no training in lovemaking. They are taught to think of all women as mothers, sisters, and daughters. When they have a wife they really do not know how to please her. In a sense you can't blame them for their shortcomings, Indian society treats sex as a secret and shameful activity. There is no training in the gentle art of seduction. It's a hit and miss thing most of the time. The male-dominated culture does not make for equal participation in the sexual act. Indian women are pleasantly surprised when the average Western male bends over backwards to please them. This then allows the woman to be less inhibited and the ensuing passion is so much more satisfying to both partners,' she says.

Savi's European boyfriend was her ecstasy and joy. 'We were meant to be together,' she says. 'When he died in a car wreck in Switzerland, some part of me died with him.'

Though she is not presently involved with anyone, her Western liaisons have left her more open to her own sexuality, both within and outside the boundaries of a marital relationship.

Indian women's sexual experiences in marriage range from the trauma of feeling raped to sheer ecstasy. They differ from person to person, but good sex seems to be rare and exceptional. Most women interviewed fell in the range of mediocre to tolerable sex, and for some there was no sex at all.

'I can show you several couples who have the perfect facade. She dresses exquisitely, they go to all the parties and arrive in an expensive luxury car. No one would ever know that at home they have separate bedrooms and never communicate,' says the worldly Monika. 'Single Indian women are sleeping with whoever is available, married or single. Come Friday night they want to go out. They are lonely. They want a nice date, a good meal, and good sex.'

When I respond that Indian women don't do that she flies into a rage, 'I can't believe that you are so goody-goody and naive,' she says. 'You've been married haven't you?' Yes I have, but Monika's observations do not support my observations within Indian-American communities.

11

Savi

Savi lives in New York with her son. She is an artist and is working on illustrating a book of Indian folk songs. Her story begins on a hot summer day in May, half a lifetime ago. Ironically, she is named for the refreshing rains which come with the dark thunder clouds of the monsoons. Savi is to be married today. It is her 17th birthday.

The old family home, a mansion formerly used by the British rulers of India, is strung with twinkling lights threaded through the towering trees and the rose bushes along the circular driveway. Red and saffron wedding tents have been set up on the manicured lawns. Pedestal fans are slowly circulating the hot air around. The bride's father is perspiring furiously under his heavy brocade wedding tunic. The flute players are sitting on an embankment under the *neem* tree, where Savi swung on the rope swing only a few months ago. Then she was a child with short stubby nails, today she is a young bride with long silver-pink nails and henna on her hands. Her skin is fragrant and dewy soft after being scrubbed with *Vatna*, a paste made from gram flour and turmeric.

Her sister hugs her. 'You look gorgeous,' she says. Savi looks in the mirror and sees someone she does not recognize. A beautiful young woman, weighed down with gold and pearls and covered with a delicately woven red and gold Banarsi wedding sari, looks back at her vacantly.

'I was numb,' says Savi. 'It was like watching a movie of someone else going through the motions. I thought I would wake up and it would be all over. It finally struck me when I was being put in the *doli* by my father. I looked at his tear-stained face and heard my own sobs. I felt that I was being abandoned. I didn't want to leave but my smiling mother-in-law claimed me as her own as she scattered coins and rupee notes over me for good luck. "Now she is our daughter," she told everyone.'

My grandfather said, 'We are giving you one of the most precious jewels in our home, look after her.'

'Little did I know that the man I was marrying would be a "mamma's boy", and that she would influence the course of my marriage to such a destructive end.'

'At 16-and-a-half I was engaged to Mahesh. Our families had been friends for generations. He had graduated from the military academy and was a captain in the army. He was 10 years older than me. I soon realized that I was a possession, something he and the family could show off. I was like a beautiful ornament, like a piece of Lalique or Baccarat crystal. He showed me off to his friends amidst many jokes of "cradle snatching", it was like saying, "Look who I married, look at the family and their home, you don't have what I have". I would start falling asleep at the various parties at the mess and everyone would laugh, "the baby needs to be put to bed".'

'Was he very tender and romantic?'

'No,' replies Savi. 'I don't think Indian men know how to treat women. In a way you can't blame them. All their lives they are kept separated from women. They do not know how to woo a woman.'

Savi recalls her husband's clumsy attempts at courtship.

'He never brought flowers or gifts. All he wanted to do when we were out, duly chaperoned by my brother, was to feel me up and kiss me. We went for a walk as my brother sat in the car. I remember the first time he attempted that I fainted. He was very frightened and as he tried to revive me he said, "Don't tell anyone, don't say anything..."'

I ask what it was like to make love to him on their wedding night.

'I don't have any recollection of it,' muses Savi, 'except being numb and getting up and having a shower.'

'Weren't you ecstatic? Didn't he remove your wedding veil romantically like in the Indian movies and tell you how beautiful you were and how much he loved you?'

'No, all I remember is a numbing sexual experience lasting about ten minutes and then it was over. I felt unclean.'

I wonder how many marital sex experience are similar to Savi's. There is no courting period in the traditional Western sense when the boy and girl get to know each other. The courting in an arranged marriage begins after the engagement.

'There were the perfunctuary calls and letters. I was expected to reply and I did. I didn't even want to be involved in picking out the traditional trousseau.'

'The honeymoon was a disaster,' recalls Savi. 'We were in a beautiful hotel on the slopes of Nainital Lake. When I playfully slid down the pine needles like I used to with my brothers and sisters, he reprimanded me and told me not to be so childish. But I was a child. He was a grown man. I was hurt and very subdued. Then he got mad again when we raced our horses to the hotel. "I beat you, I beat you," I said. His macho pride got hurt. The rest of the honeymoon was spent more or less in silence and without lovemaking.'

'How sad!' I ask if the problem was the age difference.

'Mainly it was his mother. She always bandied around how many families had offered rich dowries and money for Mahesh. She pointed out the girls and families that they could have had. Then she constantly compared him to her other son who was a dashing playboy and international business man. "All the memsahibs want to have his baby," she would brag. Mahesh never felt quite equal to him. Eventually he came to me and told me that he had this terrible desire to sleep with other women. I quickly sized up the situation and I knew I had no place to go. I couldn't tell my parents. I said, "Get it out of your system." He never did.'

'I could tell from the little things that something was going on; hotel bills, interviewing girls for clerical positions at the Presidential Hotel with his partner, his irritation with me and the child.'

Savi's life became increasingly unbearable and sad, her health deteriorated and the marriage became an empty shell. Then one day a ray of light entered her life.

'One day at a party I was sitting on a balcony by myself watching my husband flirt with a woman in the garden below, when a voice with a foreign accent asked, "Good evening, how are you?" I was startled and mumbled. "Fine".'

Savi met Peter, the love of her life, that fateful evening. He was a Swiss diplomat who loved India.

'There was something special about him. He had the clearest blue eyes,' she reminisces. Her voice grows tender as she talks about him.

'He had a crooked nose and a lopsided grin, but there was an air of great integrity and intellect about him. He was so kind and considerate that you couldn't help but love him. No one had ever treated me this way.'

Savi ran into Peter again at a diplomatic conference.

'He asked me to have lunch with him. I told him that I was married and I couldn't. He insisted on at least having a cup of tea. We never thought we would eventually make love,' she says, 'it just happened. Frankly he was surprised too.'

But observing propriety, that did not happen until she was separated from her husband. The separation occurred gradually. Mahesh, who had by now left the army, was away on business trips with increasing frequency. In one sense they had separated long before Savi took the unprecedented step of packing her bags and moving to a women's hostel.

The day it finally happened is imprinted firmly on her mind.

'He had invited me for dinner. He served fruits soaked in liquor on beautiful china. The servants left and we made love by candlelight.'

Savi compares Peter and Mahesh.

'Up to this point I had no idea what good sex was, I had nothing to compare it to. He was the most thoughtful, considerate lover. He was concerned about how "I" felt. Indian men don't do that, they don't even think about it.'

When Peter left for Zurich, Savi visited him several times. Their rendezvous were full of passion and tenderness, but something bothered her, he never asked her to marry him. One day he gave her a very expensive piece of Swiss lace. 'Have something made out of it,' he said. Savi hoped to make a wedding dress, but he never proposed.

She returned to Delhi and began seeing someone else. One day Peter turned up at her door step and she had to tell him that she could not see him anymore, she was marrying someone else. Heartbroken, he left for Zurich. The next day Savi got the news from his best friend that he had been killed in a car crash. 'He always loved you, but could not marry you because his traditional Catholic family would not accept a marriage to a divorced woman,' explained Peter's friend.

'I feel he's always around me, especially when I'm sad and in danger. It seems as though he's looking after me,' she says nostalgically. 'He taught me the meaning of love.'

She has known other men since, but, 'Peter will always be the true love of my life,' she says.

Monika

Monika's story is both poignant and graphic. She remembers her marriage as emotionally and sexually abusive, 'I felt like I was being raped every night,' she recalls. But it did not begin like that.

'I was at a family gathering when my future husband saw me. I was the catch of the season. I had won five beauty contests. He was the best boyfriend and fiancé one could ever have. He brought gifts all the time. He never came over empty-handed. He always brought roses. He called me several times a day. If he was out of town I got a card with an eloquent poem or message inside every day. He courted me for three years, and then I consented to marry him.'

'Were you allowed to go out with him during that time?'

'Yes, remember, I came from a very modern family and city. His family came from the narrow streets and courtyards of old Delhi. His parents never approved of me but I was married to him when I was 21.'

She recollects that she had this terrible sense of foreboding that she should not marry Ravi, but everyone assured her that it was just a common case of pre-wedding jitters.

'Everything changed the day I married him,' she says bitterly.

Monika's black-and-white pictures in her photo album are a little faded now, but she looks like the Indian movie stars of that time. She has sweeping black eyeliner turned up at the corners of her eyes, her hair is teased up into a bouffant, she has a lace-edged chiffon sari wrapped tightly around her which shows off her curvaceous figure and the provocative woman-child that she was.

'I was a swimming and badminton champion.' She says proudly.

Today she is just as elegant but the innocence is long gone. The mother of two grown sons, she can be graciously soft or shrewishly shrill. It seems each mood or word is carefully weighed for effect. The child-bride of yesterday has become the shrewd business woman of today. On the surface she is confident and well equipped with an arsenal of skills which should move her forward in the world smoothly, but as a relative newcomer to the United States she comes up against blocks with frustrating regularity.

We discuss the loss of influence when we move from our established circles of power in India to a new society. We do not have two or three hundred years of interaction within a community, which in effect becomes our extended family. 'I have it a little better than some other single Indian women, because my family is here,' she says.

She came to America after the breakup of her marriage in Europe five years ago. Though she is not lonely per se, she misses marriage and having a man in her life. She is a warm and passionate woman and this forced celibacy is not of her choosing. She has not met any men who are suitable husband material. Any relationship without marriage would be frowned upon.

'When people come from India for business or pleasure I meet them at family gatherings. I can see the look in the men's eyes. They survey the room and eventually position themselves close to me. They'll give their card and suggest we get together for lunch. Sometimes the intent is genuinely business, often it is not. If their wives are there I try to neutralize the situation by including them in it.'

'You mean if you are single you are expected to be looking for a man, any man?'

'Many men think you are. Or they assume that because you live in America your morals are looser. There are many Indian women in New York who, come Friday night, have to have a man. They don't care if he is married or single. They are generally middle management: bankers, real-estate, business, etc. They've been working all week and like their American counterparts, they want to go out to a nice place for dinner, have a few drinks and have fantastic sex afterwards, and maybe get a nice gift like a bottle of perfume.'

When I express my surprise at this trend, Monika reacts with excessive anger.

'What do you want? Names and phone numbers of these women and the married men they are sleeping with?'

She names a famous Indian figure in the publishing business.

'I personally heard the message he left on my friend's answering machine,' she says.

'Isn't that rather indiscreet? Everyone knows him.'

'He doesn't care. He was recently at a large Indian show and while his wife was inside socializing, he was outside in the garden, holding hands with and kissing another woman.'

'And you, do you feel the need to be with a man?' I ask.

'No!' she replies vehemently. 'Most men are dogs. Once they get what they want, that's the end of it.'

While I admire her candor, I feel and hear her pain.

'Tell me what happened to your marriage,' I ask.

'Well here I was, this young, beautiful, and talented woman, delighted to be Ravi's wife, and all he wanted was to possess me and smother me and hold back my growth and everything I was. I wasn't allowed to work, I wasn't allowed out of the house without him, while he was gone all day, wherever he wanted. I eventually found out that he was having lunches and dinners with an ex-girlfriend who was having marital problems. I called this woman and told her that now he was married and if she wanted to discuss any problems she should come to the house and discuss them with both of us. When he found out he flew into a rage and forbade me to ever talk to her again.'

'Was he sleeping with her?' I ask.

'I don't think so, it was a kick to his ego that he could see his ex-girlfriend and still dominate his wife.'

'How did you feel?' I ask.

'I didn't want him to touch me. But a close cousin-brother had warned me that I'd lose my husband if I ever denied him sex. He would come home drunk, smelling, filthy, and want sex. He would make some crude attempts at foreplay. Then he would have violent sex and it was over.'

'Didn't he take time to arouse you or seduce you?'

'No! Are you kidding? He always asserted that sex was his marital right and that I could not withhold it from him. We'd come back from a party and he would want to tear my clothes off and have sex right then and there. I wanted to bathe and put on a nice fresh nightie. If I did that he would fall asleep and refuse to have sex, "I'm too tired, it's too late," he would say.'

I listen quietly as Monika vents her anger and frustration.

'Gradually I felt like one of the servants, whose very soul was in the custody of another. One day I looked at one of the maids and I realized that I was no different from her. I was but a handmaiden for the comfort and pleasure of the master. All I did was cook and clean and look after the boys,' she says, referring to her two sons. 'He was forever sending me to his parent's home. "Go look after my parents," he would say. They never really approved of me and were rather ill-bred. I remember a vulgar remark his mother made one day. I was disgusted. My mother is so refined and soft-spoken, she would never talk like that. These people seemed like peasants in comparison.'

Monika was finally able to come into her own when her husband was transferred to Europe by the British company he worked for. She became the public relations director for a major hotel chain. This gave her husband more prestige and additional contacts. Monika was now older and more assertive. Now she could use her people skills, her charm, and her considerable business savvy. She had picked up some general business jargon from being around her husband and his business associates. Unfortunately her professional success made her marriage worse.

'My husband was so threatened by my success that he started accusing me of all kinds of things. He called me a bitch and a whore.'

I listen quietly as she continues.

'One day while he was at the office a thick envelope arrived from his father in India. I opened it instinctively. Inside were divorce papers and a note from his father saying, "See if you can force her to sign these." He didn't have to, I'd had enough. I signed them and walked out. The divorce was his father's idea. His parents had never really accepted me.'

So great was her agony that, in an act of self-preservation, she left her beautifully designed house, her sons, and her secure position as a corporate wife and walked out into the world alone. The children were young and she had no means to look after them. Her husband never forgave her for that and sent the boys back to India to be raised by his parents. Monika was painted as this awful mother who had abandoned her children and her home. When she was settled in the United States her children came to live with her. It was a long hard battle to win them back after their indoctrination by her husband and his family. She still occasionally consents to sleep with her ex-husband when he is in the country to visit the children. 'I still think of him as my husband and the father of my children. It is not a sexual need, neither is it love, it is merely an old pattern I cannot break out of. Most Indian women of my generation still find it difficult to accept divorce.'

'I was so ignorant, I used to think that sex was the best part of our marriage. Now I know better. He wasn't a good lover or a good husband. I keep hoping that in the absence of any other man in my life, this time we can get it right. But he's the same egotistical fool I married all those years ago. His social drinking buddies and his social position in Europe are more important than his children and his wife. He has never matured or changed.'

Monika lives quietly for the time being. She is aware of the impact she can have on men. She says she has no one in her life and avoids the types of casual relationships that she claims many other single Indian women have. When the right man walks in, Monika hopes she will once again become the innocent and tender 17-year-old she once was, until then she has a family to raise and a business to run.

Rani

Rani is a handsome woman, perfectly groomed with an uncommon flair for clothing. She has the half-closed eyes of women in Indian paintings. She laughs easily and is easy to feel at home with. Any man would be proud to call her his wife.

Or would he?

As we begin to talk the laughter in her voice is overtaken by her pain. Her voice breaks and she stifles back tears.

'My husband does not love me. He just told me the other day that my hips are too big. His ex-wife is tall and skinny. He insists that we go to San Francisco all the time, where she lives. Once we get there he disappears with his children (Rani's step-children) and they invite their mother to join them. They want their parents to get back together.'

'Is he unfaithful?'

'I'm sure he is!'

'Do you make love?' I ask. 'After all, you have needs. Do you still love him?'

'I have mixed feelings, I don't love him anymore. I am just a passive partner in sex.'

'Is he romantic? Does he tell you how beautiful you are?'

'No, he does not kiss or caress me. Besides, he is diabetic and cannot have an erection. We have sex every two or three months and then he may try two or three times in one day.'

She lowers her voice as though to reduce the embarrassment and shame she feels.

'When you do have sex is it satisfying?'

'No, it is nothing! To me sex without love is meaningless. And having just sex, even dogs can do that!' she says vehemently. 'Sometimes he'll be very rough. He will pinch and hurt me. The last time he did that I said, "Okay, you want to play rough? Let me pinch you and we'll see how you feel." I knew from the first day that I had made a mistake in marrying him. The day we got married, the day we arrived in America, he dropped the facade. Until then he was devoted and never left my side in India, until my parents and I consented to our marriage. All this happened in a week.'

'What happened?'

'I was a widow, living independently in my own house in Delhi with my daughter. We had a very good life. My friends and family were very supportive. I taught in a school in Delhi. My colleagues would tease, "We're going to get you married." One day this man arrived from America. He said he had many stores and businesses. He had been divorced and told me the horrors of his first marriage. Now he covers up for the same wife and children he left behind. He has taken all his assets and put them in a corporation in his children's name, so I can never touch them. He told me "Go to any court you want you won't get a cent."'

'Would you leave him if the perfect man came along?'

'Yes. When I say that my arm hurts, I want someone to say, "Show me where it hurts," when I say my hair is falling out I want someone to say, "Let me take you to the doctor." He doesn't care. I heard him tell someone the other day, "I never really married Rani. I never walked around the fire and took the sacred vows, I only had a court marriage, but I'll never let her go. I need someone to look after me when I'm old."'

Her voice at that moment conveys perfect defeat.

'I don't know what to do, sometimes I think I should go back to India, but I've been here for 10 years. My daughter is grown and married and lives here too. My grandchild is here.' She vacillates, 'Maybe I can go back and forth. You know Indian society, they won't let you live in peace if you're divorced. Maybe I just have to put up with my destiny. What bad karma could I have earned?'

'Would you have an affair with someone who loved you?' I ask.

'I've considered that. I would have to be sure he loved me,' she says, indicating that she would not make the same mistake again.

'Did your husband tell you that he loved you when he proposed to you?'

'He didn't leave my side until I agree to marry him. Later on he told me that he was never really attracted to me. In fact I got swept up in the fervor of my friends and relatives when they introduced us. I did not find him very attractive. I compare him to my first husband, who passed away, he was six foot two, very handsome, and treated me very tenderly. When I was pregnant and had morning sickness and was moody, he fed me food with his own hands, took me for walks and was so grateful that I was bringing his child into the world, and that I was going through all the pain and inconvenience of pregnancy.'

She pauses as her voice breaks.

'You've stirred up old memories,' she says tearfully. 'I didn't know what marriage was, all I knew was that I would get beautiful clothes, lots of jewelry, and a man who loved me very much.'

'Did he?'

'Yes, there was a certain innocence and purity about him. I was 17 when my parents got me engaged. He was older but I don't think that he had any practical sexual experience. He had read every book on sex that he could get his hands on and he had talked to his colleagues in the army, he was a Captain.'

'Did he use his book knowledge?'

'He tried. It took us three days to complete intercourse. We did small silly things which were very sweet. He did not know how to undress me. We laughed, we blushed and we learned together and then fell into each other's arms, exhausted.'

I ask if these memories give Rani any solace.

'Yes and no. I think of my little house on top of a hill in Sikandrabad and smile. Then I think of walking up that same hill and my husband clutching his chest and having a heart attack. Our neighbor, a Muslim doctor, rushed him to the hospital. That was the last time I saw him alive. I was given a sedative and sent home. Next morning when his family started arriving at our house I found out that he had died.'

I don't know what to say. What do you say to a woman whose heart is still buried in memories of lost love and whose new husband totally disregards her? She feels trapped in a web woven by destiny, society, and what she calls her own poor judgment.

'I should have seen through him,' she rebukes herself and continues to reminisce. 'Compared to my present husband he was a great lover. It was fun to discover the closeness of two bodies, kissing, caressing, exploring. It brought on a time of intoxication. When we did have intercourse at first it hurt, but even that was okay.'

'Were you happy and satisfied?'

'I didn't know any differently, I'd never held a sex book in my hands.'

'Was he communicative?'

'Again, relative to this one, yes. But in some ways he was secretive. He did not confide in me about the problems he was having with his business. He had a rich sister and wanted to be like her. The business failed, he had to declare bankruptcy. I think that's what killed him.'

Wrapped in old memories, Rani carries on. She calls a few days later. Her flippant remarks soon turn to tears, 'He's gone again to see his children and his ex-wife. I don't have a car, I'm stranded,' she moans.

'What am I living for?' she asks despondently.

Damini

There is rare passion in Damini's marriage. She is full of fire and fury and the light in her eyes attests to the deep satisfaction she feels in her marriage and the love with which she is surrounded.

'I'm so lucky, I have the perfect marriage,' she says enthusiastically. 'I didn't think that I would have a marriage like this, all my friends have so many problems. It was not always like this. We've been married for eleven years, we had to work at it.'

Damini's husband Krishan is tall and lanky, she is four foot ten and reminds one of a playful kitten. Most people look at her and say, 'She's a riot, she's so little, she's as cute as a bug.'

She is full of energy and works out every day, sometimes she answers the phone panting, 'Sorry, I was on the exercise bike.' Her wanting to stay in shape has much to do with her prodigious sex life. Her husband loves to see her in sexy nighties, baby doll pajamas and his favorite, sexy lingerie.

'It never stays on very long, but he'll spend any amount of money on lingerie. He does not believe in flowers and cards, he's very practical, "People like you make Hallmark rich," he tells me. Yet when I object to his spending so much money on lingerie he says, "I'm doing it for myself."'

Damini's husband fell in love with her at first sight, he says it was within 10 minutes of meeting her.

'I wasn't in love with him, but he was so nice and considerate, I thought that I couldn't do better than that.' Then she adds, 'I want people to know that there is love in arranged marriages too. What matters is that the girl wants to marry the boy. In an arranged marriage you can't fall in love with an ugly man, a fat man, a bald man.'

Damini liked Krishan right away. 'He flew from Madras to Bombay to see me. His family wanted me to come there, but I wasn't going to "show" myself. I was impressed that he made all the arrangements and did not come with an entourage and that he made his own decision. He was in India for 10 days and he wanted to get married.'

'We spent the day alone. We went to the beach, we went to Jahangir's art gallery at Samavars. My parents wondered if we were ever coming home. I had come back to Bombay after getting a degree in advertising in the United States. My parents said they would help me meet a boy. It never worked out, something was always wrong, the family. the job, or me. I was too small.'

Damini worked in a national advertising company and had the opportunity to meet several men. Most of them wanted one thing, sex. 'No one proposed to me. I also saw most of the married men having affairs with the secretaries. So when Krishan came along I was impressed with his sincerity. There was something clean about him. I asked him if he would be faithful. I was scared. We had several discussions about fidelity. He assured me, "If I have you, why would I want anyone else?"'

Now that Damini has been married 11 years and has two daughters, she muses, 'Would I ever be attracted to someone else? Yes, perhaps, but I would never do anything, I'm too committed to my marriage.'

When Damini and Krishan decided to get married she flew back to Madras with him. 'We couldn't keep our hands off each other. We cuddled and necked and pawed whenever we could, but we never had intercourse. In fact it was embarrassing, even during the traditional ceremony we couldn't keep our hands off each other.'

The courtship had essentially lasted about a week and Damini was married and returned to the United States with her husband.

'Were you scared?'

'No I would follow him wherever he went.'

The ecstasy that Damini knows in her marriage today wasn't always there.

'My husband fantasizes, "I wish I had known you in college," he thinks we would have had a long romantic courtship. I hate to burst his balloon, but I don't think I would have responded. I wasn't allowing myself to fall in love.'

She muses at the change that comes about when one decides to get married. 'It sort of enfetters you,' she says. 'You give yourself permission to fall in love. You do all sorts of things, it's like being in love with love.'

Initially Damini was frightened of sex. The cuddling and petting was fine, but she was afraid of intercourse, it would hurt.

'My husband had monumental patience, he said he would wait until I was ready. If I did not have an orgasm he was very unhappy. He would do anything, however long it took, for me to be satisfied. But he had to learn that. Initially he would plunk himself on top of me and he would be done.'

I ask how they learned to have better sex.

'It's purely instinctual. I've never read a dirty book or seen a pornographic tape. It turns me off.'

I ask how often they make love and for how long.

She laughs and blushes.

'It's not everyday, but we both know when we're ready. Foreplay begins in the morning and continues all day, culminating at night. He'll be sensual all day, a look, a touch, a word. . . .'

'How do you know when you're ready?'

'We just do. Sometimes the lovemaking is very short. Sometimes it's very long. We are like zombies the next day. The kids get up at six. We banter back and forth, "You get up, no it's your turn, You get up, I can't walk."'

She gets that faraway look in her eyes, reliving the moment of passion.

'I've never had to fake an orgasm.'

'Do you have multiple orgasms?'

'I don't even know about it. I'll have to speak to Krishan,' she says with an impudent grin.

Damini sums it up beautifully, 'We Indian women are discovering and acknowledging our own sexuality and we are not willing to settle for less. This confuses the men and frightens them. But they better get used to it, it's here to stay.'

These are the stories of Indian women, similar, yet separated by their individual experiences. They feel their experiences are unique to them, but a trend seems to emerge from these stories. They do not talk about their sex lives and therefore, until now, have suffered in silence.

All the women in this study were virgins when they married. They observed the proper traditional Indian rules of conduct which condemned premarital sexuality and relegated it to the immoral status of prostitution.

All of them began a period of courting after there was a clear understanding of commitment to marry, generally an engagement. Courting was relatively tame compared to American courtships and dating. 'Romance' was more on their minds than sex. Rani got engaged and never saw her husband until their marriage six months later. Savi had a properly chaperoned courtship. Her fiancé attempted to fondle her at which she promptly fainted. Monika's fiancé was the most romantic of all the men. Flowers, cards, and chocolate filled the three years of their courtship. Damini could not keep her hands off her future husband and kissed him whenever she could. I kissed my future husband with his valet standing guard outside the room, held his hand at the movies and did not dare dance too close to him in public for fear of appearing 'cheap'.

All the marriages except one were 'arranged'. Damini had the chance of saying yes or no to the boys presented to her for possible marriage. Monika married the man who pursued her for three years against the wishes of her parents. Rani and Savi had practically no say in the choice of their husbands. The rebel of the group, the writer of this chapter, was temporarily disowned by her family for marrying against her father's consent. A 'love marriage' was simply not permissible at the time she was growing up.

For all of them intercourse occurred either on the traditional *sohag ruat* (wedding night) or shortly thereafter. Experiences ranged from numbness, to fumbling and ultimate consummation of the marriage to sheer ecstasy and deep sexual satisfaction.

Most of the men were either inexperienced or had theoretical or little knowledge of lovemaking. One, a consummate womanizer, knew how to make love, but as it turned out knew little or nothing about loving.

The women were, for the most part, satisfied with the physical aspects of their marriages because four out of five said that they had nothing to compare it to at the time and did not know any better.

Of the five, three are now divorced, two remain married. Amongst the major causes of divorce were infidelity, neglect, being taken for granted, not being allowed to grow as an individual, and being treated as a possession rather than a peer or a partner. None of the divorces were based on sexual shortcomings. It seems the divorced women were willing to put up with mediocre sex and even impotence for the sake of preserving the marriage.

Indian women in America, now have choices about their sexuality not previously open to them. Their new home in America has given them permission to date, have relationships, and to take the initiative sexually in their marriage. These newly found privileges are not exercised with openness. Discretion, even secrecy, is deemed vital to maintaining a good image in the Indian community.

Some first generation Indians are slowly *adapting* to a new sexuality. They are letting their children date, they themselves now feel at ease with having a meal or some other social activity with a male friend, and some will even make love to a man they are attracted to.

Some second and third generation Indians are adopting an almost entirely new standard, that of the country of their birth. The women with children who were interviewed are aware of the sexual generation gap and reluctantly accept it as a fact.

As we have shared the experiences and circumstances that these women have lived through, it becomes clear that the morality dictated by the traditions of Indian culture is no longer acceptable to many of the women who now live in the United States. Foreign-born women who brought the 'old' values with them have adapted, or are struggling to adapt, to the new freedom and sense of themselves as sexual beings that Western society offers. Many of these pioneers are still restrained by the ever-expanding boundaries set forth by the Indian community here in America. They do what they want to, but remain guarded and private about who they reveal their newfound freedom to. These same women, when they return for a visit, now find that the values they had brought with them to this country no longer exist even in India, giving them some relief and alleviating some of the guilt that accompanies their new sexual personae.

10

Forged by fire: Indian-American women reflect on their marriages, divorces, and on rebuilding lives*

Sangeeta R. Gupta

Every year in early fall, married Hindu women around the world anxiously search for the rising moon. I remember when I was a child in Los Angeles, my mother would call her friends to ask if they had spotted the moon. Sometimes we drove around trying to find a place from where she could see the moon more clearly. On cloudy days, after driving for miles, we would try to convince her that it had risen. I can still picture my mother in a beautiful sari and elaborate jewelry saying her prayers as she gazed at the moon through a *chhalani* or strainer. She had been fasting since dawn in observance of Karvachoth, the most sacred day of the year for a married Hindu woman. Having seen the moon, she performed the rituals passed down through the women in her family and finally ended her fast.

Karvachoth is a festival where married Hindu women fast and pray for their husband's long life and good health. Today, in Indian-American communities, Karvachoth has become a public demonstration of spousal devotion as women create a festive atmosphere, gathering with their friends dressed in bridal finery and jewelry. One woman will narrate the story of the first Karvachoth, after which they often have a cup of tea

*I would like to thank Georgina Dodge, Christian Ghasarian, Sapna Kumar, and Valerie Matsumoto for their comments on earlier drafts of this article.

at about 4:00 p.m. and then settle down to wait for the moon to rise. Later, they will perform the rituals and prayers. Bollywood (India's Hollywood) has transformed this quiet family ritual into a movie-set celebration with hundreds of women participating in an elaborate ceremony set to popular music. A private family ritual has become an opportunity for a community to showcase the devotion of their married women and to reinforce this role. The private has become public as the second generation observes a ritual of proper wifely devotion in the name of cultural continuity.

Juxtaposed against the picture in my mind of my mother and movie scenes from Asian-Indian movies, is Sunita[1] as she discusses her sister's divorce. She tells me how she never believed in the concept of divorce and accepted the negative stereotypes associated with divorced women. 'Marriage is for life,' she emphatically states. However, she has been forced to re-evaluate this premise as she watched her elder sister struggle in a physically abusive marriage and finally make the painful and difficult decision to divorce. Sunita states that parental and community pressure forced her sister to stay in this dangerous situation, maintaining a facade of domestic bliss, for years. If the decision to divorce is so convoluted even under such harrowing circumstances, what are a woman's options if she and her husband are simply not compatible? Does the possibility of having irreconcilable differences even exist? Would adultery be 'appropriate' justification to divorce one's partner? Why is divorce such a 'crime' in these communities and why are the women who separate and divorce judged so harshly?

Divorce strikes at the very heart of the Asian-Indian patriarchal[2] system. By contemplating divorce, a woman of Asian-Indian origin is challenging the feminine gender roles established by this system—roles of submissive and subordinate daughters, wives, and mothers. She is also disturbing the perfect image of the 'model minority' which Indian-American communities are so careful to maintain by enforcing a code of silence on their members. A divorced woman is breaking this code and also stepping out of her pre-ordained role as wife. By abandoning this role, she is rejecting the communities' control over her actions. She is attempting to establish a new identity: an independent unmarried woman, an oxymoron in Indian-American society.

Even as we enter the 21st century, Indian-American women continue to encounter severe pressure to conform to specific traditional gender roles. Mythological role models of obedient, submissive, and long-suffering women such as Sita[3] of the *Ramayana* continue to be presented to young Hindu women to emulate. This ideal woman, subordinate to her husband and in-laws, is willing to compromise everything including her individual personality to fulfill her submissive role. Public figures such as actress Sridevi,[4] in a position to influence millions of young women by redefining traditional gender roles, reinforce those oppressive roles by publicly embracing them.

This chapter probes these traditional gender roles through a series of case studies of women who first 'bought into the system' but later rebelled against it by redefining themselves as women with a right to live with dignity even if that meant existing outside their traditional roles as wives. I will explore the evolution of these women through the various stages of their lives using the extensive, in-depth interviews I conducted for this study. I will examine their premarital concepts of womanhood, the predominately arranged marriages they were often coerced into, their different paths to divorce and the eventual painstaking and difficult process of rebuilding their lives. These case studies will illustrate that divorced Asian-Indian women in the US and Indian-American[5] women are more successfully and actively rejecting traditional patriarchal gender roles through the process of divorce, while their divorced sisters in India are facing a more difficult situation as they attempt to rebuild their lives. In a culture that continues to deify women who burn themselves on their husbands' funeral pyre, the decision to divorce requires a great deal of courage and conviction in one's rights as an individual. The process itself is painful—a difficult initiation into a lifestyle contrary to one's culturally ingrained sense of self. These women are pioneering a new identity for themselves. They comprise a growing number of women who not only grapple with many of the same problems other divorced women face but also carry the additional burden of the cultural taboo they have broken.

This study, the first of its kind, will contribute to a dialogue within Indian-American communities regarding the subject of divorce. It will also help the mainstream American population, the health care communities and the legal profession by increasing their awareness of the cultural nuances these women face. Divorce is considered an anomaly by both Asian-Indians and Indian-Americans and, as such, is an issue many would prefer to ignore. However, with the divorce rate increasing (in both India and within these immigrant communities), this topic can no longer be avoided. These women have gone through an *agni pariksha* (ordeal by fire) and, in spite of society's condemnation, have emerged as strong, confident, and independent women—much as steel is forged by the flame.

A better marriage?

Many individuals believe that divorce is a modern phenomenon caused by everything from industrialization, the increasing number of women in the workforce, changing gender roles, and an overall weakening of traditional family values. Although these factors have contributed to rising divorce rates, history tells us that divorce has been around for centuries. In fact, 'there has never been a society where divorce, or some functional equivalent, did not exist'.[6] In the US, divorce was first introduced by the Puritan settlers in the early 1600s.[7] The concept of divorce itself has changed over time. As it crossed national and cultural boundaries, most views on divorce fell into two belief structures: marriage is a religious sacrament which cannot be terminated and; marriage is a contract and, therefore, can be dissolved. Proponents of the second view maintain that 'divorce [is] a result rather than a cause of changes in the institution of the American marriage'.[8] In other words, the availability of divorce is not what causes a couple to separate, rather it facilitates their decision to separate. Anthropologist Margaret Mead believes that the option to divorce gives people the chance to form a better marriage.[9]

In addition to the above mentioned factors which have helped push divorce rates higher, historians have also added 'the changing nature of the patriarchal family, rising expectations of marriage, and inequalities in relationships between husbands and wives' to the list.[10] Interestingly, these 'modern' attitudes have been around for centuries. In her study of the history of divorce, historian Glenda Riley states that:

> after the American revolution, the customary view of marriage as a patriarchal structure was increasingly challenged by the emerging ideal of companionate marriage—a union based on a partnership of friends and equals. In addition to usual expectations that spouses would establish a sexual relationship, have children, and be economic partners, Americans stressed more and more the growing importance of three qualities in marriage: respect, reciprocity, and romance.[11]

The desire and ability to divorce one's partner is also not a recent phenomena in India. The Special Marriage Acts of 1926 and 1982 altered the Hindu marital union while individual states and presidencies enacted various laws from 1920 to 1952 to facilitate the dissolution of marriages. However, it was not until the Hindu Marriage Act of 1955 that Hindu women *throughout* India were able to divorce their spouses.[12]

Despite the availability of divorce, the social stigma is still so strong that many women and men will stay married rather than face society's censure, both for themselves and for their extended families. Rama Mehta's work on divorce among Hindus in India, a ground-breaking study conducted in the 1970s and 1980s, is still relevant today as the societal attitudes towards divorce and divorced individuals discussed in her work have not changed, both in India and among the Asian-Indian immigrants to the United States.[13] Although Mehta's case studies provide valuable ethnographic data, her conclusions are problematic as they reinforce patriarchal gender roles for women. The case studies, much like my own, depict emotionally abusive and physically violent marriages yet Mehta points the finger at the 'Westernized' woman who could have saved her marriage had she not 'insisted on [her] rights'. She states that many of her respondents 'felt that in spite of *irritants*, disagreement on basic issues with their husbands, they would have been better off as married women than as divorced women' (emphasis mine).[14] However, the case studies that Mehta presents chronicle the women tolerating years of adultery, physical, and mental abuse—issues that can hardly be classified as *irritants*. I would argue that Mehta could have presented a more balanced analysis by looking at why these women terminated their relationships, knowing they would face society's condemnation. Mehta states that Indian society in the 1970s was rapidly changing, however, she does not discuss how these changing social mores affected feminine and masculine gender roles and subsequently, marital roles. Instead, she states in her conclusion, that 'it was in regarding men as the superior partners in marriage that a woman would find her own happiness and fulfillment'. She also adds that 'it was the West that had given the "romantic model" for marriage. It was this false sense of romance and love that made marriage fragile in the West and would in India if women were not cautious enough to sift [through] what was real and what was only in the imagination'.[15] In these two statements Mehta is perpetuating traditional familial roles and an ideology which posits the Asian-Indian form of marriage as superior. She is reinforcing a hierarchical patriarchal system and a bipolar view of marriage—the 'Eastern' based on duty and the 'Western' based on 'a false sense of romance'. At no point does Mehta examine the role of the husbands in the breakup of these marriages. Nor does she probe a societal structure which accords men a great deal of latitude and punishes women who refuse to accept the situation. Rather, she turns the spotlight on the women and finds them lacking. Mehta also does not examine the physical and mental abuse that many of these women suffered. She provides quote after quote in which the women elaborate on the economic and social difficulties of being divorced, the mistreatment at the hands of their natal families, and their eventual realization—even among the upper-middle-class respondents—that 'if they had the chance again they would respect the wishes of their husbands and their families [thereby saving the marriage]'.[16] Mehta does not focus on the courage and strength of these women but rather on the hardships they faced after leaving their husbands. Do they really regret leaving their unhappy, often abusive, marriages or is it the lack of viable options for divorced women in India that makes them think that they were better off in their marital homes—regardless of the abuse? Would these women feel the same way if they had the opportunity and support to build happy and productive lives? Further research is needed in this area to examine society's role in insisting on the subordination of women and the carte blanche that is given to Asian-Indian men in order to present a more complete picture of divorce in India.

Sita in the 21st century

The women in my study have all been divorced under US law, and they too have faced and, sometimes, continue to face Asian-Indian communities who, in attempting to establish and sustain their cultural heritage, are often more vigilant in maintaining their traditional roots than the Indians in India itself. While their cultural peers in India have been influenced by the Western culture flowing into India, immigrant Asian-Indians often attempt to recreate and maintain the image of an India from their childhood and early adulthood—an India that no longer exists in many ways. This attempted recreation of Asian-Indian 'culture'[17] often pressures Indian-American women into specific 'gender-appropriate' roles.

As mentioned earlier, one role model still held up for Hindu women to emulate is Sita, of the Hindu epic, the *Ramayana*. She is still the personification, as per a patriarchal reading, of wifely devotion. Raghavan concludes, from her study of first generation Asian-Indians, that 'devotion to the husband is by and large, seen as the hallmark of an ideal woman'.[18] Therefore, it is evident that Sita's unique standing in the minds of most Hindus, 'regardless of region, caste, social class, age, sex, education or modernization, testifies to the power and persuasiveness of the traditional ideal of womanhood'.[19] This is not to say that Sita and her husband Rama are accepted as ideal role models in every aspect without question. There is often, for example, criticism of the *agni pariksha* she was forced to endure. However, many do still strongly support Sita's devotion to Rama as the hallmark of a good Hindu wife.

This validation and continued acceptance of Sita as the ideal role model for young wives is extremely important to understanding why the women in the subsequent case studies stayed in their marriages, tolerating years and sometimes decades of emotional and physical abuse. The women interviewed for this research had internalized, some without specifically making the connection, these expectations and attempted to fulfill them through their own marital behavior. Sudhir Kakar describes a similar internalization of gender role expectations in his research on girls in India and states that, 'In order to maintain her family's love and approval—the "narcissistic supplies" necessary for firm self-esteem—the girl tends to conform, and even *over-conform* to the prescriptions and expectations of those around her [emphasis mine]'.[20] Based on my own research, over-conformity is also a behavioral pattern for the 1.5 and second generation[21] Indian-American women. For the divorced women in this study,[22] the struggle to live up to parental and societal expectations, spoken and unspoken, has been the over-riding factor keeping them in relationships which were destructive physically, emotionally, mentally, and spiritually. However, these women, like Mehta's respondents, reached a point where they were not willing to pay such a high price to maintain their marital status and eventually left, rebuilt their lives, and their only regret, unlike Mehta's respondents, is that they did not leave sooner.

Sita's daughters and their *agni pariksha*

The five[23] women whose experiences will be discussed in this chapter are at various stages in the divorce process, from a newly separated woman to one divorced for 16 years, and at different places on the journey towards emotional recovery. While some were open and comfortable discussing the issues raised, painful as they were, others found it more difficult, such as the woman divorced for 16 years who is still angry at her husband's infidelity. The healing and recovery period of the divorce process and the subsequent rebuilding (or lack of rebuilding) of their lives is affected by many things for these women: familial and community support, internal resources, and wage-earning capacity, to name a few.

These women ranged in age from 34 to 65, came from various socio-economic and educational levels, and had been married for seven to 18 years. Four out of five had arranged marriages to an Asian-Indian, one had a marriage of personal choice to a European. Four out of five had children, now all adults. Although all expressed regret at their experiences, none expressed any strong bitterness towards their ex-spouse even in those cases where physical abuse was the basis for the divorce. Four of the women had been born and raised in India through their early twenties and one, although born in India, had spent 28 of her 34 years in the United States. All experienced some financial difficulties and are currently in different financial situations, from precarious to comfortable. The women had no regrets regarding their actions. Three had initiated the divorce and all wished they had made the decision earlier. The three who had taken the step towards divorce described a long and painful road towards this decision. Their paths were littered with doubts regarding their ability to survive on their own emotionally and economically, to raise children, to rebuild their lives, and, the biggest stumbling block of all, the ability to withstand the familial and cultural pressure to maintain the marriage even when it was a facade.

Adultery was the deciding factor in two divorces. Physical abuse occurred in two of the five cases with varying degrees of severity. Emotional abuse was present in all five cases, again in varying degrees. Some of the relationships included combinations of one or more of the above factors. All five women described years of struggle as they embraced ideological differences in order to conform to the expectations of their spouses and in-laws and maintain the marital relationship. One woman (Pooja) stated that she had changed so much during the marriage (in attempting to accommodate everyone's expectations and demands) that she no longer knew who she was as an individual and what her own personal beliefs and values were. She spent years rediscovering herself after she separated from her husband.

Prior to discussing the five general areas covered during the interviews, a brief synopsis of each woman will provide a framework from which to evaluate their experiences. Mary, a Christian in her late 50s, has a masters degree in Child Development. Educated at Christian boarding schools in India, she was exposed to the strong, single, and independent women who taught at and headed these institutions. She was very observant as a young adult and remembers seeing neighborhood women being physically and emotionally abused and recalls her determination to never be in that position herself. She began teaching in India at the age of 19 and her goal was to become a principal. She handed her paycheck over to her father as her contribution to the household. Her sense of duty led her to honor her father's dying wish and she supported her mother and two younger brothers until she came to the United States as a student in the early 1960s to escape an engagement she did not want. She eventually married her brother's college roommate, who deserted her with a toddler within a few years of their marriage. She believes he left her as he wanted a son and not the daughter she delivered. She married a second time to a Mexican-American approximately 20 years her senior eventually divorcing him due to his infidelities. At present she is happily married to an Asian-Indian. She is a strong, assertive woman who is financially independent and appears to harbor no bitterness or resentment towards either of her former partners even though she has undergone extensive hardship to rebuild her life. Her daughter is now married and is expecting her third child. Mary is financially assisting three generations of her family: her mother, her daughter, son-in-law and granddaughters, all of whom live with her. She has assimilated into the mainstream American culture and feels that being in the United States has enabled her to exercise options such as divorce—options that would have been severely limited in India.

Kalpana is in her mid-40s with a masters degree in painting. She has been divorced for 14 years from a man who was extremely physically and emotionally abusive during their 10-year marriage. The atmosphere in her parental home was very traditional and she was not consulted regarding her engagement and marriage. Her parents informed her one day, without any prior discussion, that they had selected a young man and the wedding would take place in a few months. She met her future spouse at their engagement ceremony after which they corresponded several times before they met again at the wedding ceremony. Kalpana believes that her marriage was based on the dowry her parents provided. The physical abuse began shortly after their marriage. Although her husband assaulted her severely enough to require emergency medical care, she never pressed charges—a decision she now regrets. Their separation occurred when she refused to give him $10,000 to return home after a disagreement. They have one daughter who is currently studying at a major American university. Interestingly enough, the daughter, born and raised in the US, wants an arranged marriage despite observing the abusive interaction between her parents and the struggle her mother endured to rebuild their lives. Kalpana is fully supportive of this decision stating that her daughter was raised with 'proper family values'. In an attempt to connect with other women, Kalpana initiated a support group for Asian-Indian women. Though the group is presently defunct, she plans on revitalizing it. She describes herself as a strong, assertive, and hardworking woman and states that she would like to remarry as she feels more comfortable with the 'traditional' roles for women. While this may appear to be a contradiction on the surface, I believe that given her upbringing, it is not. She is from a generation of Asian-Indian women whose gender socialization is based on the traditional concept of women as wives and mothers. Kalpana's marital situation forced her to adapt to the realities of life as a single woman, yet she appears to be more comfortable within the perceived security of those traditional gender roles.

Monica is a vibrant woman in her mid-60s who teaches Asian-Indian Cultural Studies and is a delight to her students. She has been divorced for 16 years from a European whom she married after meeting him while they were both graduate students at an American university.[24] Although she grew up in what she describes as a very traditional Asian-Indian household, she was allowed to continue her education abroad. She stated that if her parents had any objections to her marriage, they never expressed them to her. She has three adult children and has no plans to remarry because she states, 'I do not trust men and keep them at a distance with my tongue.' Her husband informed her of his affairs with several of her friends shortly before he deserted her. Her voice still echoes the outrage and pain she felt when she came home one evening and found his letter stating that he had left. Her husband, a physician, is currently married to an (ex)friend of hers. Monica says that she is struggling financially and feels rather lonely at times. Although she states that she remembers her ex-husband with affection and that he was fully supportive during their marriage, her words contradict the anger still resonating in her voice. It was clear that the interview had stirred up painful memories which were carefully buried just below the surface.

Anita, in her mid-40s, is employed at a financial institution. She was married for 18 years, has been divorced for six, and is the mother of two male college students. She, like Monica, grew up in a traditional Asian-Indian household, but immigrated to the United States after her marriage. She describes her husband as extremely frugal, cold, and very controlling. He stated that if he had wanted an independent wife, he would have married an 'American woman'. She believes that he went back to India and married her in order to have a submissive wife who would quietly exist in her husband's shadow. Our interview lasted seven hours and she described an emotional nightmare. She spoke of one physically abusive incident during which she threatened to retaliate with physical force. There was no further physical abuse following her stance as he clearly did not expect her to fight back! She regrets not ending the marriage earlier and also wishes that she had not refused alimony as she is now struggling financially. However, she clearly relishes her new independence and her ability to have a voice in her home. She happily showed me recent purchases that she had made for her home—the same home in which she was never allowed to infuse her personal taste. She wishes to remarry but states that it is difficult to meet men interested in a committed relationship—a situation not unique to these women.

Pooja is the only woman among the five who grew up in the United States. She is in her early 30s and has been legally separated from her husband for two-and-a-half years. She was pressured into an arranged marriage by parents desperate to keep their children in a 'proper Indian environment'. Looking back she realizes that her parents did not look further than the ceremony itself and never considered, despite her pleas, that there would be a cultural gap if she married a young man raised in India. She now realizes that her parents, not seeing their daughter as an individual, saw no reason why she could not make all the adjustments necessary to survive in an arranged marriage. Despite her best efforts to make the marriage work, she has become one of the growing number of young second generation Indian-American women facing divorce. It is interesting that the thought of divorce appears to be more traumatic for her than for the women raised in India. The normal trauma inherent in the divorce process may appear more vivid in her case as she is currently in the midst of it. She was married for seven years to a man who was physically abusive for the last three years of their marriage and mentally and emotionally abusive for the entire duration. Two months after their legal separation, she discovered that he had been unfaithful for a number of years—something her friends already knew. She has worked hard to rebuild her life financially and emotionally and is currently pursuing graduate studies. She is the only woman out of the five discussed in this paper who sought professional counseling and firmly believes that it has been 'extremely beneficial' in putting her on the path to complete recovery.[25] She does not have any children and has ambivalent feelings about remarriage.

Summaries of case studies

Premarital

These five women all received a traditional Asian-Indian upbringing, including Pooja who grew up in the United States. Despite this, when discussing marital relationships theoretically, all five women expressed 'progressive' views on the interaction between a husband and a wife. They described marriage as a relationship based on respect, friendship, and companionship between two equal partners. However, they admitted that this was not what they were taught as young women nor what they observed in their extended families. Rather, they were told that a woman quietly submitted to her husband and her in-laws. The sharp contrast between their romanticized ideal and the reality of their situation caused the four who immigrated to the United States to sometimes resent their partners. Furthermore, after migration, they discovered a lifestyle they could never have imagined. These four women found ever-increasing opportunities for intellectual and professional growth in a world that was opening up for women in general. These women arrived in the United States at a time when opportunities were growing for women and minorities in many areas. Therefore, the greater opportunities they experienced were not simply the result of migration to a Western country, but of changes that were occurring for many women in different parts of the world, including South Asia. Unfortunately, their husbands were not responsive to the 'new' women who were slowly evolving before their eyes.

All five women discussed in this chapter observed traditional gender roles in their natal homes, although in varying degrees. In what appears to be a contradiction, they were encouraged to pursue an education, and, at the same time, to maintain accepted modes of feminine behavior, especially acquiescence to an arranged marriage in their early 20s. When viewed in the traditional Asian-Indian context, advanced education for women is not a contradiction as it enables them to be matched with men who also possess a higher level of education. Therefore, the primary purpose of education is to enable women to make a 'better' marriage; it is not for their intellectual edification.

Four of the women had 'agreed' to arranged marriages with different levels of interaction with their future spouses. The interactions varied from seeing him for the first time at their engagement ceremony to being allowed to 'date' him in a semi-Western fashion. This progressive view prevailed for Pooja who was allowed quite a bit of interaction over several months with a young man introduced to her by her family. She admitted that she was under extreme pressure to marry an 'appropriate Asian-Indian boy'. Her previous choice of a Euro-American was flatly rejected by her parents who threatened to cut all family ties with her if she married the young man she had chosen. Apparently the only objection to her choice was that he was not of Asian-Indian origin. Interestingly enough, her younger sister later married a non-Asian-Indian and this relationship was fully accepted by the family. This brings an additional factor into play, pressure on the older sibling to conform to a stricter code of behavior in an attempt to provide a role model for younger siblings.

Of the four women who had arranged marriages, only Pooja was consulted by her parents regarding her preferences. However, she says that those preferences were not considered when the young men were screened. One criterion that was especially important to her, that the young man should have grown up in the United States, was discarded by her parents as unnecessary. Kalpana and Anita were presented with young men chosen by their fathers with no prior consultation. They did not meet their future husbands until the engagement ceremony. Mary's brother selected his college roommate as a possible spouse. Their mothers were also not consulted. In another possible alliance, Mary's father did not meet the young man he had chosen as his future son-in-law. He made this life-altering decision for his daughter based on a photograph and a discussion with the young man's older brother. However, this alliance was later discarded when Mary asserted her views regarding the expected dowry.

The parents of these four women were willing to pay a dowry, including the parents of Pooja who had been in the United States for 18 years at the time of their daughter's marriage. Pooja, however, was vehemently opposed to the practice and recalls numerous arguments with her mother on this subject. Her mother disregarded her daughter's wishes and quietly did what she felt was appropriate. Mary described an incident when her engagement had been decided by her father and the question of dowry was raised. She and her mother had been listening to the discussion in the other room, standing by the open door. After her brother-in-law-to-be asked what they could expect, Mary put her diploma and teaching certificates on a silver platter, marched into the room declaring that they constituted her dowry and that her father would not pay a cent. She was ordered out of the room by her outraged father and later admonished for her behavior. The prospective groom's brother promptly withdrew the offer of marriage due to her outspokenness and her now possible lack of a dowry. Kalpana, stating that 'they wanted the money and not the girl', firmly believes that the entire basis for her marriage was the dowry her in-laws were given.

Pooja was the only one of the five women allowed to actively participate in the decisions regarding wedding attire and the trousseau. Although Kalpana was consulted about color preferences, the final selection was made by her future sister-in-law.

Marital

All the women were in their early 20s when they were married and their spouses ranged from six months younger to approximately six years older. None of the women were able to recall the actual marriage ceremony. It was a blur for most of them. They did recall a feeling of numbness which is not surprising since four of the women felt they were marrying strangers. Several of the women remembered tears prior to the ceremony. Pooja had a crying binge the night before the ceremony and also just prior to the arrival of the *barat*.[26] The women talked about experiencing fear, uncertainty and a lack of control over their lives. Kalpana remembers feeling uneasy due to the involvement of dowry. Mary described how she spent the night before her wedding cleaning the apartment she and her fiancé would occupy after the ceremony. She then slept in the car as he had come to the apartment and she felt it was inappropriate for them to be in the apartment alone.

Except for Pooja, the women and their future spouses did not discuss or establish any particular domestic or gender roles. Pooja states that she discussed, in detail, what her expectations were and what she wanted from the marriage. She recalls how happy she felt when the young man in question agreed with her thoughts and goals. After they were married, he admitted he did not understand most of what she had said due to her American accent and that he just agreed with her at appropriate intervals. She was stunned when he also admitted to lying in response to even those questions he understood. When pressed for an explanation, he responded with the chilling statement, 'I wanted to marry you, so I told you what you wanted to hear and agreed with you so that you would marry me'. She recalls that he did not understand why his revelation upset her nor did he comprehend that a relationship based on deceit had little chance of success. The women did all the household tasks and did not question their spouses' lack of participation. In fact, all the husbands and wives assumed that household-related chores were the women's responsibility, therefore, the men's lack of participation was not an issue. Mary recalled that when she was in her last trimester of pregnancy, she would walk to the Laundromat while her husband watched TV. He refused to drive her stating that he needed to relax.

When we discussed conflict resolution, all five women admitted that they would back down or consistently try to overlook things. They all believed that they were responsible for maintaining peace in the home. Mary stated that she had been taught by her mother that the husband was the king of the house and therefore his actions were not to be questioned. Kalpana stated that her husband would listen to her comments in silence and then walk away. She felt that she had no input whatsoever in any decision. Pooja recalls suppressing her comments to the point where a submissive attitude slowly became an integral part of her behavioral pattern. It is not surprising that resentment eventually surfaced in all the marriages. During the divorce process, submissive behavioral patterns were slowly changed, to varying degrees, as the women redefined themselves.

Monica and Mary had no significant interaction with the groom's parents as Monica's in-laws lived in Europe and Mary's in-laws were estranged from their son due to his recent conversion to Christianity (after he deserted her, he converted back to Hinduism). Monica stated that her husband's parents did not accept their son's marriage. However, the distance made it possible to minimize their negative effect. Kalpana felt that her father-in-law continued to manipulate her husband and re-called her anger when she read a letter from India in which her husband was instructed not to reveal his marital status.[27] Pooja talked about the early conflict she had with her father-in-law when her husband decided weeks after their wedding that he no longer wished to immigrate to the United States. Her father-in-law stated that it was her duty as a wife to live where her husband decreed. Baffled at this abrupt reversal and finding herself alone in India with her family back in the United States, she stated her intention to leave as planned. She further made it clear that if her husband canceled his interview at the US Consulate, she would not sign his papers at a later date and he would be on his own.[28] He went through the process, following her to the United States within a few weeks. Looking back, she regrets his decision!

All the Asian-Indian in-laws, except for Mary's who had no inter-action with her husband's parents, expected the 'ideal' daughter-in-law behavior. For these women, the appropriate behavior consisted of touching the feet of all the family elders in the morning and evening (to receive their blessings), covering their heads as a sign of respect, and general submissiveness with varying degrees of traditionalism enforced. None of the women lived in their husband's extended family for more than a few months, thereby avoiding much of the day-to-day interaction with their in-laws. However, restrictions on the women's behavior were imposed during trips to India and during extended trips the in-laws made to the United States. Despite these interactions, only Kalpana and Mary felt that their in-laws actually contributed to the conflict within the marriage and the resulting divorce. Mary's in-laws went to the extreme point of denying both the marriage and their granddaughter.

All the husbands, except Pooja's, wanted children. Anita stated that her husband insisted that she immediately become pregnant despite her desire to wait for a few years. Pooja stated that her husband, the youngest in his family, did not want children as he felt that they would divert her attention from him. She had two miscarriages and is now relieved, to some extent, that she does not have children as they would necessitate a life-long connection to her former husband. However, now in her early 30s, her biological clock is ticking and she feels the pressure to have children. There was no discussion among the other couples as to when they would have children, necessary financial arrangements, or child rearing issues.

Pre-divorce

In only two cases, Mary and Monica, where the husbands walked out, was there a sudden decision to divorce. Even then, Mary gave him five years to rethink his decision although he had already written to her asking for a divorce.[29] In the remaining cases, there was a gradual decision to separate. There appears to have been constant conflict in these cases, a general feeling of unhappiness, resentment, and a desire for a more peaceful lifestyle. As stated earlier, all the cases involved adultery (on the part of the husband), physical and/or emotional abuse or desertion; some involved a combination of these factors. Pooja described how she had decided one evening that she could no longer live with her abusive husband. She kept the decision to herself as she wanted a few days to work out the next steps. A few hours later, an incident of physical abuse led to her pressing charges against her husband. His actions forced an immediate separation which now occurred under very stressful conditions.

Anita described a slow but steady process regarding the decision to leave. The catalyst was an incident which served to further illustrate that she was not considered a contributing and important member of the household. She narrated a scenario where her husband had decided they needed new furniture. Although she accompanied him to a store, he disregarded her input, selecting what he and the salesman felt was appropriate. She described this as the straw that broke the proverbial camel's back. When she filed for divorce, his only comment to their children was, 'I can't believe she actually did it'. Pooja describes similar disbelief on her husband's part; he called her from jail to post his bail after he was arrested for assaulting her. Both of these men had difficulty in accepting the fact that their previously submissive wives had rebelled.

All three women, Pooja, Kalpana, and Anita, who chose to end their marriages, stated that they had family backing for their decision, in varying degrees. However, their families were not able to cope with the onslaught of emotional upheavals that these decisions would bring—for the women and for the family members themselves. The process of divorce and recovery involves an extensive re-evaluation of self and includes a redefinition of goals, identity, and beliefs. It can be a time of tremendous anger and confusion. In the context of a society which has strict and confining gender roles for women, this self-analysis can be disconcerting for society in general and family members in particular. Asian-Indian culture dictates that 'nice' women do not express strong emotion, particularly anger. However, the depth of anger associated with the divorce process, especially one which involves abuse and/or adultery, is difficult to deny. The women who had expressed this anger, and were coming to terms with it, were the women who were able to successfully put the memories and the divorce behind them. The women who felt they had to perpetuate the image of the long-suffering Sita and repress their anger continued to exhibit traces of the unexpressed anger even years later. These women, like other divorced individuals, had to work through all the emotions that surfaced and only then, were they able to move towards rebuilding their lives.

After separating from their husbands, voluntarily or involuntarily, the women interviewed for this study experimented with a new lifestyle, in varying degrees. This exploration included everything—from a simple desire to try a new and different hairstyle to throwing caution to the winds and wanting to try skydiving and everything in-between. The important point here is not what they wanted to try but that they wanted to make some changes and have new experiences. This entire process of redefining identity and the exploration of its previously rigid boundaries was disconcerting for many of their family members and their friends. These feelings, often expressed as disapproval, made the recovery process more difficult for these women.

Familial and societal pressure were also factors in prolonging these marriages as all the women felt a need to maintain their relationships—regardless of the personal cost. In both cases where physical abuse was a factor, the families *knew* the circumstances and *still* encouraged and expected the women to work things out. Pooja states that it has taken her two-and-a-half years and extensive therapy to come to terms with what she considers as her mother's betrayal and lack of concern for her welfare. Mary, Pooja, and Anita stated that they were on their own, emotionally and financially, after they separated from their spouses.

Monica did not talk to her mother about her divorce other than to say that it was happening. She says that she is grateful that it happened after her father's death. She related how she received a letter from a 'friend' of hers with whom she had, recently, discovered her husband was involved; the letter stated, 'You've had him for twenty-five years and now its my turn'. When her husband finally told her of his infidelities, she thought they had decided to work things out. Therefore, she was shocked when she arrived home one day and found a letter saying that he had left. This memory still has the ability to make her voice tremble with pain and anger as she describes 'his cowardly act'.

Divorce and recovery

The first feeling Pooja recalls after leaving her husband was a sense of freedom. It was as if she had been 'released from prison and [she] felt free for the first time in years'. Anita confessed to a similar feeling of relief. The euphoria soon evaporated. All the women experienced feelings of pain, anger, loneliness, and abandonment. They felt a growing uncertainty about the future as the reality of their situation became apparent. Although the struggle to maintain the marriage had ended, the struggle to rebuild, and in some aspects to redefine their entire lives, had just begun.

During and after the divorce process, the women received support from family and friends in varying degrees. Pooja, who utilized professional counseling, stressed that it is very important to have the right counselor. Her therapist, an Asian-Indian woman who has successfully rebuilt her own life, understood the cultural pressure and nuances of the Indian-American communities and could, therefore, understand the difficulties of a bicultural lifestyle. The therapy gave Pooja an opportunity to evaluate her childhood, her marriage, and the rebuilding process within a supportive and non-judgmental environment. The use of professional counseling is still rare among South Asian communities, who like other Asian groups, have negative attitudes towards the process. It is widely believed that family problems should be resolved within the family. However, as divorce is a fairly recent phenomena within the Indian-American communities, neither the family nor the individual is equipped to handle the emotions that erupt when a couple separates and divorces. Skilled and timely professional intervention can provide the support necessary to handle the pain and facilitate the recovery process. Out of the approximately 20 individuals interviewed for this study, there was a marked difference in the demeanor of the two women who had utilized professional counseling. They, more so than the others, had clearly recovered from the marital conflict and the divorce process and were the most comfortable with their new lives.

All the women had to confront the prevalent feeling among Asian-Indians and Indian-Americans that couples who divorce have not 'really attempted to work things out' and have, instead, taken the 'easy way out'. None of the women in this study were happy that they were separated or divorced and felt that they had tried very hard to make the marriage work. They expressed regret that they were put in a position where they had to take this step as all strongly believed in the permanence and sanctity of marriage. However, they stated that given the nature of their spouses, divorce was the only option they had and, even then, one they took as a last resort.

The divorced mothers all stated that their children supported their decision to leave. In fact, Anita's sons had encouraged her, for years, to leave her husband. When she finally did leave, they firmly backed her decision. Her older son, so angered by his father's behavior towards his mother, has refused any financial assistance and having discarded his father's name, uses his mother's maiden name. The courts awarded custody to Anita and Monica and established visitation guidelines. For Mary and Kalpana, visitation rights were not an issue as both fathers had left the country.

Interestingly enough, the women in this study who were raised in India were less concerned about their post-divorce acceptance by their communities. They did not particularly care what people thought. They felt that they suffered enough and now, had the right to live their own lives. Their extended families were also, for the most part, still in India, and therefore, did not interact with them on a regular basis. Pooja still feels self-conscious about her divorce; she attributes this in large part to her family's attitude. Pooja's sister did not want her to discuss the divorce as she did not want her friends to know the 'sordid' details while her mother treated the divorce as a shameful secret.[30] This led Pooja to internalize her pain. Anita and Monica also stated that they did not discuss the details of their marriage or divorce with their families—they feared that they would be judged and found lacking. Pooja, in re-evaluating and redefining herself, distanced herself from Indian-Americans in general for about one-and-a-half years. She has recently started to reconnect and is becoming more comfortable with her circumstances. The remaining women stated that while they were not ostracized from community events, they were sometimes reluctant to attend them. Anita added that she will not attend her regional events unless she is accompanied by her family.

These women have clearly experienced a great deal of pain and sadness with the shattering of their marital dreams. However, they are optimistic about the future. They do not think of themselves as victims despite the sometimes harrowing circumstances of their marital relationships. They have come out of their experiences stronger, wiser, and more confident. These women are happy at their 'new found' strength, which appears to have been an untapped aspect of their personalities all along. They are comfortable with their ability to handle adversity and anything else the future may bring. The women also agreed that they feel more independent and confident as they slowly realize and develop their ability to manage their own lives. Pooja, while expressing regret that her marriage wasted her 20s, feels that she has finally come into her own in her 30s.

New relationships

All the women except for Mary and Monica expressed a desire to re-marry; this lack of interest may have to do with age. Mary and Monica are in their 50s and 60s, the others in their 30s and 40s. Pooja expressed a desire to marry someone either of Asian-Indian origin or at least very interested in the culture. Kalpana and Anita both felt that an Asian-Indian would be the best possible choice although they were open to dating men of other ethnic groups.

The three women interested in a new relationship expressed definite ideas and expectations. They wanted confident men who would not be intimidated by them; they wanted men who would see them as equals, who possessed inner strength and did not define their masculinity in a traditional and authoritative manner. However, while expressing these views, Kalpana and Anita also expressed a desire to be homemakers and appeared to be more comfortable with this scenario. They believe that a woman can be strong and assertive and express that strength with her desire to be a homemaker in a relationship which respects this choice and her contribution to the family. The role of a homemaker is often seen as a subordinate role by society which does not equate it with 'labor', currently defined as compensated production. Therefore, a homemaker's contribution is often not recognized and she is perceived to be without agency. It is within this framework that the homemaker is classified as subordinate and confined within a submissive identity. Thus, society perceives a contradiction when a woman expresses her desire to be a homemaker and still expects an egalitarian relationship. Within the scope of this paper, I am limited to stating that a homemaker with agency is unfortunately rare and so, when exercising this choice, it is usually assumed that she is subordinate to her husband. However, I would argue that a society that perceives a contradiction when a strong woman chooses to be a homemaker must take into account the reasons for the choice she has made, respect her right to make this choice, and value her labor. For when a woman or a community does not value her unpaid labor, she is placed at a disadvantage, economically and emotionally, within the balance of power inherent in the marital relationship. However, if she perceives this role and her contribution to the family as valuable and necessary, her attitude will affect the family dynamics and strengthen her position. As the self-esteem of the women in my study has increased over the years, they believe that even as homemakers, they can be equal and valued partners in any future relationships.

These women all believe that they had options, most notably the option to *successfully* leave their husbands, because they lived outside India. Although divorce is legally available in India and the divorce rate is rising, the three women who initiated their divorces believe they would have been pressured to continue to tolerate their abusive relationships if they still lived in India. The women all agreed that economic independence and a different societal perception of divorce in mainstream America facilitated these choices, enabling them to rebuild their lives. However, it was still an uphill battle for all of them. While Monica and Pooja received some short-term alimony, it just covered a few basic necessities and they struggled to provide the rest. The others were completely on their own. In addition to the monetary aspect, all the women stated that their jobs or graduate studies gave them an outlet for their energy and something to focus on. Monica believes that her teaching helped her to maintain her sanity and enabled her to channel her energies into a constructive area. She did add, however, that she was 'very lonely'. Pooja expressed her firm desire to be financially independent prior to remarrying. She states that 'she wants to make sure that she has things...like a home...that cannot be taken away from her again.' Pooja feels that the pursuit of her educational goals enables her to express her intellectual side and keep her spirits up as she revitalizes her life. She says that her education gives her hope for a better and independent future. Thus, it appears that all the women have found outlets, in varying degrees, through their careers, children, friends, and extended families.

Conclusion

After listening to their marital stories, it is apparent that these five women tolerated a great deal more than any culture should expect of a marital partner. They were willing, although sometimes not enthusiastically, to be extremely submissive and subordinate in order to placate their spouses and in-laws. They had all been taught to acquiesce to their husbands' wishes, and it is only after years of hardship that they were willing to consider an alternate solution.

Out of the approximately 20 women and men interviewed for this study, only Monica had a first marriage of personal choice. The divorces cannot be 'blamed' on the traditional arranged marriage system that is prevalent within the Asian-Indian culture as the self-arranged marriages of the Western countries incorporate a higher divorce rate. It is the *position* of women in Asian-Indian society which perpetuates patriarchal customs such as the arranged marriage system and permits the formation of an intractable male position which does not allow women to define themselves outside of narrowly constructed gender roles. It is within this context that I discuss the arranged marriage system.

The traditional arranged marriage system removes the choice of marital partner from the two people most intimately affected. They often have little or no say in the decision that permanently alters their lives. Even if consulted, the interaction between the prospective spouses is limited and certainly not enough to enable them to make such a choice. The arranged marriage system, while thrusting both people into an adult relationship, does not acknowledge their lack of preparation for such a role. The basic premise is that although these individuals are old enough to be married, they are not old enough nor experienced enough to undertake this decision on their own. In the case studies where the women involved were not even consulted, as was the case with Kalpana and Anita, the parents are basing the decision on their own criteria. They are not taking into consideration that their daughters may have some parameters of their own.

Furthermore, the insistence on strict segregation of the sexes is also problematic. Mary described an incident where she was chastised by her father when she ran into a student on the way home and walked a few blocks with him. This attitude does not prepare men or women for the intimate interaction required in the modern, primarily nuclear, marital structure now the norm for most Asian-Indian immigrants and second generation Indian-Americans. Although knowledge of gender roles is learned first and foremost in the natal home—the parents providing the primary role models and siblings providing additional insights—interaction between the sexes is necessary to fine-tune that knowledge. Therefore, pairing up two individuals who have had limited interaction with the opposite sex places both parties in a precarious position. With women attaining greater economic freedom, they are increasingly unwilling to tolerate an emotionally or physically abusive marriage. Therefore, the premise that the two people involved will adjust to their situation once they are married no longer applies, especially for the Indian-American communities. Traditionally, women have been expected to compromise and adjust. Now, women also expect their spouses to make compromises. Therefore, young women and men need to be taught that gender roles overall are changing and that women are no longer 'just' wives and mothers and men are more than providers. As many members of the 1.5 and second generation have not been exposed to these expanded gender roles in their natal homes, problems have arisen when they form their own nuclear families.

The traditional segregation of the sexes is a result of the implicit belief that women must be segregated in order to control their sexuality. This control is in effect from birth to marriage to death when responsibility for the woman has traditionally been passed from father to husband to son. It remains in effect even when the husband dies as evidenced by widow immolation or *sati* and strict rules for diet, attire, and conduct for widows. This control raises some troubling questions. Why is there such an emphasis on limiting women to the traditionally approved patriarchal roles of wife and mother? What is society afraid of? I would argue that society is clearly worried about the conduct of women not strictly confined within limited boundaries. It is to perpetuate these boundaries that the arranged marriage system is still strongly encouraged for young Indians in India and for Indian-Americans.

The concept of a father deciding on a spouse for his daughter with no input from her is difficult to justify as we approach the 21st century. If the argument is presented that elders are better equipped for this decision, why were three out of five mothers of the women discussed in this paper not consulted while male siblings, sometimes younger, were? Surely, the mothers were in a position to also judge the young man in question. It boils down to paternal authority being imposed in true patriarchal tradition. Thus we see that, in these case, true authority was based on gender not age. It should be noted that in India, many women actively participate in kinship matters and often, it is the elder women of the house who select or at least heavily influence the selection of prospective partners, however, the mothers of the women in this study were not actively involved in the selection of their future sons-in-law.

It is outside the scope of this paper to probe in detail the patriarchal foundation of the Hindu culture. Suffice to say, it is the basis for the current subordinate position of the Hindu woman. The women interviewed for this paper exhibited a great deal of courage in challenging this position and striking out on their own. They all agreed that they would have been pressured to tolerate their situations, even the abusive ones, if they lived in India. Although divorce is legally available by mutual consent in India, societal pressure to maintain the marriage is still strong. There is fear of repercussions to the woman's natal family, especially if there are unwed sisters. Economic dependence is another factor that ties Asian-Indian women to unhappy marriages. Even though there may be an internal desire to leave, there is little to no infrastructure established to facilitate this decision. For example, where would a woman go to exercise her legal options, *if* she knows that she has legal rights? Even if a few organizations exist in the urban areas, the prevailing social atmosphere often deters women from taking the final step. The culture perpetuates the theory that an unmarried individual, man or woman, is incomplete. Thus there is strong societal pressure not only to get married but to stay married.

There has been a recent trend to debate the merits of the arranged-marriage system against 'love marriage' (Western form of marriage). This debate has led to the renaming of the two systems as 'parentally arranged' or 'consensual' marriages and 'self-arranged' respectively. The term 'consensual' is being bandied about in an effort to claim that young women and men are being consulted and are, therefore, participating in the selection of their spouses. I take exception to the use of the word 'consensual' which implies the participation of two consenting adults. For within the 'consensual' marriage option, the interaction between the prospective spouses is still limited and often not enough to enable them to make an educated choice. Furthermore, with the current subordinate position of Asian-Indian women, there is little chance that they will be able to select a mate on a basis equal to that of a male in the same situation. If there were true equality between the sexes, there would be no need for dowry to be paid to the groom and his family, and women would not be considered such a liability that female infanticide in India and even among Canadian-Indians would be an issue. It is also a mistake to characterize only Western relationships as 'romantic' as Mehta does. One must question what definition of 'romantic' she is applying. There are many Asian-Indian and Indian-American relationships in which the partners truly respect and cherish each other. By portraying Asian-Indian marriages as being more 'sensibly' based on family choice and duty and Western marriages as 'romantic', Mehta is misrepresenting both forms of marriage as mutually exclusive. A strong marriage—regardless of the nationality of the spouses—consists of two individuals who have a similar set of values, a commitment to each other, and open lines of communication. Instead of debating which style of marriage is 'superior', it would be more prudent to concentrate on developing methods of interaction which are beneficial to both spouses and which enable both to live with dignity.

The phenomenon of divorce among Asian-Indians and Indian-Americans within a dominant Euro-American culture is a complicated issue. After reviewing the literature, it is evident that divorce is a life-altering experience for any ethnic group and one which requires a re-examination of self at a basic level. Women of Indian origin also undergo this restructuring of their lives and a redefinition of identity but with further complications due to their bicultural heritage. The process becomes convoluted as divorce is a new phenomenon among Indian-Americans. Therefore, there is little, if any, literature on the subject and the process as it pertains to them. Whereas mainstream bookstores have entire sections on 'interpersonal relationships' which assist Euro-Americans contemplating, in the midst of, or recovering from a divorce, no such material exists for the Indian-American undergoing this transition. While the validity of the 'self-help' genre of literature can be argued, its accessibility does provide an avenue for individuals to pursue in their efforts to rebuild their lives. Mainly it provides an understanding of the conflicting emotions they are experiencing in addition to providing some legal guidance. Another avenue which is limited for Asian-Indian and Indian-American women is that of professional counseling. It is well-documented that Asian-Americans as a group resist the concept of discussing intimate issues with a stranger despite the professional training of the counselor and the confidentiality inherent in the process. For those Asian-Indian and Indian-American women who seek counseling, there is a dearth of professionals who are trained to handle the cultural nuances these women face. The availability of counseling is an important factor in the recovery of these women. This is evidenced by the difference in the demeanor of the two women in this study who sought and utilized professional counseling as they struggled with the divorce process and rebuilt their lives. The lack of these resources results in feelings of isolation for the divorcees and may hinder their efforts to start new lives. The visible presence of divorced women who have successfully rebuilt their lives could encourage other women trapped in destructive relationships to take the first step towards that goal.

It would be a mistake to believe that arranged marriages undertaken under extreme pressure are no longer an issue, especially for the second generation. Even after the completion of this particular project, I continue to encounter young women and men in their 20s, some now with children, who were pressured into arranged marriages and are either divorced or going through the process. Despite the strong stigma attached to divorce, the divorce rate is rapidly increasing both in India and among Asian-Indians and Indian-Americans. Christian Ghasarian and Michael Levin's analysis of the 1990 United States Census indicates that 6.1 percent of Asian-Indians and Indian-Americans are currently divorced. A further breakdown of this statistic reveals that 5.9 percent of first generation Asian-Indians and 8.0 percent of Indian-Americans are divorced. The percentage of divorced women in each category is higher than the men with 3.0 percent of Asian-Indian women and 4.4 percent of Indian-American women listed as divorced while the percentage of divorced men is 2.9 percent for both categories. Therefore, women and Indian-Americans have a higher rate of divorce. The number of divorced men in both categories may be lower as there is less of a stigma attached to their divorced status, often making it easier for them to remarry. This phenomena is not limited to Asian-Indian men as, interestingly enough, the percentage of divorced men as compared to women is lower in the general US population (9.2 percent) as well as the overall foreign-born US (6.7 percent) and the Asian male (4.1 percent) populations. These numbers support the studies which reveal that divorced men in general remarry more quickly that their female counterparts.[31]

While the percentage of divorced Asian-Indian and Indian-Americans is still considerably less than the 9.2 percent of the men and 11.9 percent of the women in the overall US population who are divorced,[32] it does indicate that this is one of the critical issues of our time and, as such, must be addressed by the approximately one million Asian-Indians and Indian-Americans currently residing in the United States. Although it was very difficult for the women in this study to share their life histories, they all believed that their participation in this research may help other women trapped in unhappy, sometimes dangerous, relationships. It was clear that the women interviewed possessed inner strength and a conviction that they could survive whatever the future held in store. In an interesting development, there is a very small but growing number of young men who are observing Karvachoth with their wives, thereby changing it from a fast for the husband's long and healthy life to one asking for a long and healthy marriage for both of them. If the women in this study observe Karvachoth again, it will be for men who are true partners.

✦ Notes and References

1. In the interests of privacy, all names have been changed.
2. For the purposes of this chapter, patriarchy refers to a family structure which includes the following: patrilineal inheritance; an extended family with sons and daughters-in-law living with the parents and sometimes the grandparents; and the oldest male having authority over the younger males and the women.
3. Sita, from the Hindu epic, the *Ramayana*, was kidnapped and had to be rescued by her husband, Rama. After her rescue, she underwent an *agni pariksha* or ordeal by fire to prove that she had been faithful during her captivity.
4. 'Sridevi: Waiting For An Arranged Marriage' states the front page of the *India West* magazine. The article, written by a male writer, highlights how simple and traditional this famous Indian actress is as her life revolves around her family. Despite a solid career, financial independence and her exposure to Western culture, Sridevi states that she will leave the choice of her future spouse to her parents and refers to herself as a 'girl'. She chooses not to use the term 'woman' because this implies a lack of innocence—a fatal flaw in an unmarried Indian woman. (*India West* 1993.)
5. The term Asian-Indian will be used to refer to the immigrant population who came to the US as adults and the term Indian-American will be used to refer to those individuals who either grew up or were born in the US.

6. Mary Ann Glendon, *The Transformation of Family Law: State, Law, and Family in the United States and Western Europe* (Chicago, The University of Chicago Press, 1989), 148.

7. Glenda Riley, *Divorce: An American Tradition* (New York, Oxford University Press, 1991), 3.

8. Riley, 4. See n. 7.

9. Riley, 163. See n. 7.

10. Riley, 5. See n. 7.

11. Riley, 55. See n. 7.

12. K.M. Kapadia, *Marriage and Family in India* as cited in Rama Mehta, *Divorced Hindu Women* (New Delhi, Viking Publishing House Pvt. Ltd., 1975), 6.

13. Mehta. See n. 12, and Rama Mehta, *Socio-Legal Status of Women in India* (New Delhi, Mittal Publications, 1987).

14. Mehta, 130–31. See n. 12.

15. Mehta, 166. See n. 12.

16. Mehta, 131. See n. 12.

17. The use of words such as 'culture', 'tradition', 'traditional', 'community', 'values', etc., is problematic and therefore, these words will be highlighted by single quotes the first time they appear in this chapter.

18. Chemba Raghavan, 'Parent's Cultural Models of Female Gender Role Identity: Beliefs of Indian and American Mothers' (unpublished dissertation, 1993), 182.

19. Sudhir Kakar, *The Inner World: A Psycho-analytic Study of Childhood and Society in India*, Second Edition (New York, Oxford University Press, 1981), 63.

20. Kakar. See n. 19.

21. 1.5 refers to those individuals who immigrated to the United States of America at a very young age. Studies have shown their attitudes can be slightly different from the first and second generations. The second generation consists of those individuals born in the United States. In this chapter, I will refer to both the 1.5 and second generation as the second generation.

22. The interviews were obtained through personal contacts, referrals, advertisements in Indian magazines and newspapers, electronic news boards, and matrimonial advertisements placed by divorcees in South Asian newspapers. The interviews were conducted predominantly in the women's homes to ensure a private as well as comfortable environment. The interviews were taped with their permission and with the understanding that they could stop the recorder at any time. The tapes were transcribed verbatim and used along with interview notes to formulate the case studies.

    The women interviewed were asked general questions in five interrelated areas: premarital, marital, pre-divorce, divorce and recovery, and new relationships. The conversations were not limited to a set of specific questions but rather guided into general topics within a specific structure. I did not want to adhere to a rigid set of questions but was more interested in initiating a freewheeling discussion of experiences, expectations and a general desire to explore the Indian marital process from the viewpoint of women who had experienced both its positive and negative aspects. This method facilitated the exploration of the richness of each woman's unique account. Interpersonal relationships are by their very nature a private matter. Therefore, it was necessary to ensure that an appropriate atmosphere was created to facilitate the level of trust and privacy necessary for these conversations. The women interviewed felt reassured that as an Indian-American, I would understand the subtle nuances of the culture thereby appreciating the struggle they had endured. They would often 'interview' me for 15–20 minutes prior to agreeing to their interview.

The average age at marriage was 21 years. The average number of years married was 13.4. The average number of years that these women had been divorced was 11.8 and the average number of children was 1.2. All the women were employed at the time of their separation and possessed college degrees, with the majority holding postgraduate degrees.

Although separated and divorced men were also included in my study, due to the focus of this volume, this chapter will discuss only the experiences of the women in my research.

23. The women chosen were the first five women to be interviewed.

24. Although Monica did not have an arranged marriage, she faced the same cultural stigma when she divorced. In fact, this 'love marriage' may have been an additional burden when she divorced as she had defied society and crossed racial, cultural, and religious boundaries to marry him.

25. Out of the 20 women and men interviewed for this study, two women sought professional counseling. It was clear during their interviews that they had dealt with the issues that the marriage and divorce had raised and that they had put the past behind them. There was a difference in their demeanor as they possessed an aura of self-confidence and a sense of direction which was striking.

26. During the traditional Hindu ceremony in northern India, the bridegroom arrives on a decorated white horse with a marching band, his family and friends.

27. She suspects that her in-laws were disappointed in the dowry they had received and wanted to arrange another marriage.

28. Pooja discovered, during the divorce process, that he had twice failed the medical qualification exams that all foreign doctors had to pass. He was, therefore, hesitant to come to the US as this information may come out. He also feared his inability to pass the exam in the future. Pooja's in-laws also wanted someone who would care for them and believed that after the wedding, she could be pressured to stay in India. This attitude brings up another problem which the 1.5 generation women face. Many of these women married men raised in India. There was constant conflict with the in-laws who then expected their sons to either remain in India or return within a few years.

29. Her husband had lost his student status and was required to return to India to process a new application. Mary borrowed money from numerous friends for his airfare and gifts for his family. Shortly after he arrived in India, his family refused to acknowledge their marriage or their granddaughter and he wrote requesting a divorce.

30. Pooja's family is now more supportive. They are proud of her strength and courage as she continues to rebuild her life.

31. Christine Ghasarian and Michael J. Levin, *Asian Indians in the United States*, unpublished manuscript, 53.

32. Ghasarian and Levin. See n. 31.

11

The life waiting for me

Pooja K.

There are many ways of breaking a heart. Stories are full of hearts broken by love, but what really breaks a heart is taking away its dream.

—Pearl S. Buck

It's very difficult being an Indian woman today...especially when you're in your 30s and going through a divorce. Where do you fit in... you are no longer the 'wife of a doctor'. What is your identity now in Indian society—a society where a woman is defined by the man in her life? As a single woman, do you even have an identity? What do you tell people in a culture where divorce is still frowned upon? How do you explain to people that you had no choice...that he was physically abusive and sleeping with other women? Why do I even feel the need to explain to other people? *I* know the pain, humiliation, and heartbreak that I went through...that I am still going through. I am writing this essay because there are other people like me out there. The details may be different, but the pain and heartbreak are unfortunately too familiar. However, this is not a sad story of a tragic marriage and shattered dreams. This is a story of rebuilding and personal growth...where from the ashes of a broken heart and wounded spirit came the strength and determination to stand on my own two feet and rebuild my life. I had been let out of a prison and I was determined to use this very precious second chance at life.

The US changed its immigration policies in 1965 and as a result, thousands of Asian-Indians emigrated during the late 60s and 70s. The majority of these immigrants were highly educated professionals. Although they adjusted to the US professionally, culturally and socially, they maintained their Indian culture. Their children became young adults in the 80s and many went through arranged marriages with spouses from India. This article is the story of my arranged marriage with a doctor from India. Although I grew up in the United States, my parents felt that I would be protected from the American culture by marrying a 'nice Indian boy'. There was no question of my marrying an American as 'they did not have stable marriages'. Therefore, according to my parents, my happiness depended on marrying an Indian.

I look back, 10 years later, and wonder why and how I succumbed to the pressure. Within the last two years, I have been able to understand that I, as a naive, overly sheltered young woman, was not equipped to stand up to my father. Combine that with a sense of duty and a desire for parental approval, and you have the makings, in my case, of seven years of married hell.

I could talk about how hard I tried. . .I could tell you how much I compromised and tried to adjust. Even my mother was surprised at how much I had changed. His family and friends were amazed at how 'Indian' I was. I touched his parents' feet, got up at 5:30 a.m. to make the traditional homemade Indian bread, worked full-time, kept religious fasts and everything else I could do to be the 'ideal Indian wife'. Why was it important that I be as Indian as possible? Because I needed an identity. . .because I was caught between two cultures and since I went through a traditional Indian marriage, I had clearly chosen the Indian culture. And I chose it with a vengeance! I planned my wedding with high hopes and plenty of dreams.

It took three years for him to find a residency position. During those three years, I supported us, paid for his classes at Kaplan, helped him study for the ECFMG exams and tried to be a loving and supportive wife. Gone was the outgoing, happy, bubbly girl he had married and in her place was a woman who became more and more submissive, who tried harder and harder to please a man who was changing every day. After he got his residency position and was no longer financially dependent, the few incidents of physical abuse became more frequent and more violent. After seven years, I finally realized that there was no marriage left to save. That realization was the beginning of a five-year journey of pain, acceptance, and discovery.

I moved back home to be near my family and because I was scared to be in the same city as he was in. After all, a Protection From Abuse

Court Order is only a piece of paper. My mind grew calmer as I put more and more miles between us. For some inexplicable reason, I was not afraid of being on my own—of starting over. Maybe it was because I had hit rock-bottom and the only place I could go was up. In any case, I enrolled in college classes, got a job, and began therapy. Therapy was a big step for me as Indians, like other Asian groups, don't believe in it, but in the last few months, I had read enough books on divorce to realize that I had a rocky road ahead of me. And it has truly been hard. The road to recovery has been slow and very very painful. I remember the pain being so overwhelming at times and the tears that came from deep inside me. I felt as if all my dreams had been shattered and I wondered if I would ever stop hurting. But I have. It's true what they say about the healing effects of time. Although I do get flashbacks—the O.J. Simpson trial brought back the nightmares, but only for a few days. I've found that I heal a little more every day.

My family and friends are amazed that I am not bitter and angry. But I can't blame all men for the acts of one. Everyone assumes that I will get married again because I am very family orientated. But I don't know. I still believe in marriage. In fact, my heart yearns for a happy and stable relationship. My eyes fill with tears when I think of how I always wanted children and how I, with so much love to give, may never have even one. You see, the only thing I ever wanted in my life was a loving husband and happy children. But the thought of getting married again scares me. I never want to be controlled like that again. I realize that this is the fear in my heart talking. I know in my head that it would be different next time. This time I would choose someone capable of loving in a normal way. Sometimes I feel sad when I think of how my life turned out—I had planned something so different! Then, last summer, I saw a saying that helped me to come to terms with my life: 'You have to give up the life you planned to find the one that is waiting for you'. My new life may be different from anything I imagined as a young woman, but it's a happy one. It's a peaceful one. And it's a safe one.

A major change I see in myself is my increasing ability to march to my own beat. I see myself as an individual which is something that is not encouraged for an Indian woman. I realize that I have choices. I realize that I should and can make my own decisions—that even if I fail, its okay because, at least, I was the one to decide. I realize that I no longer have to let my life be ruled by other people's standards and opinions. These are easy words to say, but it's hard to change 30 years worth of conditioning! But I am changing—even if it's one step at a time. It's been a long road and I know that this journey has just begun, but I'm not afraid. I'm excited because suddenly, endless possibilities have opened up for me and there is nothing I cannot do!

Has the journey been worth it? Absolutely! Do I regret leaving? No. I wish that I had left earlier. Could I go back? No. I am no longer that quiet submissive girl who did everything possible to please a cruel and sadistic man. Today my male friends laugh when I tell them that I used to be submissive. . .they just cannot imagine it. Sometimes I wonder if that's good. . .I do not want the pendulum to swing too far the other way. . .I do not want to be a militant feminist. . .not because there is something wrong with that, but because that is not who I am. Many times I find myself protesting something that I may have let pass in my pre-marriage days. And I wonder. . .about the necessity to analyze everything. . .do I feel the necessity to be super-assertive as a backlash reaction to my extreme submissiveness? Where is my journey of self-exploration taking me? I really do not know. I do know that I am stronger, more independent, more assertive and more confident than at any other period of my life. And I am doing something I really believe in. . .investing in myself by pursuing an education so that I have the necessary background to give something back to the community. My goal is to prevent other women from suffering as I did by showing them that there is a way out. . .that there is life after a disastrous arranged marriage. I want to tell them that hearts can be rebuilt and dreams can be renewed.

Part III

Redefining Community

12

The habit of ex-nomination: Nation, woman, and the Indian immigrant bourgeoisie*

Anannya Bhattacharjee

Confronting accusations of having betrayed one's national cultural heritage is not an uncommon experience for members of Sakhi, a women's organization which deals with domestic violence in South Asian communities in New York City.[1] Such accusations, which have their source in the kind of identities immigrant communities assume, have inspired me to examine the problematic ways in which an immigrant community creates its own world in a country where it sees itself as different. As a co-founder of Sakhi, with which I have worked for the last three years, my encounters with South Asian immigrant worlds have enlarged my knowledge of violence against women, particularly in the lives of Indians, Bangladeshis, Pakistanis, and Sri Lankans.

Central to the creation of immigrant worlds is the idea of the nation—not the nation as a bounded geographical unit but the nation as an ideological force. In working with domestic violence, I have come to appreciate how the question of women is inextricably linked to nationness. Here, I take a close look at this link in the context of the 'Indian community' in the United States.[2] Although I came to this discussion through my position with Sakhi, my primary focus will be the construction of a 'national' culture in the Indian community rather than

*This article was originally published in *Public Culture* 5(2), Fall 1992: 19–43 (Copyright 1992), and is reproduced here with the kind permission of Duke University Press.

domestic violence in the lives of Indian immigrant women. It is in the context of such constructions of identity that the pressing issue of domestic violence must be situated.

That there is a connection between domestic violence, women, and nationality occurred to me at a celebration of a popular annual Hindu festival called Divali in New York City in the South Street Seaport. Divali is a festival of lights which celebrates the return of the epic figure of Rama to Ayodhya (in North India) after 14 years of exile in the forest. At the New York celebration, displays of handicrafts, dance, and food from different states of India were some of the many modes by which the diversity of India was exhibited. Amidst this assortment of booths there was also another style of display—one, for example, periodically demonstrated a mock Hindu wedding—that may be referred to as the 'public' displays. In this same vein but by contrast, there was another, more 'private', scene.[3] Not only was this other scene never meant to happen at this cultural extravaganza, but its participants were specifically excluded from these festivities by the organizers. It is this latter event in the context of bourgeois Indian immigrant identity that I will explore. Before I turn to this private scene, it will be useful to establish a context for this discussion by looking at some important aspects of the world of the Indian community.[4]

The habit of ex-nomination

In *Mythologies*, which is 'an ideological critique bearing on the language of so-called mass culture' in bourgeois French society, Roland Barthes explains his motivation for writing:[5]

> I resented seeing Nature and History confused at every turn, and I wanted to track down, in the decorative display of *what-goes-without-saying*, the ideological abuse which, in my view, is hidden there.[6]

Bourgeois society, as the privileged regime in which History is transformed into Nature, is his object of study.[7] He defines the bourgeoisie as the class which does not want to be named, indeed needs no name as it postulates itself as the universal. It needs no name because it names everything, or, as Barthes puts it, it is at 'the locus of an unceasing haemorrhage: meaning flows out of [it] until [its] very name becomes unnecessary'.[8] The power of bourgeois ideology, which spreads over everything, lies precisely in the bourgeoisie's ability to name but itself remain un-named. Barthes calls this characteristic of the bourgeoisie's power to remain ideologically un-named, 'ex-nomination'.[9]

Ex-nomination, which Barthes demonstrates in the case of the French bourgeoisie, is a useful idea for examining the lifeworlds of the immigrant Indian community in the United States. The persistence of this habit of ex-nomination in the bourgeoisie of this community, which is made up of immigrants/expatriates, is the focus here. But first, what/who is an immigrant/expatriate? The two terms 'immigrant' and 'expatriate' are not unambiguously synonymous. Unlike the term 'immigrant', which has come to mean 'one who migrates into a country as a settler', the term 'expatriate' in modern usage suggests 'a person who lives in a foreign country' (*Oxford English Dictionary*). Thus, the term 'expatriate' carries a trace of impermanence by leaving room for his/her return to the native country. Expatriate, then, appears to be a stage prior to the more permanent one that is designated by immigrant. However, the difference between the two is not simply a difference in linear temporal progression, where one begins as an expatriate to later become an immigrant. The expatriate always already carries the seeds of an immigrant in his/her deferred, but nevertheless prospective, immigrant's state; and the immigrant carries the seeds of an expatriate as the return to one's native place always remains a distant possibility. The difference between the two can also be seen as a deferring of commitment, an anguish over allegiances. To choose one of the words over the other is to dismiss this difference, which is central to the immigrant's experience. When I use the words 'immigrant community', I do not want to be understood as privileging the word 'immigrant' over 'expatriate'. It is difficult to unambiguously describe a collective condition as either immigrant or expatriate, and I would like to retain in my use of the word 'immigrant' the shifting grounds produced by the tension between the two terms. This tension also captures well one dimension of that crisis of identity that such a community faces.

The bourgeoisie, then, upon displacement from the nation of its origin, finds itself contained in the form of an immigrant community in a foreign country. In particular, the Third World bourgeoisie, as an immigrant group in the First World, finds itself in a position of subordination to the native bourgeoisie: a position defined partly by the experiences of Western colonialism and imperialism.[10] For the Indian immigrant community, which is considered to be predominantly highly educated and relatively wealthy, this subordination is defined more through race/nationality than through class.

As a minority community in a foreign nation, the Indian immigrant bourgeoisie experiences the loss of its power of ex-nomination. Where once it had stood for the no-name universal in the nation of its origin, it now perceives itself (and is perceived) to be in a position defined by difference. It now risks being named. The immigrant bourgeoisie's desire to overcome this condition manifests itself through its grasping for familiar essentials in whose shadows it can regain the power to remain un-named. This essay explores this desire to remain anonymous; its relation to the nation and to the past; and woman as one of the central elements in forging this relation. Even though I shall discuss woman as an element in the bourgeoisie's negotiation of its own position, I would like to emphasize that such negotiations are, as Lata Mani has pointed out, 'in some sense *not primarily* about women but about what constitutes authentic cultural tradition' (emphasis mine).[11]

Nation and ex-nomination

The landscape of the Indian immigrant bourgeois community reveals a proliferation of organizations reflecting the geographical and linguistic boundaries of India.[12] Linguistic/state/religion-identified organizations such as those of Gujaratis, Tamils, Bengalis, Muslims, and Sikhs are one kind of formation. Another kind of grouping, motivated by a desire to create a unified Indian community across the United States, is exemplified by the National Federation of Indian American Associations (NFIAA) and the Association of Asian Indians in America (AAIA).[13] These two kinds of organizations exhibit a tension where the latter attempts to create an 'all-India' community and the former attempts to express their specific unities through their state/linguistic/religious heritages.

The organizations profiled as 'all-India', which have large memberships and financial resources, are in a position to become the vehicles through which an Indian identity is articulated in the United States. A discussion of the construction of such an identity is essential, especially in light of the fact that the Indian community is among the fastest-growing Asian groups in the United States.[14]

What is the vision of these all-India organizations? The president of the NFIAA articulated the following vision for the Federation of Indian Associations (FIA) at the time of his presidency of that organization:[15]

If the Federation can justify its existence by providing a *united front of Indians* in the New York region, the next step would be to activate or form such independent Federations in other metropolitan areas so that the National Federation of Indian Associations could finally be formed to *represent the Indian community all over the United States*. We should look forward to the time when we can have... convention[s] under the auspices of the national body [emphasis mine].[16]

The phrase 'united front of Indians', in the above passage, seemingly needed little elucidation for the president, as he does not give any: it is supposedly that natural spirit of unity fundamental to Indians awaiting realization in and through an organizational body. This well of natural unity among Indians that the president invokes has historical parallels in the Indian independence movement. Post-1920 Indian nationalists constructed historical narratives that assumed 'the almost *automatic* commitment of India's inhabitants... to the Indian "nation" in the centuries past' (emphasis mine).[17] Since the 1920s, Pandey notes, 'Indian nationalism as we know it... [has taken] as its unit the individual citizen, a "pure" nationalism unsullied...'.[18]

This comparison of an organization like the FIA with Indian nationalists who have dominated 20th century Indian history, first in the freedom struggle against the British and then as the leaders of independent India, is not fortuitous. The FIA president later became the president of the NFIAA, whose description conveys the sense of being a body distanced from and above the vagaries of the community, rather like a nationalist state as it watches over its citizens. The NFIAA, we are told,

represents and advances the interests of Indians in the US... *disseminates* information on the political, economic and developmental affairs of India... *monitors and reports* on social and cultural status of Indians in the US and India... *observes and comments* on legislative activities [emphasis mine].[19]

Indeed, at one point the NFIAA could be confused with a Ministry of Cultural Affairs as it 'seeks to promote and preserve Indian culture and heritage and foster friendship and understanding between Indians and the people of North America'. The foresightedness of great leaders, who guard and propagate the essence of India, shines through in the passage. The passage's evocation of 'Indian culture and heritage', like that of the 'united front of Indians', seems to require no elaboration. In this, the words echo Pandey's characterization of 'the Spirit of India, the Essence, an already existing Oneness' as invoked by the nationalist movement, particularly since the 1920s.[20] This Essence lay in 'the ideal of Indian unity', resurrected by these nationalists, who attributed such a unity to 'the Spirit of India' from time immemorial and to 'the great rulers of the state' in the years before the arrival of the British.[21]

I point to the absence in the above passages of analysis of concepts such as the 'united front of Indians' or 'Indian culture and heritage', not in order to expose a negligence, but to demonstrate the opposite: that there is no negligence here. The absence speaks volumes. This absence can be seen as a demonstration of Barthes's 'ex-nominating operation': Indian culture and the unity of India is for all Indians to possess by the sheer magic of their being Indians; it permeates their essence. Thus, it is in the shadow of this national cultural essence, this Oneness, defined by it for its own purposes, that the Indian immigrant bourgeoisie takes refuge, under the threat of losing its power to stay un-named, in its form of an immigrant community. It is this essence, expressed here in 'the ideal of Indian unity', that Barthes described in another context as 'the haemorrhage of the name "bourgeois"... effected through the idea of nation'.[22]

While certain analogies between the nationalist spirit in India (prevalent since the 1920s) and that of the Indian immigrant bourgeoisie in the United States are worth noting, they are not meant to suggest that there is a complete synonymity between nationalists in India and a leader in a bourgeois immigrant community in the United States. The analogy is limited to the nationalist consciousness pervasive in both rather than the actualities of the Indian nation-state apparatus to which a nationalist leader in India would be connected. This nationalist consciousness seems much like a 'blueprint' of nationhood, that is to say, its elements have ossified to form a model for nationalist consciousness.[23] This model, then, becomes available for use as easily by the bourgeois immigrant as by the nationalist leader in India.

Certain elements of Indian nationalist thought help to clarify the nature of this model. It is possible to identify a dominant nationalist spirit in India which has been one of learning Western technology and economics, while protecting the culture and spiritual essence of India (which exemplifies the East). Partha Chatterjee describes this nationalist project as one which 'cultivate[d] the material techniques of modern civilization while retaining and strengthening the distinctive spiritual essence of the national culture'.[24] Such an essentialization of the West

and the East continues to be evident among the Indian immigrant bourgeoisie in the United States.

Of course, Indian nationalist thought is not a monolithic construction. Gandhi, for example, differed from the dominant nationalist
thought. He believed that 'as long as Indians continue[d] to harbour
illusions about the "progressive" qualities of modern civilization, they
would remain a subject nation'.[25] He was passionately opposed to heavy
industrialization and called for a politics that would be 'directly subordinated to a communal morality'.[26] His success in uniting the peasantry
during the Indian independence movement was unprecedented. He
was committed to localized, village democracies. However, he too, like
most nationalists, invoked the idea of an Ancient India, a changeless
and timeless India. His critique of modern civilization was based on
the original principles of this ancient India, which he took to be the
repository of civilizational values and a guide to a new future. In the
final analysis, Gandhi compromised on questions of organization and
construction of modern India with the dominant nationalist classes.[27]

By contrast, leaders like Jawaharlal Nehru were exemplary of what
has come to be seen as the dominant nationalist thought. Nehru
stood squarely behind modern industry and a centralized Indian state
supported by a mass electoral apparatus at the same time that he
idealized a society that was Indian in sentiment. Nehru understood
Gandhi's appeal for mass mobilization and successfully aligned himself
with Gandhian principles at the same time that he continued to foster
the construction of modern India.

For a diasporic organization like the NFIAA, the nationalist spirit
translates into 'advanc[ing] the interests of Indians' and 'preserv[ing]
Indian culture and heritage'.[28] The interests of Indians in the United
States, in the words of the FIA and later NFIAA president, lie in acquiring 'political clout commensurate with [their] potential economic
strength'.[29] The tension between the terms 'advance' and 'preserve'
reveals a significant opposition between political/economic interests
and cultural heritage. 'Indian immigrants to America' are exhorted to
'preserv[e] their cultural individuality while joining the mainstream of
American life'.[30] The bourgeois immigrant's role is then to learn to participate successfully in the US economy, and to protect their 'cultural
individuality'. Their success can erase their personal identification with
memories of an economically struggling India, and can demonstrate
that economically Indians are not 'essentially backward'. What emerges
in the president's comments is a satisfying resolution for the bourgeois

Indian immigrant: economic advancement through the model of the envied West and cultural preservation of the Indian Essence. In the emerging binary India signifies nation, culture, tradition, God; and the United States signifies material prosperity, participation in legislative politics, economic advancement, and industrial and technological development. In this, immigrant Indian constructions of national identity are revealed to be predictably similar to dominant nationalist thought in India.

Figure of the woman

In pursuit of the goal to 'preserve Indian culture and heritage', Indian immigrant organizations like the NFIAA and the AAIA organize celebrations of predominantly Hindu religious festivals, such as the Divali celebration that I attended. A Bharatanatyam dance performance,[31] handicrafts from Gujarat, and a food stall from Punjab were some of the featured items which served as a museum for the older generation to affirm its heritage and for the younger generation to realize its. Each such display appeared to function as an emblem for a particular state in India. The assortment was meant to represent the unity of India magically produced out of its diversities. The absence of any historical context helped to create a sense of this timeless essence of Indian unity in diversity: Punjab became a symbol for delicious food; Gujarat, for excellent mirror-work.[32] The 1arger project of the festival sought to construct the 'India of our dreams'.[33] I do not want to discount the importance of remembering one's cultural heritage, especially for immigrants. 1 do want to point out the ahistorical ways in which this is often carried out.

It helps at this point to reflect on one of Frantz Fanon's definitions of culture. Fanon warns of the dangers of a thoughtless appropriation of customs, divorced from their historical contexts, as that can lead only to an objectification that is ultimately against a positive transformation of history:

> Culture has never the translucidity of custom: it abhors all simplification. In its essence it is opposed to custom, for custom is always the deterioration of culture. The desire to attach oneself to tradition or bring abandoned traditions to life again does not only mean going against the current of history but also opposing one's own people.[34]

Fanon rejects those customs which arise out of objectification and which finally oppose 'one's own people'. The immigrant bourgeoisie's efforts to create the 'India of [its] dreams' removed from 'the current of history', results in a cannibalization of a mummified heritage. In taking culture to be an assortment of fragmentary customs, as it did in the Divali festival, it succeeds only in the construction of a reified 'India-ness'.

Now I want to return to the booth demonstrating a mock Hindu wedding. The actors were a smiling bride and groom dressed in traditional Punjabi wedding clothes, who were led by an understanding-looking and ever-smiling priest. This symbolic enactment of the Hindu ritual of marriage carried no trace of its concrete aspects such as the relations between the people concerned and their histories. This display of the wedding ritual is reminiscent of Georg Lukacs' description of the phenomenon of reification as one in which 'a relation between people takes on the character of a thing'.[35]

Such a reified display is what leaves the audience with a ritual insulated from those questions which would place it in a historical context, subject to change, protest, or overthrow; questions such as: Who is the priest? From where does his divine authority come? Who is paying him? Whom does he represent? Who is the groom? Why is he marrying the bride? To have someone to cook and clean for him? To get a servant he does not have to pay for? To maintain his respectable image in the community, while he continues the affair with his American girlfriend? To indulge his own sexual fantasies which he is not able to do otherwise? Who is the woman? Did she marry of her free will? What might become of her? Will her husband rape her, claiming consummation to be his birthright? Will he use his power over her immigration status to extract her obedience? Will she be condemned to smile like the bride in the mock wedding, even as she conceals the bruises beneath her clothes? Will he succeed in ultimately destroying her sense of self?

Admittedly, there are numerous possible interpretations of this mock wedding, some of which may be happier than mine. My choice of questions is motivated by another scene that took place at the festival. Sakhi, the South Asian women's organization that focuses on domestic violence, had requested permission to participate in the cultural events of the festival. Sakhi wanted to stage a play that would highlight select aspects of the family and women's roles in Indian society. Its request was denied by the organizers of the event on the grounds that the topics were too political and had no place in this exclusively cultural celebration.[36] We, in Sakhi, decided to attend the event anyway, to distribute fliers protesting a decision that we took to be arbitrary. We distributed information about domestic violence and about Sakhi's services for battered women. However, we had to restrict our activities to an area outside the grounds of the main event. This marginal location mirrored the marginal attention given to abuse against women in the Indian community. A few days later, a woman secretly called Sakhi: she had picked up one of our fliers but had shied away from talking to us at the festival. She had been afraid that her husband would beat her if he found Sakhi's literature in her possession or if he saw her making contact with us. She reported that she had been severely abused by her husband and wanted to know what her options were.

The woman—a wife, like the prospective bride in the mock wedding—fearfully hiding the domestic violence flier at the festival, even as she craved to read and use it, became a potential subversive at the mock wedding which drained her of her story, at the same time that it used her figure to create the myth of Indian woman-ness as a signifier for the Spirit of India from time immemorial. Her story as well as organizations like Sakhi which affirm her story became a potential threat to the preservation of the India which her womanhood signified.[37] The Indian woman is allowed no history of her own by those who adopt the spirit of Indian nationalism in a problematic way; she is allowed no content of her own. In protecting all that is meaningful, she must sacrifice her own life. There is usually a woman who pays a price for the preservation of the essential (nationalist) spirit; always a woman who must keep smiling and hide her pain so as not to betray the fragility of this spiritual heritage, the high cost of its maintenance, and the euphoric security of its myth. As Lata Mani has noted for another historical context, '[w]omen become emblematic of tradition, and the reworking of tradition is largely conducted through debating the rights and status of women in society'.[38]

A persistent theme of Indian nationalism has been the re-processing of the image of the Indian woman and her role in the family based on models of Indian womanhood from the distant glorious past. The woman becomes a metaphor for the purity, the chastity, and the sanctity of the Ancient Spirit that is India. As Chatterjee puts it, the national construct of the Indian woman attributes 'the spiritual qualities of self-sacrifice, benevolence, devotion, religiosity, and so on' to femininity, which then stands 'as a sign for "nation"'.[39] Consequently, anything that threatens to dilute this model of Indian womanhood constitutes a betrayal of all that it stands for: nation, religion, God, the Spirit of India, culture, tradition, family. Thus, Sakhi is seen as a betrayal of India's heritage and as contaminated with Western values when it challenges this model of the Indian woman. Sakhi becomes a homebreaker when it exposes abuse against women and questions the patriarchal family even though Sakhi explicitly does not advocate that any woman leave her abuser unless that is something she wants to do. Sakhi provides women information about their alternatives so that they can make an informed decision about themselves—alternatives which may vary from how she can best protect herself if she wishes to stay in her current situation to what her options are if she does choose to leave. In providing information to an Indian woman which could make it possible for her to end an abusive situation and reject a role which she is told she was to fulfill, Sakhi's presence poses a threat to the Indian community's construction of its Indian-ness.

Sakhi's presence is a continual reminder of the presence of the historical self behind the mythical Indian woman. This historical self is the 'other woman' who is never meant to be present, just as the 'other-scene' was never meant to happen. To follow this train of thought to its logical conclusion, any organization that recognizes the other woman and challenges her displacement also becomes the Other: the Other as a repository of that which threatens to crumble the imaginary world of bourgeois solidarity, and to expose the artificiality of the bourgeois landscape. Ostracization of Sakhi serves as a warning to the other woman of her fate if she tries to tell her story. It appears therefore that from the perspective of the Indian immigrant organizations, Sakhi is neither too political nor is it too social. In fact, it is whatever the Indian bourgeoisie is not, at any moment. It is simply the Other.

These comments on the Divali festival confirm my insight gained from feminist thought that the site for preservation of India, its culture, and its tradition is the family—the domestic space in which the figure of the woman stands. On the other hand, the site for economic/political advancement in the United States is the workplace, the legislature—the public space in which the figure of the man stands. This binary continues to work even for women who work outside the home, as the home still remains a place to affirm one's Indian-ness and the Indian woman is expected to be responsible for maintaining this Indian home in diaspora by remaining true to her Indian womanhood.

Construction of a model-ness

The bourgeois immigrant, like the bourgeois nationalist, sees the preservation of the nation's cultural essence as a domain that can be defended against outside intervention: this is the area where the colonial power's interference was most abhorrent; this is also the area where one must stay ever-vigilant against contamination by Western values as an immigrant. Through the changeless and timeless Spirit of India, the Indian bourgeoisie, whether immigrant or still in India, seeks to anonymously eternalize its own existence. What is ironical is that the terms of cultural preservation and negotiation are, in fact, set by the dominant power: the desire for an untouched, ancient Indian heritage can be seen to be partly a reaction to the continual threat of the universalizing nature of Western, and particularly white American, culture. Another phenomenon is also illustrative of this. In the United States, Indians, along with other Asian communities, are regarded as a model minority, exemplifying high educational status and strong financial success. The compelling and approving image of model minority can be an inducement for building an image of a model India that is commensurate with this minority standing. The timeless essence of India, derived from its distant past and unfettered by the struggles and miseries of the present, fits the model image well. This is the model that must be constructed and re-constructed. At each moment it is eternalized, preserved, and celebrated as one might eulogize an ancient artifact.

The desire for a model history, also commensurate with this model minority image, may explain the selective amnesia in the Indian immigrant bourgeoisie's memory of the history of the Indian community in the United States. The beginning of the history of the Indian community is commonly taken to date from the 1950s and 1960s, when Indian immigrants consisted predominantly of educated, urban professionals. In this historical narrative, the arrival of farmers, railroad builders, workers, and political refugees from the Indian subcontinent in the United States prior to World War I goes largely unacknowledged.[40] Sohan Singh Josh describes some of these Indian immigrants in the early 20th century, when immigration laws fluctuated with the demand and supply for cheap labor. For example, an increased demand for cheap labor to construct railroads near San Francisco around 1910 resulted in a temporary relaxation in immigration laws.[41]

Some aspects of this pre-WWI history of Indians in the United States echo a more radical immigrant culture, which was informed by an explicit anti-imperialist politics and an awareness of the international scope of Western (especially British) imperialism at that time. Their immigrant and subaltern history resonates with a consciousness of India's independence struggles, although their nationalism was problematized by an unquestioning acceptance of the Indian nation as the unit of liberation. At the same time, their perspective was diasporic: first, they seemed aware of the worldwide grip of imperialism, and second, they had an appreciation of the dispersed nature of the Indian immigrant communities in Southeast Asia, Canada, Africa, Europe, the Caribbean, and the United States. There are various explanations for their awareness: they were Indian nationalists whose country was at that time colonized; they needed diasporic support not only to facilitate emigration on ships, but also in some cases to form alternative Indian independence movements of their own; and racism in the United States in relation to immigrants was more obvious (if not brutal) then. In any case, the rhetoric and activities of pre-WWI immigrants reveal a consciousness of economic power, racial politics, and imperialism that is more radical than the consciousness that predominates today.[42]

Today the Indian immigrant bourgeoisie remembers the history of the Indian community in the United States largely in terms of its own history since the mid-20th century. Its loss of historical memory seriously limits response to other communities who continue to face more virulent forms of racism. And not infrequently intoxicated by its success as a model minority, it fails to perceive racism towards itself. In its eagerness to reach the pinnacle of economic progress symbolized by Western capitalism, the Indian immigrant bourgeoisie disregards an analysis of power and ideology which is crucial to its understanding of its own history.

The category of 'model minority', which plays an important role in the Indian bourgeoisie's construction of an 'Indian' community, is double-edged. On the one hand, the term 'model' signifies a standard of excellence, set by the dominant power, which is predominantly white and wealthy, and is presumably an invitation to the minority to join the majority once it realizes its model-ness. On the other hand, the term 'minority' signifies a relegation to the ranks of the not-majority. This contradiction between invitation and exclusion often escapes the leadership of the Indian bourgeoisie in its eagerness to join the mainstream of American life.

Towards this end, the Indian bourgeoisie, which sees itself as the custodian of the model Indian community in the United States, seems to be drawn to a certain 'worldly' discourse of diplomacy, negotiation, and officialdom. This is evident in various activities of Indian associations.[43] Activities and issues of official representation, legislative politics, congressional hearings, and banquets to honor senators on the part of these organizations reveal a desire to participate in the administrative politics of the nation-state. The Indian bourgeoisie assiduously works towards an imaginary ideal of official legislative representation in order to acquire for this model minority the coveted goal of 'political clout commensurate with its economic strength'. Thus, the politics of minority status and representation within the US government become an important focus for legislative activity.

The concerns of such a politics focus around a confusing array of racial categorizations based on biological and cultural essentialisms. Such racial categories are constructed, bolstered, and sustained by such devices as the census, which Benedict Anderson describes as fictional: 'the fiction of the census is that everyone is in it, and that everyone has one—and only one—extremely clear place. No fractions'.[44] Census categories (in relying on counting) profess but fail to capture the complex relationships between place of birth, ancestral origin, language, physical characteristics, and cultural affiliations. The inadequacy of such categories, however, does not seem to deter the leaders of Indian bourgeois organizations from participating in the official thrust towards an exhaustive racial categorization. This effort at categorization, divorced from history and politics, can only make race into a number game and a policy issue rather than an area of radical social change and action. It is further evidence of the limitations of the Indian bourgeois organizations' understanding of racial politics in the United States.

I do not mean to devalue the importance of a minority group's efforts to create a voice for itself. However, the focus on legislative politics by the bourgeois leadership of the Indian community is indicative of how its awareness of racial politics is dominated by the official discourse on race. This community's relationship with other communities, especially those of color, is dictated by competition over limited resources reserved for people of color as well as by rivalry over an imaginary standard of acceptance by the majority. Race as a problematic, with its complex manifestations in our daily lives, goes unacknowledged, let alone articulated. The result is a blind, often intense racism towards other communities, especially towards people of color.

The urge of the Indian bourgeoisie in the United States to engage in activities that have a nation-state-like character is also evident in their organization of annual celebrations of Indian national holidays such as Independence Day, which hold a sacrosanct place in official Indian discourse on the subcontinent. Independence Day is seen as the day when the timeless legacy of the nation of India is foregrounded and as the day to remember the liberation of India from a period of oppressive colonial rule to the right to freely reign over itself again in all its glory. Triumphant images of Indian nationalist leaders liberating the *mother*land from British rule often crowd out questions regarding the origin(s) of this nation-state that was liberated, questions of the identity and the methods used by the liberators to gain India's 'freedom'. Liberating a colonized country from a racist and otherwise oppressive British regime was (and is) important, as is the acknowledgment that such a struggle for independence was laudable. However, it is necessary to point out that these historic events in a nation's biography become emblems of nationhood, alongside the flag or the national anthem. They are imbued by the nation's official discourse with an unquestioning and undiluted euphoria which places any historical accountability in suspension.

The not-model community

The changing composition of the Indian immigrant community is radically altering the contours of a community that was until recently predominantly bourgeois. The bourgeoisie sees the illegal (Indian) immigrant, the unpaid (Indian) worker and the ill-paid (Indian) laborer in the United States as mere aberrations from its coveted place as a model minority. It denies the existence of gays, lesbians, and battered women as inconsistent with that Indian heritage under which it has taken refuge: for the bourgeoisie to acknowledge their existence would be an act of self-destruction.

In Sakhi, our work directly involves women in these marginalized categories, especially those of unpaid workers, battered women, and illegal immigrants. Women in abusive situations who call Sakhi come from all classes, educational backgrounds, and socioeconomic positions, much as the bourgeoisie would like to relegate them to the working class. By insisting that only cab-drivers or factory workers abuse the women in their lives, the bourgeoisie intends to develop its own image as the model minority in opposition to those it considers aberrant.

In this context, Indian owners of such commercial enterprises as magazine stalls, restaurants, or shops often have their wives work for them. Usually, the owner does not pay his wife for her work. Many times, her working conditions can be worse than those of paid workers in terms of hours and health conditions. Her unpaid labor is rationalized on the grounds that she is her husband's helpmate; indeed, her labor becomes an extension of her household duties. This situation has a historical parallel in the Indian nationalist leaders' construction of Indian womanhood as having emerged out of a golden age of the Aryans. Early nationalist historians explain that just as women in ancient India were helpmates in the Vedic sacrifice, so also women in the nationalist cause were to play helpmates' roles.[45] This translated into 'energizing the husband for the goal of regenerating the motherland'.[46] In the example of the diasporic woman, her unpaid labor is now glorified and romanticized to generate the wealth of her immigrant husband.

By our estimations at Sakhi, women form a large portion of the precariously placed/illegal immigrant population in the Indian community. An Indian woman's immigration status is often contingent on her husband's sponsorship because she usually enters the United States as his wife. Her dependence on him for legal status adds to her vulnerability, and is a threat that her husband often does not hesitate to use to his advantage.

The position of these women reveals the poverty of terms such as 'expatriate' and 'immigrant' which the United States immigration service officially uses to categorize them. Both terms usually convey a sense of agency or voluntary will on the part of the expatriate or immigrant, and assume that the presence of the 'resident' alien in the United States was (and is) a freely chosen status. For an Indian woman, who is often forced implicitly or explicitly to marry through a process over which she has little control, the question of free will may be a matter of life or death. If she arrives in the United States through a decision that she did not participate in or agree to, then her classification as an immigrant which implies agency and free will is at best inadequate. When a woman abandons her abusive spouse in order to save her life, she may be out on the streets overnight with no legal status, no home, no money, and, more often than not, no community. She is now the other woman whose presence is inconsistent with the image of the Indian community that the immigrant bourgeoisie constructs.

Naming of a space

My attempt to expose the space that the other woman occupies leads me to an area which is fraught with ambiguities and contradictions: the discourse of the private. Antonio Gramsci, in this context, identifies two major superstructural levels in society:

> the one that can be called 'civil society', that is the *ensemble of organisms commonly called 'private'*, and that of 'political society' or the 'State' [emphasis mine]. These two levels correspond on the one hand to the function of 'hegemony' which the dominant group exercises throughout society and on the other hand to that of 'direct domination' or command exercised through the state and 'juridical' government.[47]

Although Gramsci's superstructural levels need to be complicated, his use of the phrase 'commonly called "private"' suggests that private is a deliberate discursive construction. In common usage, the concept 'private' that Gramsci points to carries a sense of seclusion, isolation, and freedom from intervention and state control. Three common usages of this concept are the private world of the individual, the private world of home/family, and the private sector of the capitalist economy. All three spaces share a sacred sense of isolation in bourgeois society, especially with respect to state intervention and the public gaze.

Yet it is the bourgeoisie, by its historical creation of a regulated society, that has homogenized these three entities and imbued them with authority. Thus, the historical agency of the bourgeoisie in formalizing these entities contradicts its declarations regarding their private nature. In its assertions of the sanctity of the private spaces, the bourgeoisie succeeds in obliterating traces of its own agency. In doing so, it roots these entities—these spaces—in eternity. In fact, the production and regulation of each of these private lifeworlds is crucial to the construction of the nation-state, the emblem of bourgeois society.

In order to determine the space of the woman described above, we need to examine the private spaces constructed by the Indian immigrant community.[48] It is in this space that the immigrant bourgeoisie guards what it perceives to be the nation's cultural essence against contamination by dominant Western values. It is here that the immigrant bourgeoisie steadies itself in the face of changes in a foreign country. This private space appears to be defined at two different levels: the domestic sphere of the family, and the extended 'family of Indians' which is separate and distinct from other communities. It is in these spaces that the immigrant bourgeoisie recognizes the woman; in the private individual and the private sector it recognizes the man. Thus, we may note the different deployment of the idea of the private by the bourgeoisie in various contexts.

Community events, such as festivals, play an important role as these events become the space in which the bourgeois immigrant controls the fate of national culture in the 'family of Indian immigrants'. A restriction on the kinds of organizations which can participate (such as feminist or gay/lesbian or working-class), a careful selection of the kinds of activities that are permitted and invited, and the persistent visibility of women in certain kinds of culturally appropriate roles (such as in a stall for applying *mehendi* [henna], for teaching *bhangra* [dance], for displaying wedding ceremonies [usually Hindu]; or coordinating food-related activities) characterize the mood and organization of celebrations of national culture.

The pure, unsullied, and heterosexual family is another space that the bourgeoisie in its construction of national identities seeks to preserve. The responsibility for the preservation of this unsullied space lies with the woman, and the honor of an Indian woman is contingent upon her ability to suffer in silence and maintain this space. Her role assumes an unrivaled sanctity even as her life requires the utmost control. As Kumkum Sangari and Sudesh Vaid say, '[w]omanhood is often part of an asserted or desired, not an actual cultural continuity'.[49]

The private space of the family is, as I said above, fundamental to national constructs. Anderson points out how both family and nation denote eternal and sacred ties whose origins disappear into the mythical and distant past:

> Both idioms [family and nation] denote something to which one is naturally tied... all those things one cannot help... precisely because such ties are not chosen, they have about them a halo of disinterestedness.... For most ordinary people of whatever class the whole point of the nation is that it is interestless. Just for that reason, it can ask for sacrifices.[50]

Thus, any challenge to the family or the Indian community translates for the national bourgeoisie into a betrayal of national cultural values. For a woman (who is mother, wife, bride, daughter-in-law, or daughter-to-be-married) to disown her role(s) is to betray not just the family, but also the nation. It has been suggested that 'nation-ness is the most universally legitimate value in the political life of our time'.[51] In this respect, the woman who occupies the space outside the heterosexual, patriarchal family is in a space unrecognized by the nation, currently a highly valued construct. The displacement of her history is crucial for the construction of the nation; in re-claiming her voice, her story, she risks displacing the nation.

A twice-imagined nation

Anderson suggests that there are three paradoxes of nationalism: '[1.] The objective modernity of nations to the historian's eye vs. their subjective antiquity in the eyes of nationalists; [2.] The formal universality of nationality as a socio-cultural concept—in the modern world everyone can, should, will "have" a nationality, as he or she "has" a gender; [3.] The "political" power of nationalisms vs. their philosophical poverty and even incoherence'.[52] Anderson captures the way in which national constructions, despite their relative newness, have assumed self-evidential proportions and have lost their historicity. National identity, national allegiance, and nation all appear as an essential and eternal part of ourselves regardless of where we reside.

In the 20th century, a time when the myth of the nation has played a major and sometimes positive role in liberation struggles in the Third World, the importance of a collective identity, especially for oppressed (or colonized) peoples, cannot be overstated. Independence movements, however, are often dominated by the nationalist bourgeoisie, which unquestioningly imagines the nation to be the unit of liberation. Assertions of other loyalties have often been considered disruptive and disloyal to the cause of liberation and unity. Today, liberation struggles are frequently defined in terms of the nation: struggles which threaten national constructions are seen as random (contrary to the systematized nation), biased (not involving national loyalty), disruptive (addressing a construct other than the nation), subversive (threatening the essential national spirit), regional (not nationwide), and narrow-minded (not including the nation). Women's organizations, for example, are often called 'disruptive' in raising questions about gender, a construct other than the nation; communal loyalties are seen as 'subversive' when they challenge the idea of an essential national unity and assert regional or religious loyalties.

Through this myth of the nation, the Indian bourgeoisie in the United States establishes once again its universality and eternalizes its own existence in the soil of the community. Cloaked in nationalist consciousness by the habit of ex-nomination, it sets about recreating a community in its own image. Thus cloaked, it succeeds in eliminating any record of its agency in the making of the community—whose creation can then be attributed to the divine agency of the ancient Indian spirit.

The trope of the nation as members of the Indian community draw on it here can be seen as a strategy that they follow as they construct themselves *politically* not as a nation but as a model minority. This community finds itself caught up in the American national project as an exceptionally civil minority which, unlike its counterpart in India, does not occupy the central ground of either the nation or the state. The idea of the nation in the discourse of the Indian bourgeoisie here subserves the project of being a model minority in a culturally plural nation-state. The Indian community is thus under special pressure to present an image of homogeneity and internal discipline, which are crucial components of the 'twice-imagined nation'.

The 'figure of the woman' describes one of the foundational elements contributing to the construction of this twice-imagined nation, through which the immigrant bourgeoisie gives itself an identity. The 'figure' is the woman reified: it is a 'thing', a signifier to help unify the incoherent impoverished world of the bourgeoisie, a receptacle to be filled, by the bourgeoisie, with any static ahistorical meaning, at any given moment. In the shifting grounds of an immigrant community, the bourgeoisie uses this figure of the woman to steady itself. Sakhi, in exposing the violence behind the figure of the woman, through its concerns with the marginalized, the dispossessed, and the abused, then becomes a betrayal to the twice-imagined nation.

Resisting a habit

The importance of filling the void created by uncertain identities and changing geography, in the context of peoples of migratory movement, should not be underestimated. That Indian-ness describes a certain historical connection to a geographical area now called India, and provides a means of cohesion, also cannot be denied. However, it is only through an understanding of one's historical conditions that an immigrant can resist the appropriation of this void by ahistorical essentialisms, such as the assumption of a mythical 'Indian' identity created in antiquity existing from time immemorial. Such essentialisms can only be a denial of history.[53]

That which the Indian bourgeoisie calls 'betrayal' on the part of Sakhi is what I call a questioning of the appropriation of the Indian immigrant identity by the Indian immigrant bourgeoisie in the name of 'national' culture that it constructs for its own purposes. Indian-ness is not a natural excretion of a genealogical tree, but a continual struggle along multiple modes through a negotiation of the inescapable tension between secure definitions and a consciousness of the oppressions that such definitions rest upon. The struggle in the shifting grounds of immigrant experience holds numerous possibilities for liberation and for the invention of new social arrangements.

The immigrant Indian bourgeoisie through its habit of ex-nomination intends to render historical analysis unnecessary by creating a seamless unity called 'nation'. This seamless unity renders invisible the many violences which lie behind the figure of the woman. The invisible violence which lies hidden by the reified figure of the woman is a seam in this seamless unity. The woman who survived domestic abuse, and who decided to call Sakhi to tell her story after the Divali celebration, makes this violence visible. By reclaiming her voice and asserting her historical self, she created an opening for an intervention into the imaginary unity of the immigrant bourgeoisie's nation.

✦ Notes and References

1. The organization 'Sakhi for South Asian Women' was founded in 1989 by women of South Asian origin in New York City. It provides such services as crisis intervention, legal advocacy, and referrals to shelters and counselors. Sakhi is committed to the view that only through empowerment can women ultimately resist violence in their lives. Sakhi also actively engages in community education because it believes that the community must take responsibility for violence against women and that it is through the raising of awareness that fundamental change can occur. I am writing this article from a personal perspective and not on behalf of Sakhi. I am indebted to S. Shankar for his valuable suggestions. And I thank Purnima Bose, Supriya Nair, Jael Silliman, and Ann Cvetkovich for their thoughtful comments.

2. This link may not be unique to the Indian community in the United States, but I will restrict my discussion mainly to this community.

3. My discussion of the festival later may seem to contradict my use of the word 'public' here. However, this contradiction is only apparent and I have decided to let it remain as it is to help show that words like 'public' and 'private' carry multiple meanings. A festival defined as public in certain contexts can also be defined in very different ways in other contexts, as will become clear.

4. Some general studies of Indians in the United States include: Arthur W. Helweg and Usha M. Helweg, *An Immigrant Success Story: East Indians in America* (Philadelphia, University of Pennsylvania Press, 1990); Parmatma Saran, *The Asian Indian Experience in the United States* (New Delhi, Vikas, 1985); Roger Daniels, *History of Indian Immigration to the United States*, (New York, The Asia Society, 1989).

5. Roland Barthes, *Mythologies*, translated by Annette Lavers (New York, Noonday, 1988), 9.

6. Barthes, 11. See n. 5.

7. Barthes, 137. See n. 5.

8. Barthes, 138. See n. 5.

9. Barthes, 138. See n. 5.

10. A detailed discussion of the contradictions and paradoxes of the relationship between a recently immigrant Third World bourgeoisie in the First World and the First World bourgeoisie is beyond the scope of this article, but the topic would be appropriate for exploration.

11. Lata Mani, 'Contentious Traditions: The Debate on Sate in Colonial India'. In Kumkum Sangari and Sudesh Vaid (eds), *Recasting Women: Essays in Colonial History* (New Delhi, Kali for Women, 1989), 90.

12. The term 'bourgeois' is a complex one signifying a historical class as well as a particular culture and ideology. Thus a person can belong to the class based on his/her material conditions, but may consciously attempt to dissociate him/herself from its culture and ideology. In my use of the term, I refer to that portion of the bourgeoisie which uncritically satisfies both material and cultural and ideological conditions of the class: it is to this group that ex-nomination is attributed.

13. NFIAA is popularly known as NFIA; AAIA is popularly known as AIA.

14. Uma Segal, in 'Cultural variables in Asian Indian families' (*Families in Society. The Journal of Contemporary Human Services* 72(4), 1991, 233) says that the Indian community in the United States, whose current size is about 750,000, is estimated to grow to one million out of a total Asian population of eight million by the year 2000, and to two million by 2050.

15. I have not found documentation stating that the FIA was the precursor to the NFIAA. However, the FIA president became the NFIAA president, which suggests that possibility. It is important to point this out because I will be discussing later how the NFIAA is described in the *Encyclopedia of Associations in the United States* (Deborah M. Burek [ed.], 'National Federation of Indian American Associations', *Encyclopedia of Associations in the United States*, 26th edn, Volume 1, Part 2, Section 10 [Detroit, Gale Research, 1992]).

16. Ravindranath Guthikonda et al. (eds), *Indian Community Reference Guide and Directory of Indian Associations in North America* (New York, Federation of Indian Associations, 1979).

17. In his book (Gyan Pandey, *The Construction of Communalism in Colonial North India* [Delhi, Oxford University Press, 1990], 247) Pandey's discussion of communalism and nationalism in India spans the 19th and earlier part of the 20th century. Even though his comments refer to an earlier historical period, I find them to be relevant today in the context of the Indian community in India as well as the United States because this historical period in India is the one during which the discursive mechanisms used by Indian nationalists today evolved.

18. Pandey, 235. See n. 17. According to him, 'Before [the 1920s and 1930s] the nation of Indians was visualized as a composite body, consisting of several communities, each with its own history and culture and its own special contribution to make to the common nationality... Sometime around the 1920s... India came to be seen very much more as a collection of individuals, of Indian "citizens"'. Pandey, 210. See n. 17.

19. Burek, 1861. See n. 15.

20. Pandey, 252. See n. 17.

21. Pandey, 250. See n. 17.

22. Barthes, 138. See n. 5. Though I focus only on the idea of the nation, it is not the only essentialist category available for the purpose of ex-nomination.

23. Benedict Anderson, *Imagined Communities* (London, Verso, 1991), 80.

24. Partha Chatterjee, 'Colonialism, Nationalism and Colonized Women: The Contest in India', *American Ethnologist* 16(4,1), 1989, 623.

25. Partha Chatterjee, 'Gandhi and the Critique of Civil Society'. In Ranajit Guha (ed.), *Subaltern Studies III* (Delhi, Oxford University Press, 1989), 157.

26. Chatterjee, 164. See n. 26.

27. Chatterjee, 192. See n. 26.

28. Burek, 1861. See n. 15.

29. Guthikonda et al., 1. See n. 16.

30. Guthikonda et al., 1. See n. 16.

31. Bharatanatyam refers to what is now understood to be the classical dance of South India, and is closely identified with Tamil culture. In the 20th century, this dance genre was standardized and is now associated with the nation as a national dance form.

32. 'Unity in diversity' is a popular phrase in Indian nationalist discourse, especially today, in the midst of communal struggles that occupy center stage in challenging the very survival of both the state and the nation in India. According to Gyan Pandey, the use of this phrase has waned somewhat with the rise of a '"mainstream" (Brahmanical Hindu, consumerist) culture' which flaunts itself as *the* national culture, expecting all other 'minority' cultures to fall in line with it and to which all difference appears threatening and foreign (Gyan Pandey, 'In Defense of the Fragment: Writing about Hindu-Muslim Riots in India Today', *Representations* 37, 1992, 28). However, given the asynchronicity of social processes, we continue to see evidence of the concept of 'unity in diversity' in the immigrant community.

33. Pandey demonstrates the construction 'of a new community——the "India of our dreams"' —in the 1920s, by Indian nationalists. One of the changes, he notes, is the use of terms such as 'purely national', raising the nation to a transcendental level (Pandey, 239. See n. 17).

34. Frantz Fanon, *The Wretched of the Earth*, translated by Constance Farrington (New York, Grove/Black Cat, 1968), 224.

35. This discussion is contained in Georg Lukacs, 'Reification and consciousness of the proletariat', where he examines the structure of the commodity (Georg Lukacs, 'Reification and the Consciousness of the Proletariat', In *History and Class Consciousness*, translated by Rodney Livingstone (Cambridge, Massachusetts, MIT, 1971), 83).

36. We did not complete the script for the play but its preliminary sketches consisted of a domestic scene juxtaposing the living-room with the kitchen. A gathering of friends and family was to take place in the living-room while food preparations

were to continue in the kitchen. We were attempting to bring out the differences in interactions between the man (husband) and the woman (wife) in these two areas, in order to demonstrate the different faces of abuse and the ease with which it remains hidden.

37. Tanika Sarkar shows, in the context of Bengali nationalists, a 'constant preoccupation . . . with the figure of the woman' and with the 'conceptualisation of the country itself in her image' through a nationalist 'reconstruction of feminine roles and duties' (Tanika Sarkar, 'Nationalist Iconography: Image of Women in 19th Century Bengali Literature', *Economic and Political Weekly* 22(47), 1987, 2011).

38. Mani, 90. See n. 11.

39. Chatterjee, 630. See n. 25.

40. This was a time before the liberalization of the US immigration laws in the mid-1960s which abolished discrimination based on place of birth and national origin.

41. Sohan Singh Josh, *Hindustan Gadar Party: A Short History* (New Delhi, People's Publishing House, 1977), 60.

42. Joan Jensen describes at length the conditions of these immigrants in *Passage from India: Asian Indian immigrants in North America* (New Haven, Yale University, 1988).

43. Maxine P. Fisher, 'The Indian Ethnic Identity: The Role of Associations in the New York Indian Population'. In Parmatma Saran and Edwin Eames (eds), *The New Ethnics: Asian Indians in the United States* (New York, Praeger, 1980), 187–89.

44. Anderson, 166. See n. 24.

45. Uma Chakravarti, 'Whatever Happened to the Vedic *Dasi*? Orientalism, Nationalism and a Script for the Past'. In Kumkum Sangari and Sudesh Vaid (eds), *Recasting Women: Essays in Colonial History* (New Delhi, Kali for Women, 1989), 51.

46. Chakravarti, 53. See n. 46.

47. Antonio Gramsci, *Selections from Prison Notebooks*, edited and translated by Quintin Hoare and Geoffrey Nowell Smith (New York, International, 1971), 12.

48. In my discussion of private spaces as created by the Indian immigrant society, I would like to note a point that Dipesh Chakrabarty makes in the context of colonial India. Even as he traces the origins of the concepts of bourgeois privacy and individuality in India to British rule, he shows how these concepts were not transplanted in an uncomplicated manner into Indian society. He describes the ways in which Indians challenged and modified these ideas through their own cultural operations, and I would like to retain this thought in my discussion (Dipesh Chakrabarty, 'Postcoloniality and the Artifice of History: Who Speaks for the "Indian" Posts?' *Representations* 37, 1992, 1–26).

49. Sangari and Vaid, 17. See n. 46.

50. Anderson, 143–44. See n. 24.

51. Anderson, 3. See n. 24.

52. Anderson, 5. See n. 24.

53. In my use of the terms 'history' and 'historical' I would like to retain Dipesh Chakrabarty's point regarding the subalternity of Third World histories as long as Europe remains the sovereign subject of all histories. He stresses the importance of rethinking 'history' on the part of people of Third World origin in ways which 'displace a hyperreal Europe from the center' (Chakrabarty, 22. See n. 49).

Notes on contributors

Sabah Aafreen lives in Northern California.

Kauser Ahmed received a B.A. in Comparative Literature from Brown University and is currently a doctoral candidate in Child Clinical Psychology at the University of Denver. Her research interests focus on identity and cultural issues within minority communities. She was born in Hyderabad, India, and grew up in New Jersey. She currently resides in Denver, Colorado.

Sudha Sethu Balagopal is a Phoenix (Arizona)-based freelance writer who has published extensively in India and the United States. Although she has written about many other topics, the subjects closest to her heart relate to women's issues and business matters. She has a Master's degree in Journalism and Communications from the University of Florida.

Anannya Bhattacharjee received her M.S. in Computer Science and worked as a software engineer for four years, during which she co-founded Sakhi in 1989. Sakhi assists South Asian women with services such as crisis intervention, legal advocacy, and referrals to shelters and counselors. Sakhi is committed to the view that only through empowerment can women ultimately resist violence in their lives. Sakhi also actively engages in community education. Anannya served as the Executive Coordinator of Sakhi.

Lubna Chaudhry is a non-resident alien in the United States. She is an Assistant Professor in the Departments of the Social Foundation of Education and Women's Studies at the University of Georgia. Her dissertation research focused on the identities, marginality, resistance, and empowerment of Pakistani Muslim immigrant women in educational and community contexts. Lubna is currently collecting data on the role of the *hijab* in the lives of first and second generation Muslim women in the United States.

Mantosh Singh Devji is the author of *Strong women—weak hearts: Women and heart disease, a personal perspective*, a ground-breaking study adapted into a television documentary. Ms Singh has worked for the Arizona Governor's

Council on Aging, and the Lutheran Church to resettle refugees. She has been inducted into The Charter 100, a group of the top 100+ women leaders in business, the arts, law, medicine, and other professional fields, and is currently serving on the board. She has published extensively and was recently chosen for the prestigious Walker Woods Writers Residency Program. She is also the author of a forthcoming historical novel set in India for which she is currently negotiating a motion picture development contract.

Sangeeta R. Gupta, ABD, specializes in Asian-Indian and Indian-American history in the History department at UCLA. She is the founder and director of the South Asian Women's Conference. She won the Cary McWilliams award for her research on divorce among Indian-American women. Her research interests include cross-cultural issues, acquisition of female gender role identities and immigrant family dynamics.

Karen Leonard has a Ph.D. in Indian History and is a professor in the Anthropology department at the University of California, Irvine. She has published on the social history and anthropology of India and on Punjabi Mexican-Americans and Asian-Americans in California. She works on race and ethnicity and family and life history. She has published extensively and is the author of *Making Ethnic Choices: California's Punjabi Mexican Americans*. She is currently looking at the construction of identity in the diaspora by emigrants from Hyderabad, India, who are settling in Pakistan, Britain, Canada, the United States, Australia, and the Gulf states of the Middle East.

R. Kamna Narain is an independent writer from the San Francisco Bay Area. She is a graduate of U.C. Davis and contributes to newspapers and magazines as well as corporate and trade publications. She is the editor of the 'Focus on Youth' section of *India West*, a national newspaper for Indian-Americans residing in North America.

Pooja K. lives in New York with her new husband and has successfully rebuilt her life.

Lalita Subrahmanyan is of Indian origin. She is Assistant Professor of Education in the Department of Teacher Development at St. Cloud State University in Minnesota. She has a deep interest and involvement with gender issues in education and works with teachers who wish to be proactive in multiculturalism in education. Lalita has worked in India both in schools as well as with an urban development agency on programs for women and children.

Index

About the editor

Sangeeta R. Gupta, ABD, is currently pursuing her doctoral studies at the Department of South and Southeast Asian History at the University of California, Los Angeles. She is the founder and director of the South Asian Women's Conference, an interactive forum for the discussion of issues relating to South Asian women globally. She has conducted research and published in the areas of cross-cultural issues, gender role identities, immigrant family dynamics, and on matters relating to the second and subsequent generations.